JAMESTOWN EDUCATION

SIGNATURE READING

LEVEL
I

McGraw-Hill Glencoe

New York, New York   Columbus, Ohio   Chicago, Illinois   Peoria, Illinois   Woodland Hills, California

JAMESTOWN EDUCATION

Reviewers

Marsha Miller, Ed.D
Reading Specialist
Elgin High School
1200 Maroon Drive
Elgin, IL 60120

Kati Pearson
Orange County Public Schools
Literacy Coordinator
Carver Middle School
4500 West Columbia Street
Orlando, FL 32811

Lynda Pearson
Assistant Principal
Reading Specialist
Lied Middle School
5350 Tropical Parkway
Las Vegas, NV 89130

Suzanne Zweig
Reading Specialist/Consultant
Sullivan High School
6631 N. Bosworth
Chicago, IL 60626

Cover Image: Donald E. Carroll/Getty Images

Glencoe

The *McGraw-Hill* Companies

ISBN: 0-07-861726-X (Pupil's Edition)
ISBN: 0-07-861727-8 (Annotated Teacher's Edition)

Send all queries to:
Glencoe/McGraw-Hill
8787 Orion Place
Columbus, OH 43240-4027

2 3 4 5 6 7 8 9 113 09 08 07 06 05 04

Contents

How to Use This Book

Working Through the Lessons

The following descriptions will help you work your way through the lessons in this book.

Building Background will help you get ready to read. In this section you might begin a chart, discuss a question, or learn more about the topic of the selection.

Vocabulary Builder will help you start thinking about—and using—the selection vocabulary. You might draw a diagram and label it with vocabulary words, make a word map, match vocabulary words to their synonyms or antonyms, or use the words to predict what might happen in the selection.

Strategy Builder will introduce you to the strategy that you will use to read the selection. First you will read a definition of the strategy. Then you will see an example of how to use it. Often, you will be given ways to better organize or visualize what you will be reading.

Strategy Break will appear within the reading selection. It will show you how to apply the strategy you just learned to the first part of the selection.

Strategy Follow-up will ask you to apply the same strategy to the second part of the selection. Most of the time, you will work on your own to complete this section. Sometimes, however, you might work with a partner or a group of classmates.

Personal Checklist questions will ask you to rate how well you did in the lesson. When you finish totaling your score, you will enter it on the graphs on page 219.

Vocabulary Check will follow up on the work you did in the Vocabulary Builder. After you total your score, you will enter it on page 219.

Strategy Check will follow up on the strategy work that you did in the lesson. After you total your score, you will enter it on page 219.

Comprehension Check will check your understanding of the selection. After you total your score, you will enter it on page 219.

Extending will give ideas for activities that are related to the selection. Some activities will help you learn more about the topic of the selection. Others might ask you to respond to the selection by dramatizing, writing, or drawing something.

Resources such as books, recordings, videos, and Web sites will help you complete the Extending activities.

Graphing Your Progress

The information and graphs on pages 218–219 will help you track your progress as you work through this book. **Graph 1** will help you record your scores for the Personal Checklist and the Vocabulary, Strategy, and Comprehension Checks. **Graph 2** will help you track your overall progress across the book. You'll be able to see your areas of strength, as well as any areas that could use improvement. You and your teacher can discuss ways to work on those areas.

LESSON ① Just Once

Building Background

In the story you are about to read, the main character wants to do something very badly—so badly, in fact, that he'll be satisfied if he gets to do it only once. What have you ever wanted to do very badly? Did you get to do it, or are you still waiting for the chance? If you were given the chance to do something right now—even if you could do it only once—what would it be? Write about it on a separate sheet of paper. Then get together with a partner or a small group and share what you have written.

accolade

anonymous

elude

hapless

ponder

precedent

purist

stifle

Vocabulary Builder

1. The words in the margin are from the story you are about to read. Find those words in the sentences below. If the boldfaced word in a sentence is used correctly, write a **C** on the line next to it. If the boldfaced word is used incorrectly, write an **I.**

2. If any of the boldfaced words are unfamiliar to you, guess at their meanings for now. Then, as you read the selection, find the words and use context to figure them out. Then go back and write a **C** or an **I** next to those sentences. Double-check your earlier work, too, and make any necessary changes.

    _____ a. During the football game, they served ice cold **accolade** at the refreshment stand.

    _____ b. We knew the first and last names of the **anonymous** caller.

    _____ c. When I tried to get the mouse back into its cage, it **eluded** my grasp.

    _____ d. The **hapless** football team scored three touchdowns in a row.

    _____ e. When you **ponder** something, you hit it with a large hammer.

    _____ f. The judge had tried a case like this before, so he had a **precedent** to follow.

    _____ g. George is such a **purist** that he only wears clothes made of 100% cotton.

    _____ h. When you **stifle** a yawn, you open your mouth very wide.

3. Save your work. You will use it again in the Vocabulary Check.

Strategy Builder

Making Predictions While Reading a Story

- When you read a story, you often make predictions. A **prediction** is a kind of guess that you make based on information or clues that the author provides. Those clues are called **context clues.** They "set the scene" and help you understand what's happening. They also help you predict what might happen next.

- As you read "Just Once," you will pause twice to make predictions. At Strategy Break #1, you will write down your predictions. You also will write which clues helped you make your predictions.

- At Strategy Break #2, you will check your earlier predictions. Then you will make more predictions, and you will tell which clues helped you make them.

- After you finish reading "Just Once," you will see if any of your predictions match what actually happened in the story.

Just Once

by Thomas J. Dygard

See if you can use clues that the author provides to help you make predictions while you read.

Everybody liked the Moose. To his father and mother he was Bryan—as in Bryan Jefferson Crawford—but to everyone at Bedford City High he was the Moose. He was large and strong, as you might imagine from his nick-name, and he was pretty fast on his feet—sort of nimble, you might say—considering his size. He didn't have a pretty face but he had a quick and easy smile—"sweet," some of the teachers called it; "nice," others said.

But on the football field, the Moose was neither sweet nor nice. He was just strong and fast and a little bit devastating as the left tackle of the Bedford City Bears. When the Moose blocked somebody, he stayed blocked. When the Moose was called on to open a hole in the line for one of the Bears' runners, the hole more often than not resembled an open garage door.

Now in his senior season, the Moose had twice been named to the all-conference team and was considered a cinch for all-state. He spent a lot of his spare time, when he wasn't in a classroom or on the football field, reading letters from colleges eager to have the Moose pursue higher education—and football—at their institutions.

But the Moose had a hang-up.

He didn't go public with his hang-up until the sixth game of the season. But, looking back, most of his teammates agreed that probably the Moose had been nurturing the hang-up secretly for two years or more.

The Moose wanted to carry the ball.

For sure, the Moose was not the first interior lineman in the history of football, or even the history of Bedford City High, who banged heads up front and wore bruises like badges of honor—and dreamed of racing down the field with the ball to the end zone while everybody in the bleachers screamed his name.

But most linemen, it seems, are able to **stifle** the urge. The idea may pop into their minds from time to time, but in their hearts they know they can't do that fancy dancing to **elude** tacklers, they know they aren't trained to read blocks. They know that their strengths and talents are best utilized in the line. Football is, after all, a team sport, and everyone plays the position where he most helps the team. And so these linemen, or most of them, go back to banging heads without saying the first word about the dream that flickered through their minds.

Not so with the Moose.

That sixth game, when the Moose's hang-up first came into public view, had ended with the Moose truly in all his glory as the Bears' left tackle. Yes, glory—but uncheered and sort of **anonymous**. The Bears were trailing 21–17 and had the ball on Mitchell

High's five-yard line, fourth down, with time running out. The rule in such a situation is simple—the best back carries the ball behind the best blocker—and it is a rule seldom violated by those in control of their faculties. The Bears, of course, followed the rule. That meant Jerry Dixon running behind the Moose's blocking. With the snap of the ball, the Moose knocked down one lineman, bumped another one aside, and charged forward to flatten an approaching linebacker. Jerry did a little jig behind the Moose and then ran into the end zone, virtually untouched, to win the game.

After circling in the end zone a moment while the cheers echoed through the night, Jerry did run across and hug the Moose, that's true. Jerry knew who had made the touchdown possible.

But it wasn't the Moose's name that everybody was shouting. The fans in the bleachers were cheering Jerry Dixon.

It was probably at that precise moment that the Moose decided to go public.

In the dressing room, Coach Buford Williams was making his rounds among the cheering players and came to a halt in front of the Moose. "It was your great blocking that did it," he said.

"I want to carry the ball," the Moose said.

Coach Williams was already turning away and taking a step toward the next player due an **accolade** when his brain registered the fact that the Moose had said something strange.

He was expecting the Moose to say, "Aw, gee, thanks, Coach." That was what the Moose always said when the coach issued a compliment. But the Moose had said something else. The coach turned back to the Moose, a look of disbelief on his face. "What did you say?"

"I want to carry the ball."

Coach Williams was good at quick recoveries, as any high-school football coach had better be. He gave a tolerant smile and a little nod and said, "You keep right on blocking, son."

This time Coach Williams made good on his turn and moved away from the Moose.

The following week's practice and the next Friday's game passed without further incident. After all, the game was a road game over at Cartwright High, thirty-five miles away. The Moose wanted to carry the ball in front of the Bedford City fans.

Then the Moose went to work.

He caught up with the coach on the way to the practice field on Wednesday. "Remember," he said, leaning forward and down a little to get his face in the coach's face, "I said I want to carry the ball."

Coach Williams must have been thinking about something else because it took him a minute to look up into the Moose's face, and even then he didn't say anything.

"I meant it," the Moose said.

"Meant what?"

"I want to run the ball."

"Oh," Coach Williams said. Yes, he remembered. "Son, you're a great left tackle, a great blocker. Let's leave it that way."

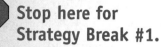 **Stop here for Strategy Break #1.**

Strategy Break #1

1. What do you predict will happen next? _____

   _____

2. Why do you think so? _____

   _____

3. What clues from the story helped you make your prediction(s)? _____

   _____

   _____

➡️ **Go on reading to see what happens.**

The Moose let the remaining days of the practice week and then the game on Friday night against Edgewood High pass while he reviewed strategies. The review led him to Dan Blevins, the Bears' quarterback. If the signal-caller would join in, maybe Coach Williams would listen.

"Yeah, I heard," Dan said. "But, look, what about Joe Wright at guard, Bill Slocum at right tackle, even Herbie Watson at center. They might all want to carry the ball. What are we going to do—take turns? It doesn't work that way."

So much for Dan Blevins.

The Moose found that most of the players in the backfield agreed with Dan. They couldn't see any reason why the Moose should carry the ball, especially in place of themselves. Even Jerry Dixon, who owed a lot of his glory to the Moose's blocking, gaped in disbelief at the Moose's idea. The Moose, however, got some support from his fellow linemen. Maybe they had dreams of their own, and saw value in a **precedent**.

As the days went by, the word spread—not just on the practice field and in the corridors of Bedford City High, but all around town. The players by now were openly taking sides.

Some thought it a jolly good idea that the Moose carry the ball. Others, like Dan Blevins, held to the **purist** line— a left tackle plays left tackle, a ballcarrier carries the ball, and that's it.

Around town, the vote wasn't even close. Everyone wanted the Moose to carry the ball.

"Look, son," Coach Williams said to the Moose on the practice field the Thursday before the Benton Heights game, "this has gone far enough. Fun is fun. A joke is a joke. But let's drop it."

"Just once," the Moose pleaded.

Coach Williams looked at the Moose and didn't answer.

The Moose didn't know what that meant.

The Benton Heights Tigers were duck soup for the Bears, as everyone knew they would be. The Bears scored in their first three possessions and led 28–0 at the half. The **hapless** Tigers had yet to cross the fifty-yard line under their own steam.

All the Bears, of course, were enjoying the way the game was going, as were the Bedford City fans jamming the bleachers.

Coach Williams looked irritated when the crowd on a couple of occasions broke into a chant: "Give the Moose the ball! Give the Moose the ball!"

On the field, the Moose did not know whether to grin at hearing his name shouted by the crowd or to frown. Because the sound of his name was irritating the coach. Was the crowd going to talk Coach Williams into putting the Moose in the backfield? Probably not; Coach Williams didn't bow to that kind of pressure. Was the coach going to refuse to give the ball to the Moose just to show the crowd—and the Moose and the rest of the players—who was boss? The Moose feared so.

In his time on the sideline, when the defensive unit was on the field, the Moose, of course, said nothing to Coach Williams. He knew better than to break the coach's concentration during a game—even a runaway victory—with a comment on any subject at all, much less his desire to carry the ball. As a matter of fact, the Moose was careful to stay out of the coach's line of vision, especially while the crowd was chanting "Give the Moose the ball!"

By the end of the third quarter the Bears were leading 42-0.

Coach Williams had been feeding substitutes into the game since halftime, but the Bears kept marching on. And now, in the opening minutes of the fourth quarter, the Moose and his teammates were standing on the Tigers' five-yard line, about to pile on another touchdown.

⬣ **Stop here for Strategy Break #2.**

Strategy Break #2

1. Do your earlier predictions match what happened? _____ Why or why not? _____

_____

_____

2. What do you predict will happen next? _____

_____

3. Why do you think so? _____

_____

4. What clues from the story helped you make your prediction(s)? _____

_____

_____

 Go on reading to see what happens.

The Moose saw his substitute, Larry Hinden, getting a slap on the behind and then running onto the field. The Moose turned to leave.

Then he heard Larry tell the referee, "Hinden for Holbrook."

Holbrook? Chad Holbrook the fullback?

Chad gave the coach a funny look and jogged off the field.

Larry joined the huddle and said, "Coach says the Moose at fullback and give him the ball."

Dan Blevins said, "Really?"

"Really."

The Moose was giving his grin—"sweet," some of the teachers called it; "nice," others said.

"I want to do an end run," the Moose said.

Dan looked at the sky a moment, then said, "What does it matter?"

The quarterback took the snap from center, moved back and to his right while turning, and extended the ball to the Moose.

The Moose took the ball and cradled it in his right hand. So far, so good. He hadn't fumbled. Probably both Coach Williams and Dan were surprised.

He ran a couple of steps and looked out in front and said aloud, "Whoa!"

Where had all those tacklers come from?

The whole world seemed to be peopled with players in red jerseys—the red of the Benton Heights Tigers. They all were looking straight at the

Moose and advancing toward him. They looked very determined, and not friendly at all. And there were so many of them. The Moose had faced tough guys in the line, but usually one at a time, or maybe two. But this—five or six. And all of them heading for him.

The Moose screeched to a halt, whirled, and ran the other way.

Dan Blevins blocked somebody in a red jersey breaking through the middle of the line, and the Moose wanted to stop running and thank him. But he kept going.

His reverse had caught the Tigers' defenders going the wrong way, and the field in front of the Moose looked open. But his blockers were going the wrong way, too. Maybe that was why the field looked so open. What did it matter, though, with the field clear in front of him? This was going to be a cakewalk; the Moose was going to score a touchdown.

Then, again—"Whoa!"

Players with red jerseys were beginning to fill the empty space—a lot of them. And they were all running toward the Moose. They were kind of low, with their arms spread, as if they wanted to hit him hard and then grab him.

A picture of Jerry Dixon dancing his little jig and wriggling between tacklers flashed through the Moose's mind. How did Jerry do that? Well, no time to **ponder** that one right now.

The Moose lowered his shoulder and thundered ahead, into the cloud of red jerseys. Something hit his left thigh. It hurt. Then something pounded his hip, then his shoulder. They both hurt. Somebody was hanging on to him and was a terrible drag. How could he run with somebody hanging on to him? He knew he was going down, but maybe he was across the goal. He hit the ground hard, with somebody coming down on top of him, right on the small of his back.

The Moose couldn't move. They had him pinned. Wasn't the referee supposed to get these guys off?

Finally the load was gone and the Moose, still holding the ball, got to his knees and one hand, then stood.

He heard the screaming of the crowd, and he saw the scoreboard blinking.

He had scored.

His teammates were slapping him on the shoulder pads and laughing and shouting.

The Moose grinned, but he had a strange and distant look in his eyes.

He jogged to the sideline, the roars of the crowd still ringing in his ears.

"Okay, son?" Coach Williams asked.

The Moose was puffing. He took a couple of deep breaths. He relived for a moment the first sight of a half dozen players in red jerseys, all with one target—him. He saw again the menacing horde of red jerseys that had risen up just when he'd thought he had clear sailing to the goal. They all zeroed in on him, the Moose, alone.

The Moose glanced at the coach, took another deep breath, and said, "Never again." ●

Strategy Follow-up

Go back and look at the predictions that you wrote in this lesson. Do any of them match what actually happened in this story? Why or why not?

_____

_____

_____

_____

_____

_____

_____

_____

_____

_____

_____

✓Personal Checklist

Read each question and put a check (✓) in the correct box.

1. How well do you understand what happens in "Just Once"?
   - ☐ 3 (extremely well)
   - ☐ 2 (fairly well)
   - ☐ 1 (not well)

2. How well did what you wrote in Building Background help you understand the Moose's feelings in this story?
   - ☐ 3 (extremely well)
   - ☐ 2 (fairly well)
   - ☐ 1 (not well)

3. By the time you finished this story, how many words were you able to identify as being used correctly or incorrectly?
   - ☐ 3 (6–8 words)
   - ☐ 2 (3–5 words)
   - ☐ 1 (0–2 words)

4. How well were you able to use context clues to predict what would happen next in this story?
   - ☐ 3 (extremely well)
   - ☐ 2 (fairly well)
   - ☐ 1 (not well)

5. How well do you understand why the Moose says, "Never again" at the end of the story?
   - ☐ 3 (extremely well)
   - ☐ 2 (fairly well)
   - ☐ 1 (not well)

Vocabulary Check

Look back at the work you did in the Vocabulary Builder. Then answer each question by circling the correct letter.

1. After the winning game, Coach Williams visits all the players who deserve an accolade. What other word in the story has a meaning similar to *accolade*?
   a. stifle
   b. compliment
   c. precedent

2. What is an example of something that you might stifle in a serious setting?
   a. a giggle
   b. a question
   c. a thought

3. Which word might describe a person for whom nothing seems to go right?
   a. purist
   b. hapless
   c. anonymous

4. The Moose is unhappy because he feels he is usually "sort of anonymous." What does *anonymous* mean?
   a. not recognized
   b. not feared
   c. not necessary

5. Which phrase best describes a precedent?
   a. something that has never been done before
   b. something that is done over and over
   c. something that serves as an example

Add the numbers that you just checked to get your total score. (For example, if you checked 3, 2, 3, 2, and 1, your total score would be 11.) Fill in your score here. Then turn to page 219 and transfer your score onto Graph 1.

► Personal
Vocabulary
Strategy
Comprehension
►TOTAL SCORE

Check your answers with your teacher. Give yourself 1 point for each correct answer, and fill in your Vocabulary score here. Then turn to page 219 and transfer your score onto Graph 1.

Personal
►Vocabulary
Strategy
Comprehension
TOTAL SCORE

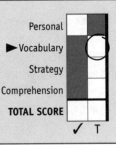

Strategy Check

Look back at what you wrote at each Strategy Break. Then answer these questions:

1. If you had predicted that Coach Williams would not let the Moose carry the ball, which clue would have best supported your prediction?
   a. "I meant it," the Moose said. . . . "I want to carry the ball."
   b. He was pretty fast on his feet—sort of nimble, you might say.
   c. "Son, you're a great left tackle. . . . Let's leave it that way."

2. If you had predicted that Coach Williams *would* let the Moose carry the ball, which clue would have best supported your prediction?
   a. "I meant it. I want to carry the ball."
   b. "It was your great blocking that did it," he said.
   c. "You keep right on blocking, son."

3. At Strategy Break #2, which prediction would have best fit the story?
   a. Coach will let Moose carry the ball.
   b. Coach will get angry.
   c. The Moose will get his chance to carry the ball but will turn it down.

4. Which clue would have best supported your prediction that the Moose would score a touchdown?
   a. He ran a couple of steps and looked out in front and said aloud, "Whoa!"
   b. This was going to be a cakewalk; the Moose was going to score a touchdown.
   c. Moose couldn't move. He was pinned.

5. What might the title have helped you predict?
   a. that Coach Williams wouldn't allow the Moose to carry the ball even once
   b. Moose would be allowed to carry the ball
   c. that Coach Williams would beg the Moose to carry the ball just once

Check your answers with your teacher. Give yourself 1 point for each correct answer, and fill in your Strategy score here. Then turn to page 219 and transfer your score onto Graph 1.

Comprehension Check

Review the story if necessary. Then answer these questions:

1. To whom does the Moose first reveal his desire to carry the ball?
   a. his father
   b. Dan Blevins
   c. Coach Williams

2. Why does the Moose want to carry the ball?
   a. He wants people to cheer when he scores.
   b. He resents the fact that no one thinks he plays well.
   c. He doesn't like the quarterback on his team.

3. What is the score when the Moose finally gets a chance to run with the ball?
   a. Both teams are tied at 42–42.
   b. The Moose's team is winning 42–0.
   c. The Moose's team is losing 42–0.

4. Why does Coach Williams finally let the Moose carry the ball?
   a. He feels that the Moose deserves a chance.
   b. His team is already winning, so the Moose can't do much harm.
   c. Both of the above answers are correct.

5. Why does the Moose say that he will never carry the ball again?
   a. He feels like a failure.
   b. He didn't enjoy it.
   c. He is badly hurt.

Check your answers with your teacher. Give yourself 1 point for each correct answer, and fill in your Comprehension score here. Then turn to page 219 and transfer your score onto Graph 1.

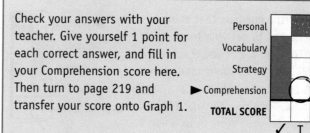

Extending

Choose one or more of these activities:

WRITE A SPORTS COMMENTARY

Write what a sports announcer might say while the Moose carries the ball into the end zone. Practice reading your commentary, and then read it into a tape recorder. Before you play the tape for others, listen to it and decide if you need to change or add anything. If necessary, record your commentary one more time, and include your changes. (You might want to use one of the football marches referenced on this page as background music for your commentary.)

SKETCH AN EXCITING MOMENT

At the end of the story, the Moose recalls the awesome sight of the opposing players advancing on him. Using details from the story to help you, make a sketch of that moment.

LEARN MORE ABOUT FOOTBALL

If you aren't familiar with American football—the rules; the number of players, their positions, and responsibilities; the equipment; and the playing field—do some research on the sport. Use some of the resources on this page for help, or interview a coach or a player on a local team. Present your findings in a multimedia presentation or an illustrated booklet about the sport.

Resources

Books

Dygard, Thomas J. *Running Wild.* William Morrow, 1996.

———. *Second Stringer.* HarperCollins, 1998.

Pincus, Arthur. *How to Talk Football.* BBS Publishing, 1995.

Theismann, Joe, with Brian Tarcy. *The Complete Idiot's Guide to Understanding Football like a Pro.* Alpha, 1997.

Web Sites

http://www.cae.wisc.edu/~dwilson/rsfc/intro/
This Web page gives you an introduction to the rules of college football in the United States.

http://www.nfl.com
This is the official site of the National Football League.

Audio Recording

Great College Football Marches. University of Michigan Band. Vanguard, 1987.

The Squid

Building Background

Although Jules Verne published most of his novels during the mid- to late 1800s, his **science fiction** stories contained many inventions that we actually use today. Some of those inventions include airplanes, guided missiles, space satellites, and submarines.

The selection you are about to read is from Verne's classic novel *Twenty Thousand Leagues Under the Sea*. The novel tells the story of Captain Nemo, a mad sea captain, who explores the oceans in a submarine. Using the title as a clue, what do you predict will happen in this selection?

astonished

caprice

formidable

repress

tentacles

vanquished

vigor

Vocabulary Builder

1. The vocabulary words in the margin are all related to the squid and the *Nautilus* crew's reaction to them. Before you begin reading "The Squid," draw a line from each word in Column 1 to its definition in Column 2.

2. If you don't know some of the words, guess for now. Then, as you read the selection, find the words in context and try to figure out their meanings. If context doesn't help, use a dictionary. Then go back and check or change your answers as necessary.

COLUMN 1	COLUMN 2
astonished	sudden impulse or urge
caprice	strength or energy
formidable	control or hold back
repress	greatly surprised
tentacles	conquered or defeated
vanquished	long, slender, armlike growth
vigor	hard to beat or fight

3. Save your work. You will refer to it again in the Vocabulary Check.

Strategy Builder

Mapping the Elements of a Story

- One of the main elements of every story is its **plot**, or sequence of events. In most stories, the plot revolves around a problem that the main characters have and the steps they take to solve it.

- Another element is the **setting**—the time and place in which the story happens. In some stories the setting is a major element. For example, in "The Squid" the underwater setting greatly influences the plot.

- A good way to keep track of what happens in a story is to record its elements on a **story map**. Study the story map below. It lists and defines the elements that you should look for as you read a story.

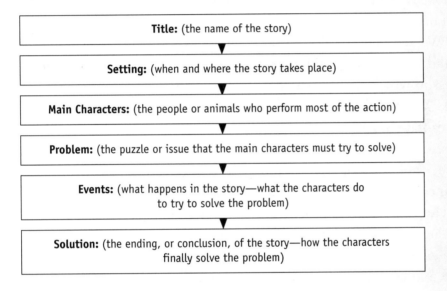

Title: (the name of the story)

Setting: (when and where the story takes place)

Main Characters: (the people or animals who perform most of the action)

Problem: (the puzzle or issue that the main characters must try to solve)

Events: (what happens in the story—what the characters do to try to solve the problem)

Solution: (the ending, or conclusion, of the story—how the characters finally solve the problem)

The Squid

by Jules Verne

As you begin reading this story, apply the strategies that you just learned. Keep track of the characters, setting, and other elements. You may want to underline them as you read.

from *Twenty Thousand Leagues Under the Sea*

For six months, Ned Land, Conseil, and I had been prisoners on board the *Nautilus*. We had now traveled 17,000 leagues, and, as Ned Land said, there was no reason why it should not come to an end. We could hope for no help from the captain of the *Nautilus*, only from ourselves.

For some time past, Captain Nemo had become graver, more retired, less sociable. He seemed to shun me. I met him rarely. Formerly, he was pleased to explain the submarine marvels to me. Now he left me to my studies and came no more to the salon. After so long a captive on this journey, I had now the knowledge to write the true book of the sea. And this book, sooner or later, I wished to publish. But still I wondered, *What change had come over Captain Nemo? For what cause?*

On April 16th, we sighted the islands of Martinique and Guadaloupe from a distance of about thirty miles out to sea. I glimpsed their tall peaks for but an instant. Conseil, who had been counting on landing at those French islands to make good our escape, was quite disheartened. So far from land, escape could not be thought of.

It was about eleven o'clock in the morning when Ned Land drew my attention to a large mass of seaweeds floating outside the panels.

"Well," I said, "these are proper hiding places for giant squid, and I should not be **astonished** to see some of these monsters."

"I will never believe that such animals exist," said Ned.

"When it is a question of monsters, the imagination is apt to run wild," I said.

"It is supposed that these squid can draw down vessels. The ancient naturalists speak of monsters whose mouths were like gulfs, and which were too large to pass through the Straits of Gibraltar."

"But how much is true of these stories?" I asked Conseil.

"Nothing, my friends; at least of that which passes the limit of truth to get to fable or legend. But one cannot deny that squid of a large species exist. According to the calculations of some naturalists, one of these animals, only six feet long, would have **tentacles** twenty-seven feet long. That would suffice to make a **formidable** monster."

"Tell me, master, its head," asked Conseil, "is it not crowned with eight tentacles, that beat the water like a nest of serpents?"

"Yes, Conseil."

"And its mouth, is it not like a parrot's beak?"

"Exactly, Conseil."

"Very well!" he replied quietly, "if this is not a squid, then it is, at least, one of its brothers."

I looked at Conseil. Ned hurried at the window. "What a horrible beast!" Ned said.

I looked in my turn and could not **repress** a gesture of disgust. Before my eyes was a horrible monster, worthy of the ancient legends. It was eight yards long. It swam crossways in the direction of the *Nautilus* with great speed, watching us with its enormous staring green eyes. Its arms, or rather feet, fixed to its head, were twice as long as its body, and were twisted like the Furies' hair. One could see the air-holes on the inner side of the tentacles. The monster's mouth, a horned beak like a parrot's, opened and shut vertically. Its tongue, a horned substance, furnished with several rows of pointed teeth, came out quivering from this veritable pair of shears. Its body formed a fleshy mass that might weigh four thousand to five thousand pounds. The varying color changed with great rapidity, and passed successively from livid gray to reddish brown.

What irritated this monster? No doubt the presence of the *Nautilus*, more formidable than itself, and on which its suckers or its jaws had no hold. Yet, what monsters these giant squid are! What **vigor** there is in their movements! Chance had brought us in its presence and I did not wish to lose the opportunity of carefully studying this specimen. I overcame the horror that inspired me, and,

taking a pencil, began to draw it.

By this time other squid appeared at the port light. I counted seven. They formed a procession after the *Nautilus*, and I heard them against the iron hull. I continued my work. These monsters kept pace with us in the water with such precision, they seemed immovable.

Suddenly the *Nautilus* stopped. A shock made it tremble in every plate.

"Have we struck anything?" I asked.

"We are still floating," said Ned.

The *Nautilus* was floating, no doubt, but it did not move. A minute passed. Captain Nemo, followed by his lieutenant, entered the drawing room. I had not seen the captain for some time. He seemed dull. Without noticing or speaking to us, he went to the panel, looked at the squid, and said something to his lieutenant. The latter went out. Soon the panels were shut. The ceiling was lighted.

I approached the captain. "A curious collection of squid?" I said.

"Yes, indeed, Mr. Naturalist," he replied, "and we are going to fight them, man to beast."

I looked at him. I thought I had not heard aright.

"Man to beast?" I repeated.

"Yes, sir. The screw is stopped. I think that a squid is entangled in the blades. That is what prevents our moving."

"What are you going to do?"

"Rise to the surface, and slaughter this vermin."

"A difficult enterprise."

"Yes, indeed. The electric bullets are powerless against the soft flesh, where they do not find resistance enough to go off. But we shall attack them with the hatchet."

"And the harpoon, sir," said Ned, "if you do not refuse my help."

"I will accept it, Master Land."

"We will follow you," I said and together we went toward the central staircase.

There, about ten men with boarding hatchets were ready for the attack. Conseil and I took two hatchets. Ned Land seized a harpoon. The *Nautilus* rose to the surface.

 Stop here for the Strategy Break.

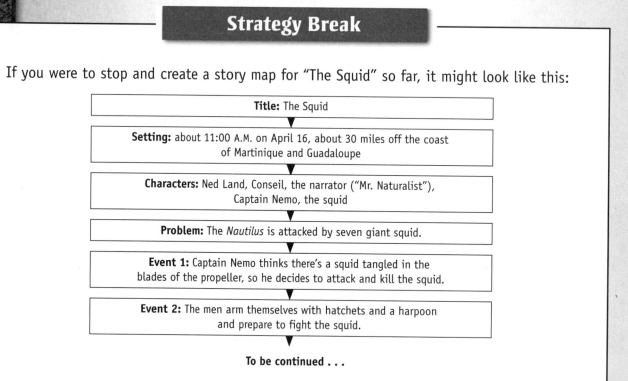

Strategy Break

If you were to stop and create a story map for "The Squid" so far, it might look like this:

Title: The Squid
Setting: about 11:00 A.M. on April 16, about 30 miles off the coast of Martinique and Guadaloupe
Characters: Ned Land, Conseil, the narrator ("Mr. Naturalist"), Captain Nemo, the squid
Problem: The *Nautilus* is attacked by seven giant squid.
Event 1: Captain Nemo thinks there's a squid tangled in the blades of the propeller, so he decides to attack and kill the squid.
Event 2: The men arm themselves with hatchets and a harpoon and prepare to fight the squid.

To be continued . . .

As you continue reading, pay attention to the events in this selection. You will complete the story map in the Strategy Follow-up.

 **Go on reading to see what happens.**

One of the sailors, posted on the top ladder step, unscrewed the bolts of the panels. But hardly were the screws loosed, when the panel rose with great violence, evidently drawn by the suckers of a squid's arm.

Immediately one of these arms slid like a serpent down the opening, and twenty others were above. With one blow of the ax, Captain Nemo cut this formidable tentacle; it slid wriggling down the ladder.

Just as we were pressing one on the other to reach the platform, two other arms, lashing the air, came down on the seaman placed before Captain Nemo, and lifted him up with irresistible power. Captain Nemo uttered a cry, and rushed out. We hurried after him.

What a scene! The unhappy man, seized by the tentacle and fixed to the suckers, was balanced in the air at the **caprice** of this enormous monster. He rattled in his throat, attempting to cry, "Help! Help!"

Those words, *spoken in French*, startled me! I had a fellow countryman on board, perhaps several. That heart-rending cry! I shall hear it all my life.

The unfortunate man was lost. Who could rescue him from that powerful grasp? However, Captain Nemo had rushed to the squid, and with one blow of the ax had cut through one arm. His lieutenant struggled furiously against other monsters that crept on the flanks of the *Nautilus*. The crew fought with their axes. Ned, Conseil, and I buried our weapons in the fleshy masses. A strong smell penetrated the atmosphere. It was horrible!

For one instant, I thought the unhappy man, entangled with the squid, would be torn from its powerful suction. Seven of the eight arms had been cut off. One only wriggled in the air, brandishing the victim like a feather. But just as Captain Nemo and his lieutenant threw themselves on it, the animal ejected a stream of black liquid. We were blinded by it.

When the cloud dispersed, the squid had disappeared, and my unfortunate countryman with it. Ten or twelve squid now invaded the platform and sides of the *Nautilus*. We rolled pell-mell into the midst of this nest of serpents that wriggled on the platform in the waves of blood and ink. It seemed as though these slimy tentacles sprang up like Hydra's heads. Ned Land's harpoon, at each stroke, plunged into the staring eyes of the squid. But my bold companion was suddenly overturned by the tentacles of a monster he had not been able to strike.

Ah! how my heart beat with emotion and horror! The formidable mouth of a squid was open over Ned Land. The unhappy man would be cut in two. I rushed to his aid. But Captain Nemo was before me. His ax disappeared between the two enormous jaws, and, miraculously saved, Ned, rising, plunged his harpoon deep into the giant squid's heart.

"I owed myself this revenge!" said the captain to Ned.

Ned bowed without replying. The combat had lasted a quarter of an hour. The monsters, **vanquished** and mutilated, left us at last, and disappeared under the waves.

Captain Nemo, covered with blood, nearly exhausted, gazed upon the sea that had swallowed up one of his companions, and great tears gathered in his eyes. None of us would forget that terrible scene, but Captain Nemo's grief was great. He wept while watching the waves. It was the second companion he had lost since our arrival on board, and what a death! That friend, crushed, stifled, bruised by the dreadful arms of a giant squid, pounded by his iron jaws, would not rest with his comrades in the peaceful coral cemetery!

Captain Nemo entered his room, and I saw him no more for some time. That he was sad and unsettled I could see by the vessel, of which he was the soul, and which received all his impressions. The *Nautilus* did not keep on its settled course. It floated about like a corpse at the will of the waves. It moved at random. Evidently, the captain could not tear himself away from the scene of the last struggle, from this sea that had devoured one of his own. ●

Strategy Follow-up

Now complete the story map for "The Squid." (Use a separate sheet of paper if you need to.) Start with Event 3. Parts of the events have been filled in for you.

Problem: The *Nautilus* is attacked by seven giant squid.

Event 3: After one sailor unscrews the bolts of the panels,

Event 4: After Captain Nemo cuts off the squid's tentacle, the squid

Event 5: The crew fight the squid until the one holding the sailor

Event 6: As the men fight 10 or 12 squid,

Solution: After 15 minutes of fighting,

✓Personal Checklist

Read each question and put a check (✓) in the correct box.

1. How well do you understand what happens in this selection?
    - ☐ 3 (extremely well)
    - ☐ 2 (fairly well)
    - ☐ 1 (not well)

2. How well were you able to use the title and the information in Building Background to predict what would happen in this selection?
    - ☐ 3 (extremely well)
    - ☐ 2 (fairly well)
    - ☐ 1 (not well)

3. In the Vocabulary Builder, how well were you able to match the vocabulary words and their definitions?
    - ☐ 3 (extremely well)
    - ☐ 2 (fairly well)
    - ☐ 1 (not well)

4. How well were you able to complete the story map in the Strategy Follow-up?
    - ☐ 3 (extremely well)
    - ☐ 2 (fairly well)
    - ☐ 1 (not well)

5. At the end of the selection, how well do you understand why the *Nautilus* did not keep on its settled course?
    - ☐ 3 (extremely well)
    - ☐ 2 (fairly well)
    - ☐ 1 (not well)

Vocabulary Check

Look back at the work you did in the Vocabulary Builder. Then answer each question by circling the correct letter.

1. Which other word from the selection has a meaning similar to *formidable*?
    - a. dreadful
    - b. irresistible
    - c. unsettled

2. The narrator says he "should not be astonished" to see some giant squid hiding among the seaweeds. What is another word for *astonished*?
    - a. calmed
    - b. cheered
    - c. surprised

3. With which part of its body does the squid grab the sailor?
    - a. its tentacle
    - b. its teeth
    - c. its tongue

4. Which phrase describes the word *caprice* as it is used in this selection?
    - a. part of a squid's body
    - b. sudden impulse or urge
    - c. large, luxurious car

5. What does it mean to repress something?
    - a. to hold something back
    - b. to press it until it's flat
    - c. to make something sad

Add the numbers that you just checked to get your Personal Checklist score. Fill in your score here. Then turn to page 219 and transfer your score onto Graph 1.

Check your answers with your teacher. Give yourself 1 point for each correct answer, and fill in your Vocabulary score here. Then turn to page 219 and transfer your score onto Graph 1.

Strategy Check

Review the story map that you completed in the Strategy Follow-up. Then answer these questions:

1. What happens after a sailor unscrews the bolts of the panels?
   a. He slowly lifts a panel up and climbs out of the submarine.
   b. A squid lifts a panel off and slides a tentacle down the opening.
   c. He spots a squid and closes the panel again very quickly.

2. What happens after Captain Nemo cuts off the first squid's tentacle?
   a. It grabs one of the sailors and lifts him up in the air.
   b. It shrinks back and swims away as fast as it can.
   c. It ejects a stream of black liquid and blinds the men.

3. What does the squid do to make the men stop cutting off its tentacles?
   a. The squid grabs one of the sailors and lifts him up in the air.
   b. The squid shrinks back and swims away as fast as it can.
   c. The squid ejects a stream of black liquid and blinds the men.

4. What is the final solution to the crew's problem?
   a. They manage to kill all of the squid.
   b. They all escape the squid unharmed.
   c. The defeated squid disappear.

5. Why is this solution not entirely satisfying?
   a. Although the crew successfully kill all the squid, they lose one of their men.
   b. Although the crew successfully fight off the squid, they lose one of their men.
   c. Although the crew successfully fight off the squid, they kill all but one.

Comprehension Check

Review the selection if necessary. Then answer these questions:

1. At the beginning of the selection, what change has taken place in Captain Nemo?
   a. He has become more friendly and outgoing.
   b. He has become quieter and less sociable.
   c. He has become sickly and very weak.

2. Who is the first person to spot the giant squid outside the window?
   a. Conseil
   b. Ned Land
   c. the narrator

3. Why does Captain Nemo decide to fight the giant squid?
   a. He's a hunter who thinks that killing the creatures will be enjoyable.
   b. He wants to rescue one of his men from the giant squid.
   c. He thinks one of the squid has caused the *Nautilus* to stop moving.

4. When does the narrator realize that the captured sailor is truly lost?
   a. when Captain Nemo weeps while watching the waves
   b. when the squid blinds the men and disappears with the sailor
   c. when the men cut off seven of the squid's eight tentacles

5. Which word best describes the actions of Captain Nemo and the crew?
   a. carefree
   b. cowardly
   c. courageous

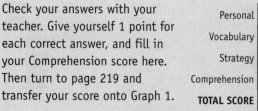
Check your answers with your teacher. Give yourself 1 point for each correct answer, and fill in your Strategy score here. Then turn to page 219 and transfer your score onto Graph 1.

Check your answers with your teacher. Give yourself 1 point for each correct answer, and fill in your Comprehension score here. Then turn to page 219 and transfer your score onto Graph 1.

Extending

Choose one or more of these activities:

LEARN MORE ABOUT JULES VERNE

Jules Verne is often considered one of the first science fiction writers. Work alone or with a small group to learn more about this influential author. Present your findings in the form of a talk, a mock interview, or a panel discussion.

READ MORE BY JULES VERNE

"The Squid" is only a part of the novel *Twenty Thousand Leagues Under the Sea.* Read or listen to this novel or another one that Verne wrote. (See the resources listed on this page.) Give a book talk in which you discuss the book with some or all of your classmates. If other students have read or listened to different books by Verne, compare and contrast the books in a group discussion.

MAKE A SUBMARINE MODEL

The characters in "The Squid" explore the ocean in a crude submarine. Find out what early submarines were really like, and create a simple model or models for display. (Some of the resources on this page might help you get started.) Then, in a brief oral or written report, compare the early submarines with ones that are used today.

RESEARCH THE GIANT SQUID

The giant squid is a real animal, but no one knows much about it. Using some of the resources on this page as well as ones you discover yourself, find out as much as you can about this mysterious monster.

Resources

Books

Cousteau, Jacques Yves. *The Ocean World.* Danbury Press, 1975.

Verne, Jules. *Around the World in Eighty Days.* Scholastic, 1996.

———. *Journey to the Center of the Earth.* New American Library, 1995.

———. *Twenty Thousand Leagues Under the Sea.* Puffin, 2002.

Web Sites

http://americanhistory.si.edu/subs/history/subsbeforenuc/index.html
This Web site offers a history of submarines before nuclear power. Click on the "Early American Submarines" link to learn about the first submarines in the United States.

http://seawifs.gsfc.nasa.gov/OCEAN_PLANET/HTML/squid_links.html
This Squid Links page provides links to many Web resources related to squids.

Audio Recordings

Verne, Jules. *Around the World in Eighty Days.* Blackstone Audiobooks, 1993.

———. *Journey to the Center of the Earth.* Bookcassette Sales, 1993.

———. *Twenty Thousand Leagues Under the Sea.* Naxos AudioBooks, 1995.

Video/DVD

Vanishing Wonders of the Sea. Carousel Film and Video, 1998.

LESSON ❸ Survival at Sea

Building Background

True stories of disasters and rescues are always exciting. We all want to know how real people survive in the face of incredible dangers. Think about a dangerous situation that you have read about in a newspaper or seen on the news. Describe the situation by writing a paragraph or two, explaining the five *W*'s: who, what, when, where, and why. Get together with a group of classmates and share what you have written. Then work together to predict what kinds of problems Ariane Randall might describe in the her true account of "Survival at Sea."

acknowledge

amnesia

congregated

hallucinate

indefinitely

reluctant

Vocabulary Builder

1. Each boldfaced vocabulary word below is followed by three other words. One of the three words is an **antonym** (opposite) of the boldfaced word.

2. Underline the antonym of any boldfaced word that you already know. Then, as you read the selection, use context to help you figure out the other boldfaced words. Return to this exercise, if necessary, and underline the rest of the antonyms.

3. Save your work. You will use it again in the Vocabulary Check.

acknowledge	admit	agree	deny
amnesia	forgetfulness	mindfulness	loss of memory
congregated	scattered	gathered	grouped
hallucinate	imagine	see realistically	fantasize
indefinitely	uncertainly	not clearly	surely
reluctant	eager	unwilling	hesitant

Strategy Builder

How to Read an Autobiographical Sketch

- An **autobiography** is the story of a real person's life, written by that person. An **autobiographical sketch** is the story of a part of a real person's life.

- An autobiographical sketch is always written in the **first-person point of view**. That means that the narrator tells his or her own story using the words *I, me, my,* and *mine.*

- Like every other type of nonfiction, an autobiographical sketch follows a particular pattern of organization. Since autobiographical sketches describe events in the order in which they happened, they follow the pattern of **sequence.**

28   SIGNATURE READING, I

- To make the sequence as clear as possible, writers often use **signal words**. Examples of signal words are *yesterday, several hours later,* and *early the next morning.*

- As you read the following paragraph, pay attention to the sequence of events. Use the underlined signal words to help you.

> Yesterday I searched through my grandmother's trunk in the attic. First I opened the trunk with a special key that hung on a hook by the steps. After I lifted the lid, I studied a photograph of Grandmother as a young woman. Then I searched through her old clothes and found a pretty sweater. When I tried it on, I looked at myself in the mirror. "Jayne, you don't look like yourself in this sweater," I said to myself, "but you *do* look like someone familiar." I glanced at the photo again. Finally, I realized who I looked like—Grandmother.

- If you wanted to show the sequence of events in the paragraph above, you could use a **sequence chain.** It would look like this:

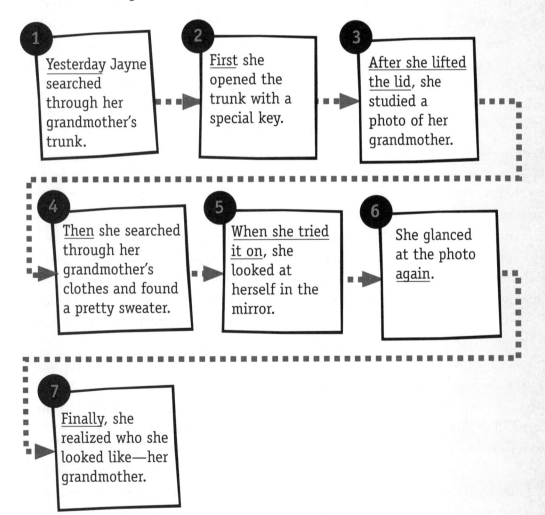

Survival at Sea

by Ariane Randall

As you read the first part of this autobiographical sketch, apply the strategies that you just learned. Look for signal words as you read. They will give you a more exact picture of when things happened.

The nightmare began July 4, when Ariane Randall and her father crashed in a small plane off the coast of Haiti. For thirty-six hours they battled fear, waves and the specter of death. Here is the story of her amazing ordeal.

My trip to Club Med in Haiti began at New York's La Guardia Airport, two weeks after my fourteenth birthday. All the people going to Club Med had **congregated** around the check-in counter. While waiting around, I met Anna Rivera and Delia Clarke, who would be passengers on the doomed plane, and Delia's daughter, Krista. Anna was concerned about how she could get malaria pills.

I had a great time during my week at Club Med, waterskiing, snorkeling, swimming, and suntanning—things I don't get to do much in New York City. During the week, the Haitians went on strike a number of times to protest against the government. At the end of week American Airlines, on which we were supposed to fly, canceled all flights to and from Haiti **indefinitely** because of the political unrest.

Club Med gave those of us who were supposed to fly home Saturday a choice: Either stay in the village for free until the airline restored service, or go by chartered airplane to Santo Domingo, in the Dominican Republic, and catch a connecting flight from there. I wanted to stay since I was having such a good time and there would be a July Fourth celebration, but my father decided that we should get out of the country while we still could. This story proves that all parents should listen to their children.

The next day, July 4, twelve guests gathered to wait for the bus. As it turned out, we wouldn't be leaving for another two hours, so I took the opportunity to sunbathe and go for a last dip in the pool. Finally the bus arrived, and I said good-bye to the friends I'd made.

At the airport the plane never came, due to engine trouble. Finally Club Med chartered four small planes, and a few hours later four of us—Delia Clarke, Anna Rivera, my father, and I—boarded the last of them. It was a dinky-looking plane, a Piper Cessna, with only three rows of seats. My father and Anna sat backward in the second row, and Delia and I faced them in the third row. Delia was slim and pretty with short brown hair. She told me she'd lost seventy pounds a few years before. (Later I guessed that kind of willpower helped give her strength after we crashed.) Anna was also nice-looking. She was going home to New York.

We took off at 8:36 P.M. It was soon after that my dad looked out the window and noticed the stars were all wrong. From the location of the Big Dipper and other stars, he could tell that we were going west, toward Cuba, as opposed to east, toward Santo Domingo. He asked Anna, who spoke Spanish, to ask the pilot why we were going in the wrong direction, but she was **reluctant**. She didn't want to question authority. I don't know why I didn't use my Spanish to question him myself. The plane was getting cold, but I went to sleep for two hours, during which time, I have been told, we continued going 180 degrees in the wrong direction.

When I woke up, I noticed that we were over water, with no land in sight. The lights on the wings were not functioning properly. They started and stopped—and then stopped altogether. Most of the instruments on the dashboard were not lit up. This was something I hadn't paid too much attention to before but now scared me. The pilot was not getting a response on his radio, and Anna noticed we were running out of gas. The next thing I knew the pilot was saying, "Mayday! Mayday!" into the radio. Anna cried, "Oh, my God, we're going to crash!" I started looking desperately for my life jacket behind and under the seat, but I couldn't find it. Anna found hers. Delia did not. The last thing I saw the pilot doing was tossing his life jacket to my father, who gave it to me and then pulled me on his lap. The plane circled three times around an oil tanker and began the swift descent, gliding toward the sea.

 Stop here for the Strategy Break.

Strategy Break

If you wanted to record the main events in Ariane's autobiography so far, your sequence chain might look like this:

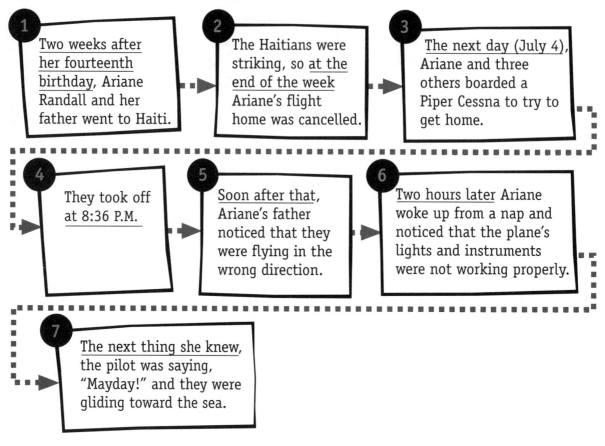

1 Two weeks after her fourteenth birthday, Ariane Randall and her father went to Haiti.

2 The Haitians were striking, so at the end of the week Ariane's flight home was cancelled.

3 The next day (July 4), Ariane and three others boarded a Piper Cessna to try to get home.

4 They took off at 8:36 P.M.

5 Soon after that, Ariane's father noticed that they were flying in the wrong direction.

6 Two hours later Ariane woke up from a nap and noticed that the plane's lights and instruments were not working properly.

7 The next thing she knew, the pilot was saying, "Mayday!" and they were gliding toward the sea.

As you continue reading, pay attention to the sequence of events. Also look for signal words. At the end of this selection you will use some of them to complete a sequence chain of your own.

 **Go on reading.**

We hit the water, and there is a terrible crashing sound as my side of the plane breaks off and water rushes in. I climb out onto the wing. As I stand there I realize my glasses are gone. I fish around in the water and come up with half the frame. I toss it away. The plane is sinking, and my father comes out with the two ladies but no pilot. We swim away from the wreck as the tail disappears beneath the water. Now we are four people and two life jackets in the vast, dark Caribbean Sea. The pilot is nowhere to be seen.

The water is warm, and we swim together, realizing it's the safe thing to do and it's comforting. I am the least hurt, having received a blow to the head, probably from my dad's chin.

He has a gash on his chin and is bleeding heavily (later we found out he'd lost a quart of blood). And he has bruises, especially on his legs. Delia seems to have broken her nose, and there is blood coming from it. She is not in pain, though. Anna has several cuts about her face, a broken arm, and a concussion that has caused partial **amnesia**. She keeps asking what has happened, and we tell her that the airplane has crashed. She will ask again the next minute.

Anna and I have inflated our life jackets. They have lights on them that shine brightly. We all hold on to each other, mainly so that the two without life jackets can remain afloat but partly for security. I'm wearing boxer shorts, a T-shirt over my new red bikini, and Chinese slippers, which I keep on the whole time. My father's pants and shoes are bogging him down, so he takes them off.

We think we see a boat light, but it soon disappears. I wonder if we will ever be rescued. The thought of floating out here until I die is horrifying. I think about sharks and ask Anna and Delia not to splash about so much because it will attract "the wrong kind of fish." Sharks can smell blood a mile away, and three of us are bleeding. There is a silent agreement not to mention the pilot or sharks.

Pretty soon we are all telling each other how glad we are to be together and how much we love each other. We talk about ourselves. Anna is single (we find out later she has a sister). She works with bilingual children and has a new job waiting for her on Monday. She is worried that her job

won't be kept for her if we are not rescued soon. Delia has two boys back in Connecticut, where she works in a real-estate office. She's happy that her daughter, Krista, was not on our flight. My father, Francis, a Russian history professor, will be teaching in the fall. I'll be a sophomore in high school, and if I make it back, I'll have the best what-did-you-do-for-your-summer-vacation essay to hit my teachers in a long time.

All of a sudden a light appears. It looks like a boat light, and we are filled with hope. It appears to be coming steadily toward us. Delia is the only one who can really see since both my father and I have lost our glasses and Anna is fading toward unconsciousness. Anna's injuries are so serious I think she's going to die, but she seems to get better as time goes on. After a half hour (I have my waterproof watch on) the boat light starts to fade. If no boat comes, I decide that I'll swim for land in the morning . . . if there's land anywhere in sight.

We think we see another boat light, but it turns out to be the planet Venus. I feel sick and throw up a lot, which makes me feel better. I drift off into something like sleep. Around 4:30 A.M. Delia spots something that looks like land but might be mist. We wait for dawn to be certain.

When dawn comes, we see it is definitely land. We talk about what to do. Delia and Anna cannot swim well, if at all. If we all go at their pace, there's no way we will reach shore by night. We must make a decision: If my father and I swim for shore, it seems likely we'll make it and be able to tell the Coast Guard where to find Anna and Delia. Or my father might be able to find a boat and come back himself, and in the meantime they could continue to swim. The alternative is to stick together and hope for rescue. My father and I think that splitting up will increase our collective chances of survival. Anna and Delia are reluctant—they feel safer in a group—but they **acknowledge** that splitting up would be better. Anna and Delia have the better life jacket. We separate, not really saying good-bye because we expect to see each other again soon. Even after we swim far away and can't be seen, we hear their voices carrying over the waves.

I keep my father posted on the time. Hours pass, and the nearer we get, the more we realize that we still have many miles to cover. We stop every twenty minutes or so for a rest break, during which I float on my back, which is not so hard to do with a life jacket. I'm not feeling very strong, and I hold on to my dad's shirttails and kick or just let him pull me.

It is noon, and we are still a good distance from land. I no longer hear the voices of Delia and Anna. Every now and then my father tells me he loves me a million, trillion times. I say I will tell him how much I love him when we get to land. I'm too tired to speak just now.

It is two o'clock. I have more energy now and a determination to get to land before dark. My dad is getting weaker but still pushes on. I get salt in my mouth all the time, and my tongue is numb from it. It also gets in my eyes, but I have learned to open them quickly afterward, and for some reason this gets rid of the sting. My hair is all matted. We have not had fresh water or food in thirteen hours, but I'm not hungry, or thirsty.

It is three o'clock, and I'm starting to **hallucinate**. I see dolphins, seals, an occasional shark or two, sailboats, and buoys. I say to my dad, "We can do it." And he says, "Yes . . . we can do it." We keep telling each other "I love you" and that we'll make it to shore. I'm guiding my father now, because he keeps his eyes closed most of the time because of the brine and starts to go in the wrong direction unless I correct him. Two pieces of sugarcane float by us, and like the twig brought back to Noah's Ark, they seem like a sign of hope. I think I see palm trees behind me, but they are not really there. At six o'clock we are maybe a mile from shore and feel certain we will make it before nightfall.

But an hour later, with the shore in sight, the sky has become gray with thunderclouds. We think we see thousands of tiny sailboats, and my dad yells for me to swim fast to them. I try hard as the wind blows and it gets stormier. I look back. I can't see my dad. "Daddy! Where are you?" I scream. No one answers, and I'm crying for the first time. "Help! Somebody please help! Daddy, where are you?" The rain is coming down hard and fast. I stick my tongue out to see if I can get some. It doesn't work too well. I fight with the waves to keep moving toward land. I ask God why He has put this test before me. I tell Him it won't work: I will come through this with flying colors; I'll ace this test.

When the storm passes, I just want to sleep. The problem is that I then drift with the current, which seems to be going out to sea. Sea snails are biting my legs, but I don't have the strength to brush them off. I don't know what has happened to my father. I try the signal we planned—a high shriek—in case we got separated, but he doesn't answer. I fight to keep awake but slowly drift off.

All the girls I hung out with at Club Med are inside my head telling me to swim this way or that. I'm trying to swim toward a hotel, where I can go to sleep. I just want to relax, but I can't because I'll drown. The straps of my life jacket are cutting into me, so I take it off and let it float away. My mouth is burning from the salt—I don't want to die now—if I have to die, can't I at least have a Coke to drink?—something nice-tasting before I drown.

I dream I am destined to drown. Everyone says so, but I'm still trying to find a way out. I dream I inhaled something that burned out my lungs and throat. Then I'm being pulled. I'm being pulled out of the water into a dugout canoe. By two men. Are they capturing me? I must get out. I pick up a piece of wood from the bottom of the boat and try to clobber one of them with it. But he stops me and hits me back.

What a nice way for me to greet my Haitian rescuers—for that's who they were. I saw that they had picked up my dad, too, in another canoe. I heard my dad asking them to start a search for Anna and Delia. The villagers of Bariadelle fed us mangoes and fresh water and crowded around us to watch. They were trying to talk to us in Creole. I could scarcely talk and was confused, but I did manage a *merci beaucoup.*

From Bariadelle we were driven to Dame Marie and deposited in a French Canadian mission station. By this time my body had gone into shock. I had a high fever, a severe sunburn, and a throat infection that made it difficult to swallow anything without coughing. We were taken to a doctor, but by morning my fever was gone. I found out that I'd lost three pounds. (What a crash diet!) My father had lost fifteen. We were driven to a hospital in Anse d'Hainault and eventually, passing through fourteen roadblocks and over sixty miles of bumpy mountain roads, to the city of Jérémie. There my father was able to phone my mother and brother and tell them that we were all right. There was still no news of Anna and Delia.

Back in New York the phone never stops ringing. People call to find out if all this really happened to us. Sometimes I ask myself the same question. But what about Anna and Delia? I think of their voices over the waves as we swam away. What happened to them? What will happen to their families?

It is a miracle my father and I survived. When people ask me what I feel about the whole experience, I say that when you've almost missed life, you see it differently. To be with my family and friends, just to be able to go shopping to replace my lost clothes, each day seems like an amazingly good thing.

Editor's note: On July 8 Ariane Randall and her father returned home to New York. An extensive three-day search was carried out by the U.S. Coast Guard, but Anna Rivera (of New York), Delia Clarke (of Ledyard, Connecticut), and the pilot, Elia Katime (of the Dominican Republic), were never found. ●

Strategy Follow-up

Work with a partner or a small group to complete this activity. On a large sheet of paper, create a sequence chain for the second part of this selection. Begin with event 8, and include only the most important events. Underline any signal words that you include.

LESSON 3: SURVIVAL AT SEA

✓Personal Checklist

Read each question and put a check (✓) in the correct box.

1. In Building Background, how well were you able to predict the kinds of problems that Ariane might describe in "Survival at Sea"?
   - ☐ 3 (extremely well)
   - ☐ 2 (fairly well)
   - ☐ 1 (not well)

2. In the Vocabulary Builder, how well were you able to choose an antonym for each vocabulary word?
   - ☐ 3 (extremely well)
   - ☐ 2 (fairly well)
   - ☐ 1 (not well)

3. How well were you able to help your partner or group complete the sequence chain in the Strategy Follow-up?
   - ☐ 3 (extremely well)
   - ☐ 2 (fairly well)
   - ☐ 1 (not well)

4. How well do you understand why Ariane says that her story "proves that all parents should listen to their children"?
   - ☐ 3 (extremely well)
   - ☐ 2 (fairly well)
   - ☐ 1 (not well)

5. How well do you understand why Ariane tries to "clobber" one of her rescuers?
   - ☐ 3 (extremely well)
   - ☐ 2 (fairly well)
   - ☐ 1 (not well)

Vocabulary Check

Look back at the work you did in the Vocabulary Builder. Then answer each question by circling the correct letter.

1. Which of the following is *not* an example of the word *congregated*?
   a. people lined up outside a theater
   b. the night watchman at a factory
   c. people celebrating at a party

2. What might a high fever cause a person to do?
   a. congregate
   b. hallucinate
   c. acknowledge

3. Anna develops partial amnesia after the crash. What is amnesia?
   a. a loss of vision
   b. a loss of memory
   c. a loss of time

4. Which word is described by the definition "showing unwillingness"?
   a. celebration
   b. indefinitely
   c. reluctance

5. What does it mean when a flight is cancelled indefinitely?
   a. The flight will never take off.
   b. The flight will take off as scheduled.
   c. No one knows when the flight will take off.

Add the numbers that you just checked to get your Personal Checklist score. Fill in your score here. Then turn to page 219 and transfer your score onto Graph 1.

	Personal
Vocabulary	
Strategy	
Comprehension	
TOTAL SCORE	✓ T

Check your answers with your teacher. Give yourself 1 point for each correct answer, and fill in your Vocabulary score here. Then turn to page 219 and transfer your score onto Graph 1.

	Personal
Vocabulary	
Strategy	
Comprehension	
TOTAL SCORE	✓ T

Strategy Check

Review the sequence chain that you completed in the Strategy Follow-up. Also review the selection if necessary. Then answer these questions:

1. At one point, Ariane and the others think they see a boat light. Which signal words describe when the light starts to fade?
   a. all of a sudden
   b. in a long time
   c. after a half hour

2. When does Delia spot something that looks like land?
   a. around 4:30 A.M.
   b. at noon
   c. at 3:00 P.M.

3. Which signal words describe when Ariane and her father take rest breaks while they are swimming?
   a. every twenty minutes or so
   b. around 4:30 A.M.
   c. pretty soon

4. How many days after their ordeal began did Ariane and her father make it back to New York?
   a. 1 days
   b. 2 days
   c. 4 days

5. Which sentence summarizes the main events in this selection?
   a. A plane crashes, two passengers are related, and two others aren't.
   b. A plane crashes, all the passengers are hurt, but they all survive.
   c. A plane crashes, two passengers survive, but two others don't.

Comprehension Check

Review the selection if necessary. Then answer these questions:

1. Why do Ariane and her father take the Piper Cessna to get back home?
   a. They want a more exciting ride than the regular flight can offer.
   b. A strike has caused American Airlines to cancel all its flights.
   c. They decide that riding in a smaller plane will be much safer.

2. What concerns Ariane's father soon after the Piper Cessna takes off?
   a. The plane is traveling in the wrong direction.
   b. The pilot speaks Spanish, but no one else does.
   c. The pilot is not getting a response on his radio.

3. How does Ariane know that Anna has developed partial amnesia?
   a. Anna has broken her arm.
   b. Anna keeps asking what has happened.
   c. Neither of the above answers is correct.

4. Which action shows that Ariane is not thinking clearly at the end of her ordeal?
   a. She loses track of her father and doesn't seem to care.
   b. She doesn't try to brush off the sea snails that are biting her legs.
   c. She thinks she's being captured and tries to hit one of her rescuers.

5. What does Ariane say she has learned from her experience?
   a. She will never go on vacation with her father again.
   b. Piper Cessnas are extremely uncomfortable planes.
   c. When you've almost missed life, you see it differently.

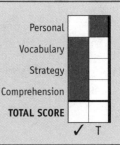

Extending

Choose one or more of these activities:

READ MORE TRUE STORIES OF SURVIVAL

Use the resources listed on this page or ones you find yourself, and read or listen to other true stories of survival. Get together with a small group of class-mates and discuss what you have read or heard. Do all the survivors share any common qualities or char-acter traits? If so, what are they? Have one group member list them as you brainstorm.

INTERVIEW EMERGENCY PERSONNEL

Many people in your community are ready to respond when someone is in danger. Interview one of these emergency workers, such as a member of the fire department, police department, or coast guard. Write several questions to ask that person about the type of rescues he or she has participated in or has been trained to handle. Find out what dangerous situations are common in your area and how the workers help those in need.

PREPARE A TRAVEL BROCHURE FOR HAITI

Create a travel brochure about Haiti. The Web sites on this page can help you get started. In your brochure include a brief history, a map that shows Haiti's location, and a list of its main tourist attrac-tions. In addition, include pictures of people and places on the island. Try to make the idea of travel to Haiti as attractive as possible to a potential visitor.

Resources

Books

Arias, Ron. *Five Against the Sea: A True Story of Courage and Survival.* Onyx, 1990.

Callahan, Steven. *Adrift: Seventy-six Days Lost at Sea.* Mariner Books, 2002.

Doswell, Paul. *Tales of Real Survival.* Real Tales. EDC Publishing, 1995.

Web Sites

http://www.discoverhaiti.com
This Web site provides information on topics such as Haitian art and history.

http://www.lonelyplanet.com/mapshells/caribbean/haiti/haiti.htm
For links related to Haiti, click on the map on this Web page.

Audio Recordings

Callahan, Steven. *Adrift.* Brilliance Audio, 1989.

Reader's Digest Presents Drama in Real Life (abridged). Dove Books Audio, 1997.

Freaky Food

Building Background

What is your favorite food? Whatever it is, there's a good chance that it's different from the favorite food of the person sitting next to you. That's because food preferences are very personal. Often, you like what you are used to. For example, if your family regularly eats pasta, you probably enjoy eating it. If you were used to munching on fried ants, however, chances are good that you'd like those instead. Just because a food is familiar, however, doesn't always mean you have to like it.

Fill in the chart below with your favorite and least favorite foods. Then compare your chart with those of other classmates. Which foods did most students list as their favorite and least favorite?

Kind of Food	Favorite	Least Favorite
Meats, Poultry, and/or Fish		
Vegetables		
Fruits		
Dairy Products		
Breads and Grains		

delicacy

endangered

intestines

larvae

saliva

Vocabulary Builder

1. Choose one of the words in the margin to complete each sentence below. Use a dictionary if you need help.

2. Save your work. You will refer to it again in the Vocabulary Check.

   a. It is illegal to hunt and eat animals that are _____.

   b. When people smell appetizing food, their mouths sometimes begin to produce _____.

   c. Because snails are considered a _____, they are served only in the finest restaurants.

   d. The immature forms of many kinds of insects are called _____ .

   e. Food passes through the esophagus, the stomach, and the _____ on its journey through the body.

Strategy Builder

How to Read an Informational Article

- An **informational article** is nonfiction that gives readers information about a particular subject, or topic. The **topic** is what the article is all about and is usually stated in the **title**. For example, the topic of the article you are about to read is food—especially food that you might find "freaky," or unusual.

- Every piece of nonfiction follows a particular pattern of organization. The most common patters are listed in the margin. The pattern of "Freaky Food" is description. **Descriptions** usually tell what things are, what they do, or how and why they work.

- Descriptions are usually organized according to **main ideas** and **supporting details.** Read the following paragraph and try to locate its topic, main ideas, and supporting details.

CLIPBOARD

Most Common Organization Patterns of Nonfiction

Jellyfish are sea animals that are made of jellylike material between two layers of cells. The "jelly" supports the cell layers and helps the jellyfish float. Some people think that a jellyfish looks like an umbrella. It has a short tube with frilly projections hanging from the center of its body. Tentacles hang from the edges of its body. To move, a jellyfish expands its body, then quickly pulls it closed. This action squeezes water away from the body and helps the jelly-fish move in the opposite direction from the water jet.

- If you wanted to arrange this paragraph's topic, main ideas, and supporting details on a graphic organizer, you could use a **concept map,** or web. It might look like this:

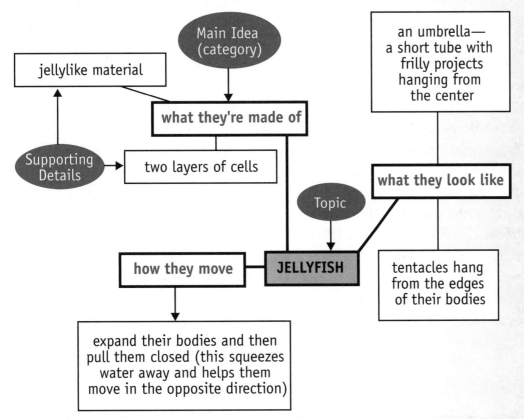

Freaky Food

by Nancy Shepherdson

As you read the following article, apply the strategies you just learned. Look for the main ideas and the details that support them.

So you think spinach is yucky? Try some fish eyes or sheep's stomach. People around the world eat some interesting things.

Have you ever thought about eating ants? Kids in southern Mexico like to munch on fried winged ants, sold in paper bags like popcorn. That probably makes you say, "*ewww.*" But it's perfectly normal for them. People naturally eat the foods of their country. They like them.

Even bird spit.

Around the world, *including* America, people enjoy what others might call "weird" foods. Snakes, bats, bugs, camel's hump. Think about that the next time your mom fixes you spinach or broccoli or liver. Wouldn't you rather have roasted termites instead?

Fish for Breakfast

In Japan, many kids eat fish first thing in the morning. Makes sense, in a country surrounded by water.

Later in the day, they might have jellyfish. The sting from these jellyfish can kill, so the poison must be removed first. That takes four to eight days of soaking in cold water. After that, all that's left is a crunchy treat, like chicken nuggets, usually eaten with a dipping sauce.

Other fishy meals around the world include fermented shark, or *hakarl,* eaten in Iceland. To make hakarl, just bury a shark in sand for three years, then dig it up and dig in.

In Alaska, a well-loved Native American dish is fish eyes. (Think tiny tomatoes. *Squish.*)

You're Bugging Me!

Ounce for ounce insects are a great source of energy. When food supplies ran low, American pioneers ate Mormon crickets and other bugs on the journey west. In more than half the world today, including Africa, Australia, Europe, Asia and America, insects are on the menu.

Most bugs taste like shrimp, nuts or the spices they are cooked in. Especially tasty, it is said, are beetle **larvae**, ant eggs and termites.

You might even be eating bugs without knowing it. Red candy is sometimes colored with dye made from the cochineal beetle. And strange but true: The Federal government allows a certain percentage of insect parts in foods like hot dogs.

If you run out of food in the wilderness, insects can save your life.

"Just steer away from bright-colored insects," warns Dr. Gene Defoliart, who studied bugs at the University of Wisconsin. That's nature's way of saying, "Don't eat me."

 Stop here for the Strategy Break.

Strategy Break

If you were to create a concept map for the section of this article called "You're Bugging Me!" it might look like this:

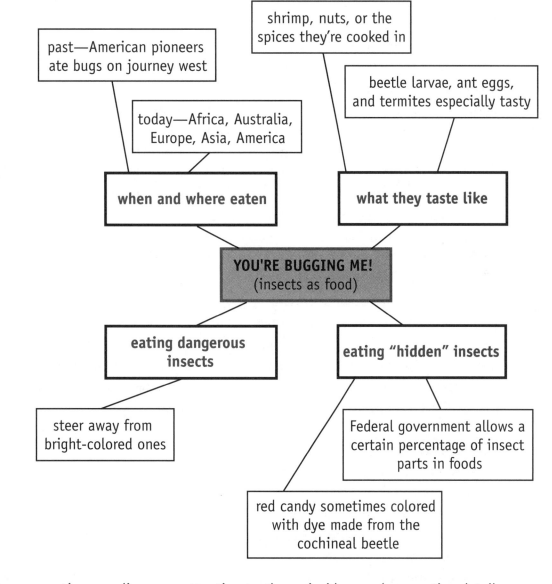

As you continue reading, pay attention to the main ideas and supporting details. At the end of this article, you will use some of them to create a concept map of your own.

➡ Go on reading.

Chicken Paws

Our grocery stores are full of food. But there are a lot of things we won't find there. Ever wonder what happens to chickens' feet, for instance? Every week, the United States sends 15 million pounds of meaty "chicken paws" to Asia. They are mostly made into soup.

Bird's nest soup is a Chinese favorite. It's made from the **saliva** that tiny birds called swifts use to make their nests. When the nests are boiled and cleaned, the swifts' spit looks just like noodles. This dish is sometimes served with hundred-year-old eggs. They're not actually 100 years old. They are simply raw eggs soaked in salty water for about three months, then buried in the ground. The yolks turn green but are supposed to be delicious.

People on the Pacific island of Samoa once ate baked fruit bats before the creatures became **endangered**. Rats (and mice) are sometimes eaten for dinner in West Africa, Asia and France. In our country, hunters may serve opossum, squirrel, raccoon, deer and even skunk to their families.

Insides Out

Meat is more than just steaks and hamburgers and fish sticks. It could be the brains or heart or tongue of a cow or other animal. Look carefully in your store's meat department and you'll probably find some "organ meats." (You can't miss the tongue. That's exactly what it looks like.) You've already eaten organ meats if you like hot dogs or lunch meat. They're in there.

Other cultures are much more adventurous than Americans when it comes to chowing down on every part of the animal.

In Scotland, a sheep's stomach is filled with oatmeal, organ meats, fat, spices and fruits, then boiled. That's called *haggis*. In Saudi Arabia, roast camel's hump is a tender **delicacy**. And in southern Africa, the large **intestines** of antelopes called elands are barbequed to make *vet derm*, or "fat gut."

Eat a Weed

Did you know you can eat dandelions? Europeans and Americans have been eating them for centuries. The fresh, young leaves make a healthy salad. And the yellow flowers can be deep fried, like French fries. Just be sure to wash them well.

American soldiers in the Persian Gulf War learned how to survive on wild prickly pear cactus. You can eat its fruit raw, but be careful of the spines. The "pads" or branches can also be roasted over a fire. And when water is short, you can peel the skin off the pads and suck moisture out of the pulp inside.

Acorns are another wild source of food. They can be used in bread, soups, stews and to make coffee. Catnip can be made into tea. And seaweed is now part of many of the foods we eat every day. Your fast-food hamburger, for instance, might contain some seaweed. So might your ice cream. Bet you can't taste it.

No Thank You!

Eating a burger may seem normal to you. But a person from India might get sick thinking about it. A major religion in India, called Hinduism, forbids killing cattle. So Hindus don't eat beef.

Beliefs about food occur in every culture. Traditional Navajo will not eat bear because they believe they share a kinship with the soul of the bear. The Zulu people in southern Africa avoid plentiful local lizards because they believe them to be the souls of their ancestors. And some residents of Sardinia, an Italian island, hate seafood. They were invaded by pirates hundreds of years ago and have avoided the sea ever since. ●

Strategy Follow-up

Now create a concept map for the section of this article called "Eat a Weed." Part of the map has been filled in for you.

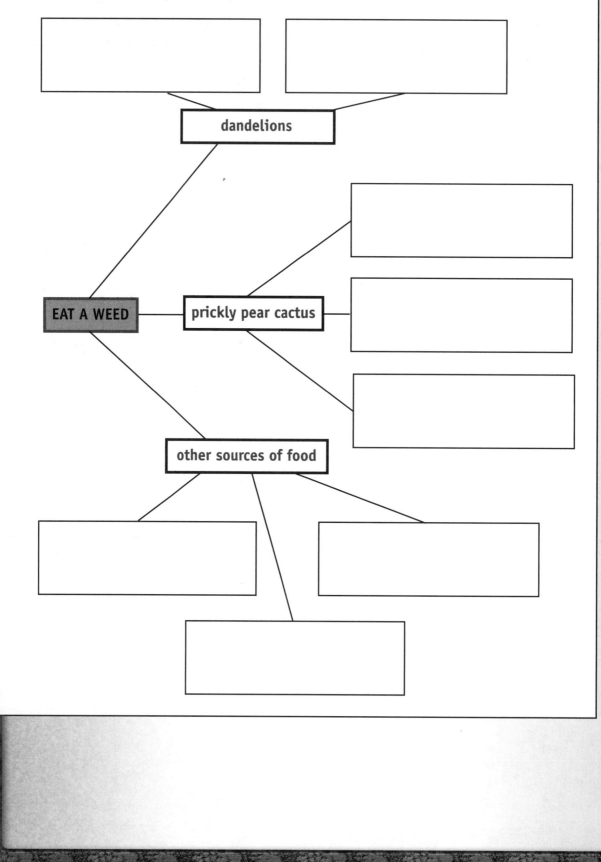

✓Personal Checklist

Read each question and put a check (✓) in the correct box.

1. How well do you understand the information presented in this article?
   - ☐ 3 (extremely well)
   - ☐ 2 (fairly well)
   - ☐ 1 (not well)

2. After reading this article, how well would you be able to describe what some "freaky foods" are?
   - ☐ 3 (extremely well)
   - ☐ 2 (fairly well)
   - ☐ 1 (not well)

3. How well were you able to fill in the chart in Building Background?
   - ☐ 3 (extremely well)
   - ☐ 2 (fairly well)
   - ☐ 1 (not well)

4. How well were you able to complete the sentences in the Vocabulary Builder?
   - ☐ 3 (extremely well)
   - ☐ 2 (fairly well)
   - ☐ 1 (not well)

5. How well were you able to complete the concept map in the Strategy Follow-up?
   - ☐ 3 (extremely well)
   - ☐ 2 (fairly well)
   - ☐ 1 (not well)

Vocabulary Check

Look back at the work you did in the Vocabulary Builder. Then answer each question by circling the correct letter.

1. What other word from this article has the same meaning as *saliva*?
   - a. larvae
   - b. intestines
   - c. spit

2. Which animals are most likely to be considered endangered?
   - a. ants
   - b. tigers
   - c. houseflies

3. Which of the following is an organ of the body?
   - a. larvae
   - b. saliva
   - c. intestines

4. Which meaning of the word *delicacy* fits this selection?
   - a. something good to eat
   - b. state of being dainty or fine
   - c. state of needing special care

5. Immature insects are often called
   - a. worms
   - b. maggots
   - c. larvae

Add the numbers that you just checked to get your Personal Checklist score. Fill in your score here. Then turn to page 219 and transfer your score onto Graph 1.

Personal
Vocabulary
Strategy
Comprehension
TOTAL SCORE
✓ T

Check your answers with your teacher. Give yourself 1 point for each correct answer, and fill in your Vocabulary score here. Then turn to page 219 and transfer your score onto Graph 1.

Personal
Vocabulary
Strategy
Comprehension
TOTAL SCORE
✓ T

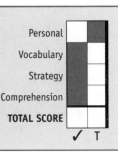

Strategy Check

Review the concept map that you completed for "Eat a Weed." Also review the rest of the article. Then answer these questions:

1. Which supporting detail does *not* describe how to prepare dandelions for eating?
   a. Europeans and Americans have been eating dandelions for centuries.
   b. Dandelion leaves can make a healthy salad.
   c. Their yellow flowers can be deep fried.

2. Under which main idea would you list the detail that catnip can be made into tea?
   a. dandelions
   b. prickly pear cactus
   c. other sources of food

3. If you were to create a concept map for "Insides Out," which food would you *not* include as a supporting detail?
   a. steak
   b. haggis
   c. vet derm

4. Which detail describes the way some people eat organ meats?
   a. You can eat wild prickly pear cactus raw.
   b. In Scotland, people eat boiled sheep's stomach.
   c. Hakarl, eaten in Iceland, is fermented shark.

5. What helps you identify the main ideas discussed in this article?
   a. the title
   b. the headings
   c. the italic words

Comprehension Check

Review the article if necessary. Then answer these questions:

1. According to the article, what do many kids eat for breakfast in Japan?
   a. fried winged ants
   b. chicken nuggets
   c. fish

2. Why did American pioneers eat Mormon crickets and other bugs on the journey west?
   a. Their food supply was running low.
   b. They thought crickets were a delicacy.
   c. They couldn't keep crickets out of their food.

3. What is the main ingredient in bird's nest soup?
   a. swifts' saliva, or spit
   b. hundred-year-old eggs
   c. green eggs

4. Why do Hindus refuse to eat beef?
   a. because they get sick when they eat beef
   b. because their religion forbids the killing of cattle
   c. because they don't enjoy the taste of beef

5. The Federal government allows a certain percentage of insect parts in foods. What does this suggest about insects?
   a. It is dangerous to eat insect parts.
   b. Eating insect parts doesn't harm people.
   c. Insect parts make a great seasoning.

Check your answers with your teacher. Give yourself 1 point for each correct answer, and fill in your Strategy score here. Then turn to page 219 and transfer your score onto Graph 1.

Personal
Vocabulary
Strategy
Comprehension
TOTAL SCORE
✓ T

Check your answers with your teacher. Give yourself 1 point for each correct answer, and fill in your Comprehension score here. Then turn to page 219 and transfer your score onto Graph 1.

Personal
Vocabulary
Strategy
Comprehension
TOTAL SCORE
✓ T

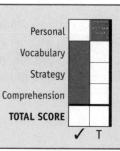

Extending

Choose one or both of these activities:

TAKE A SURVEY

"What is the strangest food you have ever eaten?" Ask that question of everyone in your class. Then assemble their answers on a chart or a graph. Count how many different foods were mentioned. If you can, put the foods into different categories. Then have the class vote on the food that they think is the strangest, or most exotic.

PREPARE A "FREAKY FOOD" COOKBOOK

Work with other members of your class to plan and create a "freaky food" cookbook. Do some research, and then list which foods you want to include. (Use the resources provided on this page, or check the Internet for its many recipe sites.) Assign partners to find and copy the recipes for one or more of the foods on your list. Then compile all the recipes into a cookbook. You might organize the book's sections by countries of origin. Or you might organize them by different plants, animals, or insects—or body parts. Really brave students might want to prepare and sample one or more of the recipes.

Resources

Books

Menzel, Peter, and Faith D'Aluisio. *Man Eating Bugs: The Art and Science of Eating Insects.* Ten Speed Press, 1998.

Ramos-Elorduy, Julieta. *Creepy Crawly Cuisine: The Gourmet Guide to Edible Insects.* Park Street Press, 1998.

Web Sites

http://www.ent.iastate.edu/misc/insectsasfood.html
You can find "Insect Recipes" on this Web site.

http://www.geocities.com/EnchantedForest/9702/snacks.html
This Web page describes crawling snacks.

The Quick Little Fellows

Building Background

Have you ever tried eating with chopsticks? If so, how successful were you? The selection you are about to read provides a brief history of chopsticks, as well as instructions on how to use them. If you have never tried using chopsticks, this selection might help you learn to use them with grace, speed, and skill.

agility

inefficient

manipulating

tapered

uniquely

Vocabulary Builder

1. The questions below contain words from "The Quick Little Fellows." Those words are boldfaced. Before you begin reading the selection, try to answer as many of the questions as possible.

2. As you read the selection, find the boldfaced words and use context to figure them out. Then, after you've read the selection, go back and check or change your answers.

3. Save your work. You will refer to it again in the Vocabulary Check.

    a. What are some foods that are **uniquely** Chinese? _____
    _____

    b. What utensils do you have an easier time **manipulating**—chopsticks or a fork and knife? _____

    c. Why might some people think that a spoon with a rounded bottom is **inefficient**? _____

    d. Who would show greater **agility**—someone who uses chopsticks or someone who uses a fork? _____ Why? _____
    _____

    e. Some kinds of chopsticks are **tapered** on the end. What does that mean?
    _____

Strategy Builder

Following the Steps in a Process

- When writers describe the process of how to do or make something, their main purpose for writing is to **inform**. They usually use the organizational patterns of both **description** and **sequence** as they describe the steps in the process.

- To make the sequence of steps as clear as possible, writers often use **signal words**. Some examples of signal words are *first, next, then,* and *finally.*

- The following paragraph describes how to make chow mein. Use the underlined signal words and phrases to follow the sequence.

Vegetable chow mein is a healthful and delicious dinner. To make it, follow these steps: <u>First</u>, wash and cut all the vegetables you will need, and <u>then</u> put them aside. <u>Next</u> get a pan and sauté all the vegetables in oil. <u>After the vegetables are lightly cooked</u>, add a sauce. <u>Then</u> cook about five more minutes. <u>Finally</u>, serve the dish over rice, and dig in!

- If you wanted to track the steps in the process above, you could use a **sequence chain**. It might look like this:

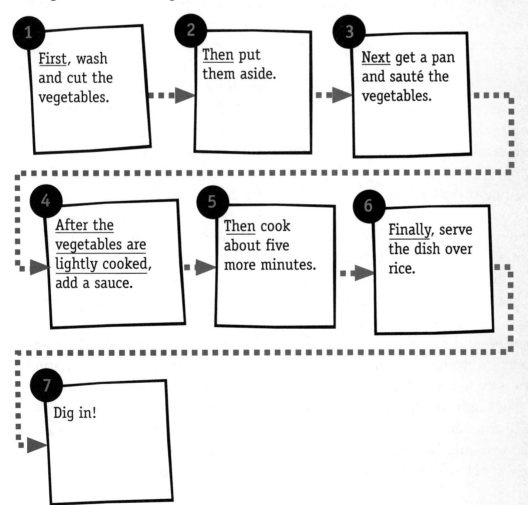

The Quick Little Fellows

by James Cross Giblin

In this part of "The Quick Little Fellows," the author first provides a brief history of chopsticks. Then he describes the steps involved in setting a Chinese table and eating a meal. See if you can use the signal words to help you follow the steps.

No one knows exactly when the Chinese began to use chopsticks. But some say it was greedy people who thought of them first.

According to this story, it happened at the beginning of Chinese written history, around 3000 B.C., when most people cooked their food in tripods. These were metal pots that stood on three squat legs and could be set directly over a fire.

The large pots took an hour or so to cool after the food was cooked, and some people were too greedy to wait. Grabbing a pair of sticks, they poked at the steaming food and lifted out the best pieces for themselves. Others copied them, and within a short time people all over China were eating with chopsticks.

Another explanation credits the Chinese preference for chopsticks over knives to the philosopher Confucius, who lived from 551 to 479 B.C. Confucius once remarked that honorable and upright people would rather see an animal alive than dead. And if they heard the noise and screams of an animal being killed, they would not want to eat its flesh.

For Confucius, knives were a constant reminder of such killings. Consequently, he wrote in one of his books: "The honorable and upright man keeps well away from both the slaughterhouse and the kitchen, and he allows no knives on his table."

Whether or not Confucius was responsible, we do know that by 400 B.C. people throughout China were using chopsticks. Hand in hand with their adoption came the development of a **uniquely** Chinese style of cooking. Meat and vegetables were either cut into bite-size pieces or cooked until they were so tender that they required no cutting. Even when poultry and fish were served whole, the meat was so tender that it could be picked easily off the bones with a pair of chopsticks.

Besides chopsticks, the Chinese from very early in their history also used spoons. They were made of hard earthenware called porcelain and had flat bottoms so that a diner could set one down on a tabletop without spilling the contents. The Chinese thought the round-bottomed European spoon was very **inefficient!**

Unlike Europeans, the Chinese never used their spoons to eat any food except soup. For everything else they used chopsticks, **manipulating** the two sticks smoothly and quickly as they plucked bits of food from first one dish and then another. In fact, the word for chopsticks in Chinese means "the quick little fellows."

Most Chinese chopsticks are ten to twelve inches long and about as thick as a pencil. Those for children can be as short as five inches. Those used by the hostess or host to pass special delicacies to their guests are sometimes as long as twenty inches.

Chopsticks have been made from many different materials over the centuries: bamboo, wood, jade, ivory, gold, and silver. Many upper-class families in old China used ivory chopsticks tipped with silver. Since ancient times the Chinese had believed that silver was a protection against poison. If the silver-tipped chopsticks came into contact with food that had been poisoned, they would turn black—or so people said.

In setting a Chinese table, the chopsticks are placed either to the right or below a small, central plate. The soup bowl is located to the upper right of the plate with the flat-bottomed soupspoon in it. A bowl of rice, served with every Chinese meal, is put directly on the plate.

At Chinese banquets, the meat and vegetable dishes are served one after another, and the guests help themselves to portions of each, putting them on their small plates. The soup is served last. At family dinners, all the dishes are in the middle of the table at the beginning of the meal, with the soup tureen in the center.

A single pair of chopsticks is used to eat all the dishes, even at banquets. Often the diners are provided with small rests of porcelain on which they can lay their chopsticks between courses so that they won't soil the tablecloth.

Chopsticks serve as signals during a Chinese meal. At the start, the host raises his chopsticks over his rice bowl to invite the guests to begin eating. Then he puts his rice bowl to one side of the plate, and all the other diners do the same. At the end of the meal, the diners set their chopsticks even and parallel across the tops of their rice bowls to indicate that they've finished.

 Stop here for the Strategy Break.

Strategy Break

If you were to arrange the steps that describe what happens during a Chinese meal, your sequence chain might look like this:

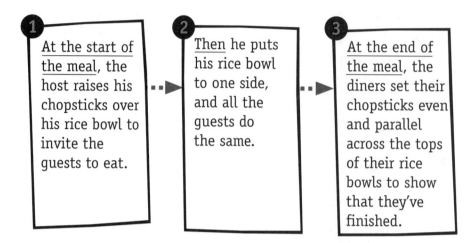

1 At the start of the meal, the host raises his chopsticks over his rice bowl to invite the guests to eat.

2 Then he puts his rice bowl to one side, and all the guests do the same.

3 At the end of the meal, the diners set their chopsticks even and parallel across the tops of their rice bowls to show that they've finished.

As you continue reading, keep track of the steps involved in the process of using chopsticks. Also look for signal words. You will use some of them later to create a sequence chain of your own.

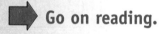 **Go on reading.**

Chopsticks often seem awkward to handle at first, even for Chinese children. But when you learn how to hold them firmly but lightly, there's no strain at all, and their use quickly becomes second nature.

To begin, hold your right hand (or your left, if you're left-handed) in a relaxed position. Place the first chopstick between the tip of your fourth, or ring, finger and the base of your thumb. Be sure you pick up the chopstick the right way: the top half, which you hold in your hand, is squared; the tip, which takes up the food, is rounded. Your thumb should be around the squared section and your ring finger at the midpoint of the chopstick.

Brace the chopstick against the fourth finger with the middle of the thumb, but keep the tip of the thumb free. You'll need it to help hold the second chopstick. Place the second stick between your thumb tip and the tips of your index and middle fingers. Grasp the stick lightly so that you can move it up and down against the other chopstick, which remains still.

When you want to pick up a piece of food, push upward on the second chopstick with your middle finger. This will open the tips of the chopsticks. To grasp the food, push down on the second stick with the same middle finger. The two chopsticks will come together with the food pinched securely between the two tips. Then you can raise the bite swiftly to your mouth.

It's important to keep the tips of the chopsticks even with one another at all times. If one is higher and one is lower, the chopsticks will not work.

Rice is hard to eat with chopsticks because the individual grains are so small. However, the Chinese have found a solution to this problem. They lift the rice bowl with their thumb resting on the rim and their index and middle fingers grasping the bottom. Then, holding the bowl quite close to the mouth, they use their chopsticks to transfer globs of rice from bowl to mouth. When they get near the bottom of the bowl, they raise it up to the lips in a drinking position and scoop out the last few grains.

The use of chopsticks spread from China to the neighboring countries of Vietnam and Korea. Eventually, like many other Chinese customs, it also reached Japan. This occurred sometime before A.D. 500, and within a short time people throughout the Japanese islands were eating with chopsticks.

The Japanese call their chopsticks *hashi*, meaning "bridge," because the sticks acted as a bridge between bowl and mouth. Japanese chopsticks differed somewhat from the Chinese variety. They had **tapered** rather than rounded ends and were most often made of lacquered wood instead of bamboo or ivory.

Basically, the Japanese handle their chopsticks in the same way the Chinese do. And they've done so for centuries. When a merchant from Italy, Francesco Carletti, visited Japan at the end of the 1500s, he wrote in his journal about the natives' skillful use of chopsticks. "They are the length of a man's hand and as thick as a quill for writing," wrote Carletti. "With these two sticks, the Japanese are able to fill their mouths with marvelous swiftness and **agility**. They can pick up any piece of food, no matter how tiny it is, without ever soiling their hands." ●

Strategy Follow-up

Work with a partner or a small group to complete this activity. On a large sheet of paper, create a sequence chain the shows the steps in the process of holding and using chopsticks. Underline any signal words that you use. If you'd like, add drawings or photographs to your sequence chain to help clarify each step.

✓Personal Checklist

Read each question and put a check (✓) in the correct box.

1. How well do you understand the information presented in this selection?
    - ☐ 3 (extremely well)
    - ☐ 2 (fairly well)
    - ☐ 1 (not well)

2. After reading this selection, how well would you be able to show and tell someone how to use chopsticks?
    - ☐ 3 (extremely well)
    - ☐ 2 (fairly well)
    - ☐ 1 (not well)

3. By the time you finished reading this selection, how well were you able to answer the questions in the Vocabulary Builder?
    - ☐ 3 (extremely well)
    - ☐ 2 (fairly well)
    - ☐ 1 (not well)

4. How well do you understand the different explanations about why the Chinese use chopsticks?
    - ☐ 3 (extremely well)
    - ☐ 2 (fairly well)
    - ☐ 1 (not well)

5. How well were you able to help your partner or group complete the sequence chain in the Strategy Follow-up?
    - ☐ 3 (extremely well)
    - ☐ 2 (fairly well)
    - ☐ 1 (not well)

Vocabulary Check

Look back at the work you did in the Vocabulary Builder. Then answer each question by circling the correct letter.

1. Which of these phrases defines the word *unique*?
    a. up to date
    b. one of a kind
    c. quite ordinary

2. Of these three activities, which requires the most agility?
    a. sitting and reading a book
    b. typing a report for school
    c. watching a movie on TV

3. If you manipulate chopsticks well, what do you do with them?
    a. control and use them easily
    b. break them successfully
    c. make them skillfully

4. What is an example of an inefficient way to eat rice?
    a. Pick it up and eat it one grain at a time.
    b. Scoop up globs of it from bowl to mouth.
    c. Use a spoon to bring it to your mouth.

5. Japanese chopsticks are tapered. What is a synonym for *tapered*?
    a. quick
    b. narrowed
    c. wooden

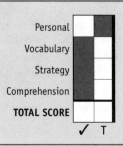

Add the numbers that you just checked to get your Personal Checklist score. Fill in your score here. Then turn to page 219 and transfer your score onto Graph 1.

Personal
Vocabulary
Strategy
Comprehension
TOTAL SCORE
✓ T

Check your answers with your teacher. Give yourself 1 point for each correct answer, and fill in your Vocabulary score here. Then turn to page 219 and transfer your score onto Graph 1.

Personal
Vocabulary
Strategy
Comprehension
TOTAL SCORE
✓ T

Strategy Check

Review the sequence chain you that helped complete in the Strategy Follow-up. Also review the rest of the selection. Then answer these questions:

1. Which of the following is *not* an example of signal words?

   a. in China

   b. to begin

   c. at all times

2. In the process of using chopsticks, which of these steps comes first?

   a. Pinch the food between the two sticks.

   b. Hold your hand in a relaxed position.

   c. Brace the chopstick against the fourth finger.

3. What must you do when you want to pick up a piece of food with your chopsticks?

   a. Push upward on the second chopstick with your middle finger.

   b. Place the first chopstick between your fourth finger and your thumb.

   c. Push down on the second stick with the same middle finger.

4. In what order does the selection say that the use of chopsticks spread from country to country?

   a. Vietnam, Korea, Japan, China

   b. China, Vietnam, Korea, Japan

   c. China, Japan, Korea, Japan

5. Which signal words could you use to describe how long the Japanese have been using chopsticks?

   a. for years

   b. for decades

   c. for centuries

Comprehension Check

Review the selection if necessary. Then answer these questions:

1. According to one old story, when were chopsticks invented?

   a. around 3000 B.C.

   b. around A.D. 500

   c. at the end of the 1500s

2. Why is Chinese food well suited to the use of chopsticks?

   a. It is so tender it doesn't need to be cut.

   b. Its ingredients are usually bite-size.

   c. Both of the above reasons are correct.

3. Why did the Chinese think that round-bottomed European spoons were inefficient?

   a. because they were not made of porcelain

   b. because they would spill if they were set on a table

   c. because they were only useful for eating soup

4. What does the Chinese word for *chopsticks* mean?

   a. sticks used for chopping food

   b. the quick little fellows

   c. bridge between bowl and mouth

5. In what main way were Japanese chopsticks different from Chinese ones?

   a. They had tapered ends rather than rounded ones.

   b. They always had tips made of silver.

   c. They looked like bridges instead of sticks.

Check your answers with your teacher. Give yourself 1 point for each correct answer, and fill in your Strategy score here. Then turn to page 219 and transfer your score onto Graph 1.

Personal		
Vocabulary		
Strategy		
Comprehension		
TOTAL SCORE		

✓ T

Check your answers with your teacher. Give yourself 1 point for each correct answer, and fill in your Comprehension score here. Then turn to page 219 and transfer your score onto Graph 1.

Personal		
Vocabulary		
Strategy		
Comprehension		
TOTAL SCORE		

✓ T

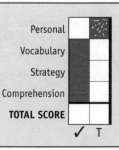

Extending

Choose one or both of these activities:

TAKE A FIELD TRIP TO A CHINESE RESTAURANT

With the help of your teacher or parents, arrange a trip to a Chinese restaurant. Before the meal, ask the owner of the restaurant to demonstrate the proper use of chopsticks. (How do his or her instructions match the ones in this selection?) Also ask someone to explain the different foods you will be eating, as well as how they are prepared. If you feel comfortable enough, eat part or all of your meal with chopsticks. Which foods are the easiest to manipulate with them?

MAKE A DEMONSTRATION VIDEO

Practice using chopsticks until you can handle them well. Then work with one or two partners to make a demonstration video. Using the resources listed on this page, prepare a Chinese dish, or order one from a restaurant. Then show how to hold the sticks and manipulate them to pick up the food quickly and easily. If you don't feel comfortable being filmed yourself, interview and film someone who has used chopsticks since childhood (possibly the restaurant owner from the previous activity), so that viewers can see how "swift and agile" the process can be.

Resources

Books

Brown, Carrie C. *Asian Vegetables: Chinese Style Cooking.* Jain Publishing, 1996.

Callery, Emma, ed. *Chinese Cooking for Everyone.* Crescent Books, 1991.

Yan, Martin. *A Wok for All Seasons.* Doubleday, 1988.

Web Sites

http://www2.gol.com/users/issott/JRHome/Convention/Chopsticks.html
This Web page has diagrams and instructions related to using chopsticks.

http://www-2.cs.cmu.edu/~mjw/recipes/ethnic/chinese/chinese.html
You can find several recipes for Chinese dishes on this site.

Learning New Words

VOCABULARY

From Lesson 3
- indefinitely

From Lesson 5
- inefficient

Prefixes

A prefix is a word part that is added to the beginning of a root word. (*Pre-* means "before.") When you add a prefix, you often change the root word's meaning and function. For example, the prefix *un-* means "not" or "the opposite of." So adding *un-* to the root word *even* changes the word to its opposite, *uneven.*

in-

The prefix *in-* has the same meaning as *un-*: "not" or "the opposite of." In Lesson 5 you learned that the Chinese thought European spoons were inefficient because their contents spilled when they were set on a table. *Inefficient* means "not efficient" or "wasteful."

Match each word with its definition.

1. inconsistent   not convincing or final

2. inconclusive   not allowable

3. inaccurate   not the same

4. indecent   not correct or precise

5. inadmissible   not proper

re-

From Lesson 2
- repress

The prefix *re-* can mean "again," or it can mean "back." For example, the word *reheat* means "heat again." In "The Squid," however, the narrator cannot *repress,* or hold back, his disgust when he first sees the giant squid.

Write the word for each definition.

1. pay back   _____

2. wind again or over   _____

3. act back   _____

4. adjust again   _____

5. start over or again   _____

Suffix

A suffix is a word part that is added to the end of a root word. When you add a suffix, you often change the root word's meaning and function. For example, the suffix *-ful* means "full of," so the root word *joy* changes from a noun to an adjective meaning "full of joy."

-ly

The suffix *-ly* can turn words into adverbs meaning "in a _____ way, or manner." Or it can turn words into adjectives meaning "like a _____." In Lesson 5 you learned that the Chinese first used chopsticks to eat hot foods quickly. *Quickly* is an adverb meaning "in a speedy manner." You also learned that they developed a style of cooking that was uniquely their own. *Uniquely* is an adjective meaning "like no other."

Write the definition for each word below.

1. brotherly _____

2. cautiously _____

3. cheerfully _____

4. neighborly _____

Prefixes and Suffixes

Some root words have both a prefix and a suffix added to them. For example, in the word *indefinitely*, the prefix *in-* means "not" and the suffix *-ly* means "in a _____ way." So *indefinitely* means "in a way that is not definite or clear."

Write a word for each definition below.

1. in a way that is not complete _____

2. in a way that is not direct _____

3. in a way that is not expensive _____

4. in a way that is not convenient _____

VOCABULARY

From Lesson 3
• indefinitely

From Lesson 5
• uniquely

From Lesson 3
• indefinitely

LESSON 6 The Tale of the Tiger's Paintbrush (Part 1)

Building Background

Art surrounds us all. Paintings in museums are art, of course. But so are the ads that you see on billboards and in magazines. Every building is the work of an architect, another kind of artist. The dances you see on music videos, as well as the music you hear on the radio—all are forms of art.

Think for a moment about all the art forms that you see and enjoy. Then complete the concept map below. Compare you ideas with those of your classmates.

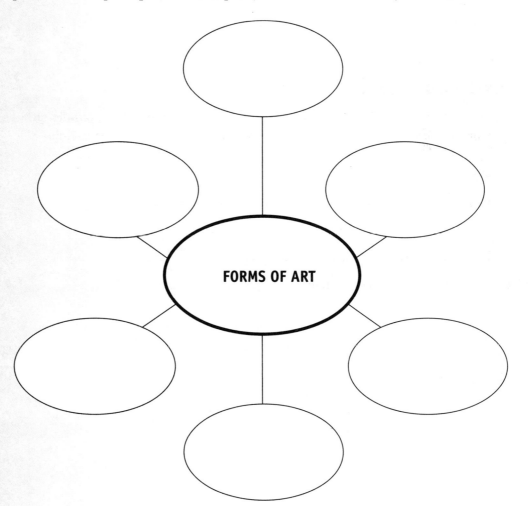

FORMS OF ART

Vocabulary Builder

1. The words in the margin are all related to art and artists. Use a dictionary to find any of the words that you don't know. Then, on a separate sheet of paper, use each word in a paragraph about art. Be sure to use each word at least once.

2. Save your work. You will refer to it again in the Vocabulary Check.

Strategy Builder

Making Predictions While Reading a Fantasy

- The story you are about to begin in this lesson is a type of fiction called fantasy. A **fantasy** is an imaginary story in which the normal rules of life do not always apply. Its lack of realism is shown in its setting, its characters, and its plot.

- To enjoy a fantasy, you have to let go of your everyday expectations. A fantasy may take place in a **setting** such as outer space or a time machine bound for a prehistoric age. The **characters** can be talking tigers or timid giants. The **plot** can include events that you will never see in real life, such as a character falling into a hole and coming out on the other side of the world.

- The **author's purpose** for writing a fantasy may be simply to entertain the reader. However, many fantasies also have a hidden purpose—to teach. Often the author wants to teach a lesson or moral through one or more of the characters.

- As you read any story, you are likely to make predictions. You know that a **prediction** is a guess based on clues that the author provides. Because fantasy stories contain elements that the author makes up in his or her imagination, predicting what will happen in a fantasy story can be a bit more fun and challenging. As you read Part 1 of "The Tale of the Tiger's Paintbrush," look carefully for any clues that the author provides—no matter how large or small. Also use what you know about fantasy stories to help you make your predictions.

artist

envision

handiwork

hue

landscapes

paintbrush

strokes

surface

vermilion

The Tale of the Tiger's Paintbrush (Part 1)

by Lloyd Alexander

As you begin reading this fantasy story, keep the title in mind. It just might provide a clue that will help you make predictions later.

In his wanderings through the countryside, Chen-cho the painter comes upon a young man being attacked by robbers. Chen-cho helps the man fight off the robbers, but his paints and brushes are ruined. In gratitude, the stranger gives Chen-cho a sandalwood box. Upon opening it, Chen-cho finds a wonderful collection of brushes, paints, and other tools.

Chen-cho the painter was a good-natured, easygoing sort. He liked his food and drink, though as often as not he did without either. Not because he suffered any lack of customers. He was, in fact, a most excellent **artist**, and many who saw his pictures wished eagerly to buy them. To Chen-cho, however, parting with one of his **landscapes** was like having a tooth pulled. Sometimes, of course, he was obliged to do so, when he needed a few strings of cash to keep body and soul together—although usually he spent the money on paper and paint. On the other hand, out of sudden impulse or foolish whim, he was just as likely to give away one of his pictures to a passerby who wistfully admired but could ill afford to purchase it.

For the rest, he was a little absent-minded, his head so filled with colors and shapes that he lost track of time, forgot to wash his face or change his clothes. With his collapsing umbrella, his felt cap, his bespattered trousers flapping around his ankles, he became a familiar sight in towns and villages where he stopped in the course of his wanderings. Children tagged after him, fascinated to peer over his shoulder as he worked. Local officials, however, felt more comfortable after he left.

Now, with the sandalwood box on the table in front of him, paying no attention to the rejoicing villagers crowding the inn, Chen-cho gleefully scrutinized his gift. As an artist, he had immediately recognized the excellence of the materials, but he studied them again to confirm his first opinion.

He picked up the stick of black ink and rolled it around in his fingers. He sniffed at it, even tasted it, and licked his lips as if it were some delicious morsel.

"Marvelous!" Chen-cho said to himself. "Perfect! No question, this ink's made from the ashes of pine trees on the south slope of Mount Lu, the very best."

Next, he turned his attention to the ink stone, with its shallow little basin for water at one end and its flat **surface** for grinding the solid ink at the other. The stone was fine-grained, flawless; and, in color, an unusual reddish gray. Chen-cho rubbed his thumb over it lovingly and shook his head in amazement.

"Here's a treasure in itself! I've heard of stones like this. They come only from one place: a grotto in Mount Wu-shan. I never believed they were more than legend. Yet, I have one right in my hand."

Checking over his good fortune, blessing the stranger he had fondly nicknamed Honorable Ragbag, the painter picked up the last object in the box: a **paintbrush** with a long bamboo handle.

"This is odd," Chen-cho squinted at the brush hairs, tested them on the palm of his hand and the tip of his nose. "Soft? Firm? Both at once? What's it made of? Not rabbit fur, not wolf hair, not mouse whiskers."

The painter could not restrain himself another moment. He called the landlord for a cup of water, poured a little into the basin of the ink stone, then carefully rubbed the tip of the ink stick against the grinding surface. No matter how much he rubbed, the stick showed no trace of wear.

"At this rate," he said to himself, "it will last forever. One stick, and ink enough for the rest of my life. There's frugality for you!"

He pulled out a sheet of paper. Moistening the brush, rolling the tip in the ink he had ground, he made a couple of trial **strokes**. As he did, a thrill began at the tip of his toes, raced to his arm, his hand, his fingers. The sensation turned him giddy. He glanced at the paper. His jaw dropped. The brush strokes were not black. They were bright **vermilion**.

"I'd have sworn that ink was black," Chen-cho murmured. "Was I mistaken? Yes, no doubt. The light's dim here."

He made a few more brush strokes. They were no longer vermilion, but jade green. Chen-cho put down the brush and rubbed his chin.

"What's happening here? That ink stick's black as night, through and through. What's doing it? The stone? The brush? No matter, let's have another go."

Chen-cho daubed at the paper, which was soon covered with streaks of bright orange, red, and blue. Anyone else might have grown alarmed or frightened at such an uncanny happening. But Chen-cho enjoyed surprises, mysteries, and extraordinary events. And so he laughed with delight to find himself owner of these remarkable materials.

"Well, old fellow," he said to himself, "you've come onto something you never expected and probably better than you deserve. Let's try something else. Those are marvelous colors, but what if I wanted a sort of lilac purple-green with a reddish cast?"

No sooner did Chen-cho imagine such a **hue** than it flowed from his brush. He quickly discovered that he need only **envision** whatever shade he wanted, and there it was, from brush to paper.

"That's what I call convenient and efficient," exclaimed the joyous Chen-cho. "No more paint pots and a dozen different pigments. Here's everything all at once."

With that, he clapped his felt hat firmly on his head, seized a handful of papers, packed up the box, and hurried out of the inn. He ran all the way to the stream where he had first met Ragbag. There he settled himself, ignoring the weather, forgetting to put up his umbrella, and worked away happily, letting the brush go as it wished, hardly glancing at what he was doing.

It was dusk and the light had faded before he could make himself leave off. But the picture was finished, better than anything he had ever painted. Chen-cho laughed and slapped his leg. "Old boy," he told himself, "keep on like this and you might even do something worthwhile."

He went back to his room at the inn. Excited by his wonderful new possessions, he forgot to eat his dinner. He barely slept that night, eager to start another picture.

Next morning and for several days thereafter, Chen-cho went into the countryside looking for scenes to paint. Each landscape that took shape under his hand delighted him more than the one before.

It snowed heavily on a certain morning. Chen-cho usually paid no mind to bad weather. That day, the wind blew so sharply and the snow

piled up so deeply that he decided to stay in his room. Nevertheless, his fingers itched to take up the brush. Ordinarily, he painted outdoors, according to whatever vista caught his eye. This time, he thought to do something else.

"Why not make up my own landscape? I'll paint whatever pops into my head and strikes my fancy."

Taking one of his largest sheets of paper, he set about painting hills and valleys, forests and streams, adding glens and lakes wherever it pleased him. He painted rolling meadows he had never seen; and bright banks of flowers he invented as he went along; and clouds of fantastic shapes, all drenched in sunlight, with a couple of rainbows added for good measure.

"What this may be, I've no idea," Chen-cho said when he finished. He blinked happily at the picture. "All I know is: I've astonished myself. That's something that never happened before."

Chen-cho could not take his eyes from his **handiwork**. He peered at it from every angle, first from a distance, then so close he bumped his nose.

"If I didn't know better," he said, "I'd swear I could smell those flowers. In fact, if I hadn't painted them, I'd believe I could pick one."

He reached out, pretending to pluck a blossom. Next thing he knew, the flower lay in his hand.

⬛ **Stop here for the Strategy Break.**

Strategy Break

Think about what has happened in this story so far. What elements of fantasy has the author introduced? How do you think those fantasy elements will affect what happens next? Get together with a partner and predict two or three different directions that this story could take. Answer the questions below as you brainstorm each possibility.

1. What do you predict will happen next? _____

   _____

2. Why do you think so? _____

   _____

3. What clues from the story helped you make your prediction(s)? _____

   _____

4. What else helped you make your prediction(s)? _____

   _____

➡ **Go on reading to see what happens.**

Chen-cho gaped at the flower. He swallowed hard, then grinned and shook his head. "What you've done, you foolish fellow, is go to sleep on your feet. You're having a dream. A marvelous one, but that's all it is."

He pinched himself, rubbed his eyes, soaked his head in a basin of water, paced back and forth. The flower was still where he had set it on the table. Fragrance filled the room.

"I'm wide awake, no question about it," he finally admitted. He went again to the picture. "That being the case, let's examine this reasonably. It seems I've put my hand into it. What, for example, if I did—this?"

Chen-cho poked his head into the painted landscape. Indeed, he could look around him at the trees and lakes. The sunshine dazzled and warmed him. He sniffed the fragrant air. He heard the rush of a waterfall somewhere in the distance.

"This is definitely out of the ordinary," Chen-cho murmured, pulling back his head. "Dare I explore a little farther?"

With that, Chen-cho plucked up his courage and stepped all the way into the picture. ●

Strategy Follow-up

First, go back to the concept map that you created in Building Background. Think about the kind of art that Chen-cho creates, and add that art form to your concept map if it is not already there.

Then get together with your partner again, and discuss what happened in Part 1 of "The Tale of the Tiger's Paintbrush." Do any of the predictions that you made at the Strategy Break match what has happened so far? Why or why not?

_____

_____

_____

_____

_____

_____

_____

_____

_____

_____

_____

✓Personal Checklist

Read each question and put a check (✓) in the correct box.

1. How well do you understand what has happened so far in "The Tale of the Tiger's Paintbrush"?
   - ☐ 3 (extremely well)
   - ☐ 2 (fairly well)
   - ☐ 1 (not well)

2. How well were you able to complete the concept map in Building Background?
   - ☐ 3 (extremely well)
   - ☐ 2 (fairly well)
   - ☐ 1 (not well)

3. In the Vocabulary Builder, how many vocabulary words were you able to use in your paragraph about art?
   - ☐ 3 (7–9 words)
   - ☐ 2 (4–6 words)
   - ☐ 1 (0–3 words)

4. At the Strategy Break, how well were you and your partner able to predict what might happen next?
   - ☐ 3 (extremely well)
   - ☐ 2 (fairly well)
   - ☐ 1 (not well)

5. How well have you been able to find the elements of fantasy in this story so far?
   - ☐ 3 (extremely well)
   - ☐ 2 (fairly well)
   - ☐ 1 (not well)

Vocabulary Check

Look back at the work you did in the Vocabulary Builder. Then answer each question by circling the correct letter.

1. When artists paint landscapes, what do they paint?
   a. mountains, lakes, trees, and other scenery
   b. the facial expressions of different people
   c. flowers in vases and fruits in bowls

2. Which of these things could be described as vermilion?
   a. freshly fallen snow
   b. the sky on a sunny day
   c. a sparkling ruby

3. Which meaning of the word *strokes* fits this story?
   a. sounds made by hitting something
   b. movements made by a pen or brush
   c. times of good luck or bad luck

4. Which vocabulary word is defined by the phrase "creation or design"?
   a. envision
   b. handiwork
   c. surface

5. What is another word for *hue*?
   a. color
   b. shape
   c. stroke

Add the numbers that you just checked to get your Personal Checklist score. Fill in your score here. Then turn to page 219 and transfer your score onto Graph 1.

Personal / Vocabulary / Strategy / Comprehension / **TOTAL SCORE** ✓ T

Check your answers with your teacher. Give yourself 1 point for each correct answer, and fill in your Vocabulary score here. Then turn to page 219 and transfer your score onto Graph 1.

Personal / Vocabulary / Strategy / Comprehension / **TOTAL SCORE** ✓ T

Strategy Check

Review the predictions that you and your partner wrote in this lesson. Also review the selection if necessary. Then answer these questions:

1. If you had predicted that Chen-cho would be able to step into the painting, which clue would *not* have supported your prediction?
   a. He can always step into his paintings, which is why people want them.
   b. The materials he got from Honorable Ragbag seem to be magical.
   c. He merely mentions picking a flower, and one appears in his hand.

2. What clue might have supported your prediction that Chen-cho was dreaming?
   a. "What this may be, I've no idea."
   b. The snow piled up so deeply that he decided to stay in his room.
   c. It was dusk and the light had faded before he could make himself leave off.

3. What can you conclude about the person Chen-cho calls Honorable Ragbag?
   a. He is a magician or other fantasy character.
   b. He wants to punish Chen-cho.
   c. He is playing a trick on Chen-cho.

4. Which sentence from the story was a clue that Ragbag's paintbox might be magical?
   a. As an artist, he had immediately recognized the excellence of the materials.
   b. He picked up the stick of black ink and rolled it around in his fingers.
   c. The brush strokes were not black. They were bright vermilion.

5. What do you predict might happen in Part 2?
   a. Chen-cho will realize he's been dreaming.
   b. Chen-cho will have a wonderful experience.
   c. Chen-cho will have a frightening experience.

Comprehension Check

Review the selection if necessary. Then answer these questions:

1. Why does Chen-cho often do without food and drink?
   a. He is such a bad artist that he never sells his work.
   b. He would rather spend his money on paper and paint.
   c. He had a tooth pulled and finds it too difficult to eat.

2. Why do you think Chen-cho doesn't like to part with his paintings?
   a. He likes them too much and feels they're a part of him.
   b. He doesn't think they're good enough to ask money for them.
   c. He can't get the money for them that he thinks they are worth.

3. What is most unusual about the ink that Ragbag gives Chen-cho?
   a. It disappears when Chen-cho tries to paint with it.
   b. It is extremely easy to mix and use.
   c. Its color is determined by Chen-cho's thoughts.

4. Why does Chen-cho decide to stay inside and paint one day?
   a. He doesn't want anyone to see his magical paint.
   b. It is too windy and snowy to go outside.
   c. Chen-cho is too tired and decides to paint in bed.

5. Why does Chen-cho first believe that he was able to pluck a flower from his painting?
   a. He believes he has had too much to drink.
   b. He believes he is having a marvelous dream.
   c. He believes he is ill and is hallucinating.

Check your answers with your teacher. Give yourself 1 point for each correct answer, and fill in your Strategy score here. Then turn to page 219 and transfer your score onto Graph 1.

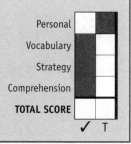

Check your answers with your teacher. Give yourself 1 point for each correct answer, and fill in your Comprehension score here. Then turn to page 219 and transfer your score onto Graph 1.

Extending

Choose one or more of these activities:

DRAW OR PAINT YOUR OWN LANDSCAPE

When Chen-Cho decides to paint his own landscape, he pictures hills, valleys, forests, streams, and whatever else pleases him. Take a large sheet of paper and draw or paint a landscape that pleases you. Make your landscape a place in which you would enjoy spending time. The objects in your landscape can be real or imaginary, according to your own desires.

FIND OUT ABOUT CHINESE PAINTING

Traditional Chinese painting often focuses on peaceful scenes and landscapes. Alone or with a partner, search through some art books and find several examples of this type of painting. (See the book listed on this page for a place to start.) If possible, discover how painting, poetry, and calligraphy have been related to one another for centuries.

READ MORE BY LLOYD ALEXANDER

Lloyd Alexander is well-known for his wonderful fantasy writing. Find more of his books—or books on audio cassette—beginning with the ones listed on this page. Prepare an oral or written report in which you discuss the elements of fantasy that Alexander uses. If you read or listen to more than one book, you might list the fantasy elements on a comparison chart.

Resources

Books

Alexander, Lloyd. *The Book of Three.* Yearling, 1999.

———. *The Cat Who Wished to Be a Man.* Puffin, 2000.

———. *The First Two Lives of Lukas-Kasha.* Puffin, 1998.

———. *The Fortune-tellers.* Puffin, 1997.

———. *Gypsy Rizka.* Puffin, 2000.

Lai, T. C. *Chinese Painting.* Images of Asia. Oxford University Press, 1992.

The Tale of the Tiger's Paintbrush (Part 2)

Building Background

From "The Tale of the Tiger's Paintbrush" (Part 1):

"I'm wide awake, no question about it," he finally admitted. He went again to the picture. "That being the case, let's examine this reasonably. It seems I've put my hand into it. What, for example, if I did—this?"

Chen-cho poked his head into the painted landscape. Indeed, he could look around him at the trees and lakes. The sunshine dazzled and warmed him. He sniffed the fragrant air. He heard the rush of a waterfall somewhere in the distance.

"This is definitely out of the ordinary," Chen-cho murmured, pulling back his head. "Dare I explore a little farther?"

With that, Chen-cho plucked up his courage and stepped all the way into the picture.

Read on to find out how things turn out in this fantasy story. Keep looking for clues that help you predict what will happen next.

apprehension

clamoring

miraculous

nitpicking

tedious

Vocabulary Builder

1. Complete each sentence with one of the vocabulary words in the margin. Use a dictionary if you need help.

2. Save your work. You will refer to it again in the Vocabulary Check.

   a. Watching a chess match can be _____ if no one moves for hours.

   b. Before the contest, my hands were cold, and I felt some _____ .

   c. When the store ran out of its best-selling CD, disappointed customers were _____ for more.

   d. Hannah's constant criticizing and _____ made it hard to be around her.

   e. The fact that Matt could walk again after his accident was simply _____ .

Strategy Builder

Using Story Summaries to Make Predictions

- Sometimes when you read a long story, it helps to stop once in a while and summarize what you've read. When you **summarize**, you briefly describe who is in the story, where it is taking place, and what has happened so far.

- Summarizing helps you keep track of what is happening in a story. It also helps you predict what might happen next. Think back to Part 1 of "The Tale of the Tiger's Paintbrush." Here is a sample summary of it:

After Chen-cho helps a young man fight off some robbers, the man gives him a sandalwood box. As Chen-cho examines the box's contents, he discovers that all he has to do is imagine colors and he can paint them with the brush.

One day, Chen-cho paints a beautiful landscape. When he pretends to pick one of its flowers, the flower appears in his hand. After he realizes he's not dreaming, he sticks his head into the painting. Finally he plucks up his courage and steps all the way into the picture.

- Now use the summary of Part 1 and your knowledge of fantasy elements to help you predict what might happen in Part 2. Don't worry if your predictions don't match what actually happens. You'll have a chance to make new ones at the Strategy Break.

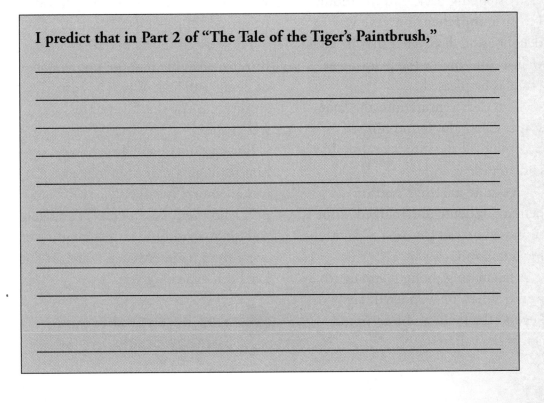

I predict that in Part 2 of "The Tale of the Tiger's Paintbrush,"

_____

_____

_____

_____

_____

_____

_____

_____

_____

_____

The Tale of the Tiger's Paintbrush (Part 2)

by Lloyd Alexander

As you read Part 2 of "The Tale of the Tiger's Paintbrush," look for clues the author provides to help make your predictions.

He was not certain how he did it. The painting was large, but far from as large as the artist himself. Yet, it must have grown spacious enough to take him in, for there he was, standing knee-deep in the soft grass of a meadow.

"So far, so good," he said. "But now I've gone in—how do I get out?"

He answered his own question by easily stepping back into the room. His first **apprehension** gave way to delight as he discovered that he could walk in and out of the painting as often as he pleased.

With each venture into the landscape, Chen-cho found himself becoming all the more comfortable and confident.

"It's quite amazing, hard to believe," Chen-cho remarked. "But I suppose one can get used to anything, including miracles."

A fascinating thought sprang to mind. What, he wondered, lay beyond the fields and forests and across the valleys?

"I've no idea what's there," he said, "which is the best reason to go and find out."

Chen-cho picked up the sandalwood box and a sheaf of paper in case he found some especially attractive scene. Stepping into the landscape, he set off eagerly along a gentle path that opened at his feet. He soon came to a high-arched bridge over a stream lined with willows. The view so charmed him that he spread his paper and began to paint.

He stopped in the middle of a brush stroke. He had the impression of being watched. When he turned around, he saw that his impression was correct.

Sitting on its haunches, observing him through a pair of orange eyes, was an enormous tiger.

"Hello there, Chen-cho." The tiger padded toward him, stripes rippling at every fluid pace. "My name is Lao-hu. I've been expecting you."

 **Stop here for the Strategy Break.**

Strategy Break

On the lines below, write a brief summary of what has happened so far in Part 2. Be sure to mention only the most important details and events.

_____

_____

_____

_____

_____

Now write what you predict will happen next, and why.

_____

_____

_____

_____

➤ **Go on reading to see what happens.**

"A pleasure to make your acquaintance," replied Chen-cho. Having by now grown accustomed to marvelous happenings, the arrival of a tiger did not unsettle him too much, especially since the big animal had addressed him in a friendly tone. "However, I can't truthfully say I was expecting you."

"You must have, whether you knew it or not," Lao-hu said. "Otherwise, I wouldn't be here. Ah. I see you've been using my brush."

"Yours?"

"My hairs," Lao-hu said. "From the tip of my tail. I hope it pleases you."

"A remarkable brush," Chen-cho said. "I'd go so far as to call it **miraculous**. From the tip of your tail? Yes, but in that case, I'm a little puzzled. I hope you don't mind my asking, but if you weren't here until I painted this picture, where were you before I painted it? If you were someplace else, how did you get here? And who plucked out those hairs in the first place?"

"Why concern yourself with details?" Lao-hu yawned enormously. "It's a **tedious**, boring matter you wouldn't understand to begin with. Let me just say this: You're not the first to paint such a picture, nor the last. Many have done still finer work. And you're certainly not the first to use my brush."

"Tell me, then," Chen-cho said, "can others find their way into my picture? A question of privacy, you understand."

"Of course they can," replied Lao-hu. "It's your painting, but now that you've done it, it's open to anybody who cares to enter. But leave that idle speculation and **nitpicking** to scholars who enjoy such occupation. You've hardly seen the smallest part of all this"—Lao-hu motioned around him with his tail—"so let me show you a little, for a start. Climb on my back."

Chen-cho gladly accepted the tiger's invitation. Lao-hu sprang across the stream in one mighty leap. Chen-cho clamped his legs around the tiger's flanks and his arms around Lao-hu's powerful neck. The tiger sped across meadows, through forests, up and down hills. Chen-cho glimpsed garden pavilions, farmhouses, towns and villages, sailboats on rivers, birds in the air, fish leaping in brooks, animals of every kind. Some of what he saw looked vaguely familiar; the rest, altogether strange and fascinating. Lao-hu promised they would continue their explorations and carried the painter back to where they had started.

As easily as he had stepped into the painting, Chen-cho stepped into the room. Lao-hu followed, much to the surprise and delight of the painter, who was reluctant to part from his new companion.

"I can go wherever I please," Lao-hu replied when Chen-cho asked about this, "just as you can."

"Can other people see you?" asked Chen-cho, wondering what his landlord might say if he came into the room and found a tiger.

"Of course they can," Lao-hu said. "I may be a magical tiger, but I'm not an invisible one."

With that, Lao-hu curled up at the foot of Chen-cho's bed. The tired but happy painter flung himself down and went to sleep, thinking that, all in all, it had been an interesting day.

Next morning, when the storm had passed, Chen-cho packed his belongings and set off on his way again. Lao-hu had jumped back into the picture, which the artist had rolled up and carried under his arm. Once away from the village, Chen-cho unrolled the painting. He saw no sign of Lao-hu. Dismayed, the artist anxiously called for him. The tiger appeared an instant later, sprang out, and padded along beside Chen-cho.

From then on, whenever he was sure they were unobserved, Chen-cho summoned Lao-hu, and the two of them wandered together, the fondest companions. When Chen-cho stopped to paint some scene or other, the tiger would stretch out next to him or disappear into the picture on some business of his own. Nevertheless, Chen-cho had only to call his name and Lao-hu would reappear immediately; and Chen-cho always kept the painting beside him when he worked.

As for his other paintings, thanks to the tiger's brush, the marvelous ink stick, and the grinding stone, they became better and better, as did Chen-cho's reputation. Whenever he lodged in a town or city, he could expect any number of customers to come **clamoring** for his pictures. However, as always, he parted with few. Nor would he even consider selling his marvelous landscape, no matter what price was offered. So, more often than not, would-be purchasers left disappointed at being refused.

Only once did Chen-cho have a disagreeable encounter. In one town, a merchant came to inspect Chen-cho's paintings, but as soon as he saw them, he shook his head in distaste.

"What dreadful daubs are these?" he exclaimed. "Not one suitable to put in my house! And this"—he pointed at the landscape, where Lao-hu had prudently hidden himself out of sight—"worst of all! An ugly, blotchy, ill-conceived scrawl! I've had nightmares prettier than this."

Chen-cho, glad to see the merchant stamp off, flung a few tart words after him. He was, nonetheless, puzzled. He called Lao-hu, who popped out instantly.

"Easily understood," Lao-hu said, when Chen-cho told him the merchant's opinion. "As a painter, you should know this better than anyone. We see with eyes in our head, but see clearer with eyes of the heart. Some see beauty, some see ugliness. In both cases, what they see is a reflection of their own nature."

"Even so," replied Chen-cho, "a painting's a painting. Colors and shapes don't change, no matter who looks at them."

"True enough," said Lao-hu. "Very well, then, let me put it this way: You can't please everybody."

"That, I suppose," Chen-cho said, "is a blessing." ●

Strategy Follow-up

First go back and look at the predictions that you wrote in this lesson. Do any of them match what actually happened in Part 2? Why or why not?

Next, write a brief summary of the end of Part 2. Include only the most important characters, settings, and events.

_____

_____

_____

_____

_____

_____

_____

_____

_____

_____

_____

✓Personal Checklist

Read each question and put a check (✓) in the correct box.

1. How well were you able to predict what might happen in Part 2 of "The Tale of the Tiger's Paintbrush"?
   - ☐ 3 (extremely well)
   - ☐ 2 (fairly well)
   - ☐ 1 (not well)

2. How well were you able to complete the sentences in the Vocabulary Builder?
   - ☐ 3 (extremely well)
   - ☐ 2 (fairly well)
   - ☐ 1 (not well)

3. How well were you able to write summaries for Part 2 of "The Tale of the Tiger's Paintbrush"?
   - ☐ 3 (extremely well)
   - ☐ 2 (fairly well)
   - ☐ 1 (not well)

4. How well do you understand why the merchant doesn't like Chen-cho's work?
   - ☐ 3 (extremely well)
   - ☐ 2 (fairly well)
   - ☐ 1 (not well)

5. How well do you understand what Lao-hu means when he tells Chen-cho that you can't please everybody?
   - ☐ 3 (extremely well)
   - ☐ 2 (fairly well)
   - ☐ 1 (not well)

Vocabulary Check

Look back at the work you did in the Vocabulary Builder. Then answer each question by circling the correct letter.

1. Which word from this story is a synonym of *tedious*?
   a. spacious
   b. fascinating
   c. boring

2. When you are always finding fault with things, what are you doing?
   a. clamoring
   b. nitpicking
   c. praising

3. In which situation might you feel apprehension?
   a. while waiting to take a test
   b. while playing with your kitten
   c. while reading a humorous book

4. What does it mean that customers were clamoring for Chen-cho's pictures?
   a. They were criticizing them.
   b. They were demanding them.
   c. They were praising them.

5. Which event from this story can best be described as miraculous?
   a. Chen-cho's painting keeps on improving.
   b. Chen-cho can step in and out of his painting.
   c. A merchant criticizes Chen-cho's paintings.

Add the numbers that you just checked to get your Personal Checklist score. Fill in your score here. Then turn to page 219 and transfer your score onto Graph 1.

Personal	
Vocabulary	
Strategy	
Comprehension	
TOTAL SCORE	
	✓ T

Check your answers with your teacher. Give yourself 1 point for each correct answer, and fill in your Vocabulary score here. Then turn to page 219 and transfer your score onto Graph 1.

Personal	
Vocabulary	
Strategy	
Comprehension	
TOTAL SCORE	
	✓ T

Strategy Check

Review the summaries and predictions that you wrote in this lesson. Then answer these questions:

1. At the Strategy Break, which detail should you have included in your summary?
   a. Chen-cho examines the contents of the sandalwood box.
   b. Chen-cho pretends to pick a flower, and it appears in his hand.
   c. Chen-cho decides to explore the landscape.

2. At the Strategy Break, which new character should you have included in your summary?
   a. Chen-cho the painter
   b. Lao-hu the tiger
   c. a disagreeable merchant

3. At the Strategy Break, which prediction would *not* have fit this selection?
   a. Chen-cho and Lao-hu will become very good friends.
   b. Chen-cho will put Lao-hu in a zoo.
   c. Chen-cho will ask Lao-hu if he can paint him.

4. In the Strategy Follow-up, which important event should you have included in your summary?
   a. Chen-cho turns around and sees a tiger sitting behind him.
   b. A merchant has a nightmare about one of Chen-cho's paintings.
   c. Lao-hu tells Chen-cho that you can't please everybody.

5. How might the title of this story have helped you make predictions as you read?
   a. The title was a clue that Chen-cho's brush was made from Lao-hu's tail.
   b. The title was a clue that Chen-cho stole Lao-hu's paintbrush.
   c. The title was a clue that Lao-hu actually painted Chen-cho's paintings.

Comprehension Check

Review Part 2 of "The Tale of the Tiger's Paintbrush" if necessary. Then answer these questions:

1. From what is Chen-cho's paintbrush made?
   a. hairs from Lao-hu's tail
   b. whiskers from Lao-hu's face
   c. eyelashes from Lao-hu's eyes

2. Why does Chen-cho ask Lao-hu if anyone else can enter his picture?
   a. He is afraid of enemies entering.
   b. He wants to maintain his privacy.
   c. He doesn't want nasty neighbors.

3. What happens to Chen-Cho's way of life after he meets Lao-hu?
   a. Chen-cho stops painting altogether.
   b. Chen-cho becomes very wealthy.
   c. Chen-cho becomes a popular painter.

4. Why doesn't Chen-cho ever sell his magical landscape?
   a. It is too precious to ever consider selling.
   b. No one is willing to pay the price he's asking.
   c. Both of the above answers are correct.

5. Why does the merchant see only ugliness in Chen-cho's paintings?
   a. The merchant is practically blind.
   b. He's seeing a reflection of his nature.
   c. He's looking at Chen-cho's practice paintings.

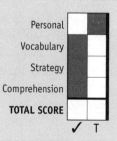

Check your answers with your teacher. Give yourself 1 point for each correct answer, and fill in your Strategy score here. Then turn to page 219 and transfer your score onto Graph 1.

Personal
Vocabulary
Strategy
Comprehension

TOTAL SCORE

✓ T

Check your answers with your teacher. Give yourself 1 point for each correct answer, and fill in your Comprehension score here. Then turn to page 219 and transfer your score onto Graph 1.

Personal
Vocabulary
Strategy
Comprehension

TOTAL SCORE

✓ T

Extending

Choose one or both of these activities:

WRITE A PERSUASIVE ESSAY

At the end of this story Lao-hu tells Chen-cho, "We see with eyes in our head, but see clearer with eyes of the heart. Some see beauty, some see ugliness. In both cases, what they see is a reflection of their own nature." Do you agree with Lao-hu's words? Why or why not? Write a persuasive essay in which you explain why you agree or disagree with Lao-hu. Be sure to give examples that help support your opinion—and convince others to agree with you too.

MAKE A PRESENTATION

Every era has its artists who become popular just as Chen-cho did. With a partner, do some research and find out who some popular artists of today are. What techniques, materials, and subjects do they use? Why do people want to buy their work? To begin your research, you might want to use some of the resources listed or talk to your school's art teacher. Another resource might be your local art museum. Prepare your findings in an oral presentation. If possible, hold up pictures or show slides of some of the artwork you are discussing.

Resources

Books

Krystal, Barbara. *100 Artists Who Shaped World History.* Bluewood Books, 1997.

Lewis, Samella. *African American Art and Artists,* rev. ed. University of California Press, 2003.

Marschall, Richard, ed. *America's Greatest Comic-Strip Artists: From* The Yellow Kid *to* Peanuts. Stewart Tabori and Chang, 1997.

Pomegranate. *30 Contemporary Women Artists.* Pomegranate, 1992.

Sweet Machines

Building Background

The modern world is filled with different modes, or methods, of transportation. Long ago, the only ways to get around were on foot or by horse-drawn cart. Now, however, people use cars, buses, subways, trains, planes, and even rocket ships to travel across town, around the planet, or into outer space.

Think about the various modes of transportation available today. Then fill in the comparison chart below. When you finish, put a check next to the forms of transportation that you predict will appear in "Sweet Machines."

Mode of Transporation	Advantages	Disadavantages
Walking		
Horse, Mule, Camel, etc.		
Bicycle		
Motorbike and/or Motorcycle		
Automobile		
Bus		
Train		
Airplane		
Spacecraft		

ball bearings

bellowed

booming

chains

chatter

punctures

roar

scream

spokes

whir

Vocabulary Builder

1. The words in the margin are all from "Sweet Machines." Study the words, and then decide which ones are related to sounds. Write those words on the first clipboard on page 83.

2. Write the words that are related to bicycles on the second clipboard on page 83.

3. As you read the story, look for other words to add to both clipboards. Save your work. You will use it again in the Vocabulary Check.

Strategy Builder

Identifying Problems and Solutions in Stories

- In some stories, the main character or characters have a **problem**. Throughout the story, the characters try to solve the problem. Sometimes they try more than one **solution**. By the end of the story, they usually come up with the solution that works—the **end result**.

- As you read the following paragraph, notice the girls' problem and what they do to solve it.

CLIPBOARD 1
Sounds

> Jamie and Elaine met for lunch at their usual table. "Oh no," said Elaine when she saw what her mother had packed. "Peanut butter and jelly again!"
>
> "You think you've got it bad," said Jamie. "I have a tuna-salad sandwich, and everyone knows I hate tuna. I'd rather have a peanut butter-and-jelly sandwich any day."
>
> The girls studied their lunches for a moment. Then they had an idea. Elaine took Jamie's tuna-salad sandwich. Jamie took Elaine's peanut butter-and-jelly sandwich. As the girls ate, they both agreed that their sandwiches were delicious.

CLIPBOARD 2
Bicycle Words

- If you wanted to show the girls' problem and solutions, you could put them on a **problem-solution frame**. It would look like this:

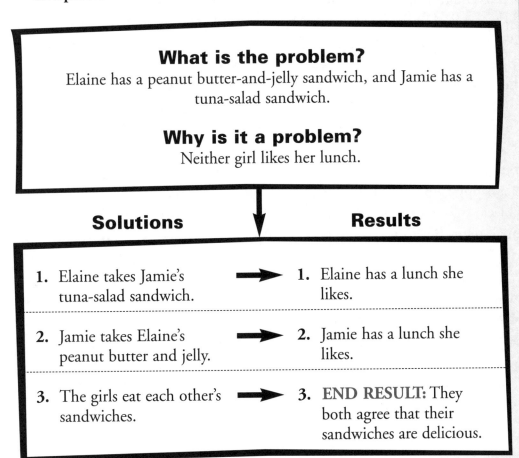

What is the problem?
Elaine has a peanut butter-and-jelly sandwich, and Jamie has a tuna-salad sandwich.

Why is it a problem?
Neither girl likes her lunch.

Solutions

Results

1. Elaine takes Jamie's tuna-salad sandwich. → 1. Elaine has a lunch she likes.

2. Jamie takes Elaine's peanut butter and jelly. → 2. Jamie has a lunch she likes.

3. The girls eat each other's sandwiches. → 3. **END RESULT:** They both agree that their sandwiches are delicious.

Sweet Machines

by Anna Sigard

As you read the first part of this story, apply the strategies you just learned. Look for the problem that Panos the repairman has—and why.

Once upon a time there was a little town in Greece where people got around on foot, on donkeys, on mules, on horses.

Or on bicycles.

When the bicycles needed to be repaired, the people took them to Panos, the bicycle repairman.

Panos was a small man with black hair and a black, silky mustache. He fixed the brakes and tightened the **chains**; he replaced the **ball bearings**, mended the **punctures**, and straightened the **spokes** of the bikes people brought to his shop.

Panos could make a bike run as swiftly as a bird in flight. He could make it run as quietly as a square of silk pulled through a ring. He'd smile as he watched the bikes he'd fixed **whir** out of his shop.

"Sweet machines," he'd say to himself.

But if you had asked Panos, "Are you a happy man?" he'd have stroked his black, silky mustache and replied, "I'm all right. But things could be better."

Then one day Yannis Daskalos came to the little town. Yannis was a teacher of English, and *daskalos* means "teacher" in Greek. Yannis Daskalos was a big man, well over six feet tall. He had a red beard and mustache, fierce blue eyes, and a deep, **booming** voice. He had traveled all over the world and spoke English like an American. He rode around on a big yellow motorbike that trailed a plume of exhaust fumes and made a noise like a million infuriated hornets.

The children in the little town admired the big teacher. They all wanted to learn English from him. Soon Yannis Daskalos was busy from morning to night, riding from house to house on his big yellow motorbike to give lessons.

The grownups in the town admired the big teacher as well. They were too old to learn English, but they all wanted motorbikes like Yannis Daskalos. Pretty soon most of the bicycles were put away in sheds or left to rust in backyards, and everyone who was old enough to get a license was riding a motorbike.

The narrow streets of the little town were thick with the smell of exhaust fumes and loud with the **chatter** and **roar** and **scream** of motorbike engines.

"How modern and up-to-date we are!" said the people. "Just like Yannis Daskalos! How modern and up-to-date our town is! It's just as noisy and every bit as smelly as the big city!"

Pretty soon all these motorbikes began to break down. And when they did, the people took them to Panos to fix. There was nowhere else to go.

Poor Panos was a terrible motorbike mechanic, and all his customers told him so. They made his life miserable. And worse than all the others put together was Yannis Daskalos.

Daskalos drove well, but he drove hard. And his yellow motorbike was always breaking down. Whenever this happened, the big teacher would fly into a rage and bring the motorbike to Panos. He'd stand over the little repairman with his red beard bristling and his eyes shooting blue fire. With trembling fingers, poor Panos would try to fix the bike.

Sometimes Panos would fix the yellow motorbike so it would run again for a month or two, sometimes it would go for a week or two, and sometimes he'd fix it so it would carry Yannis just a mile or two down the road—far enough to give Panos time to shut up shop and head out of town for his little plot of land where he kept some chickens and goats, and where he hoped Daskalos would not come and find him.

If you'd asked him now, "Panos, are you a happy man?" he'd have stroked his silky mustache and replied, "I suppose I'm all right. But things would be a whole lot better if I didn't have those angry customers—especially Yannis Daskalos—on my back!"

 Stop here for the Strategy Break.

Strategy Break

If you were to create a problem-solution frame for the story so far, it might look like this:

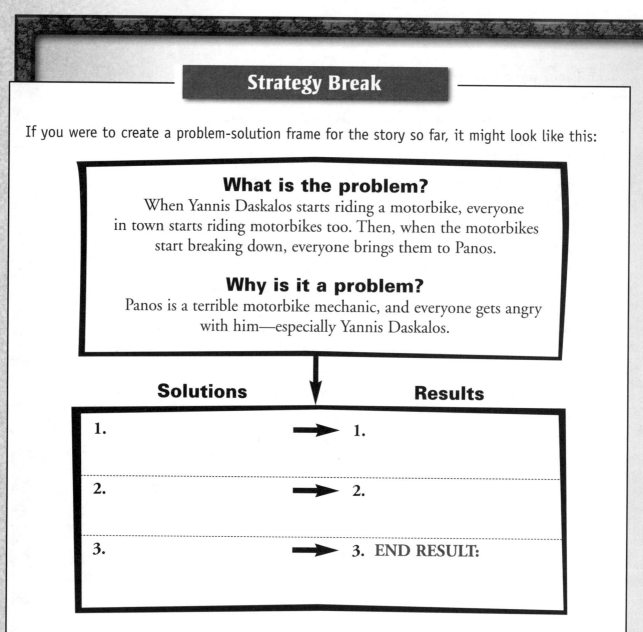

What is the problem?
When Yannis Daskalos starts riding a motorbike, everyone in town starts riding motorbikes too. Then, when the motorbikes start breaking down, everyone brings them to Panos.

Why is it a problem?
Panos is a terrible motorbike mechanic, and everyone gets angry with him—especially Yannis Daskalos.

Solutions   **Results**

1.   ➡   1.

2.   ➡   2.

3.   ➡   3. END RESULT:

As you read the rest of this story, pay attention to how Panos tries to solve his problem. Keep track of his solutions, the results, and the end result. When you finish this story, you will complete the problem-solution frame.

➡ **Go on reading to see what happens.**

Then one black night on a dark dirt road, Yannis Daskalos drove into a dark, black runaway mule.

Nothing much happened to the mule. But the yellow motorbike ended up in Panos's workshop. And Yannis Daskalos ended up in the hospital with a lot of broken bones.

How peaceful life was in Panos's workshop while Yannis was in the hospital! Panos put up with the complaints of all his other customers, a smile under his black, silky mustache. It was wonderful not to have the big teacher glaring at him, red beard bristling, blue eyes shooting cold fire.

Panos did a lot of thinking while Yannis was away and when at last Daskalos limped into the workshop, Panos was ready for him.

"Well," said the big teacher, "have you fixed my motorbike?"

"No," said Panos, "not yet."

"Why not?" Yannis's eyes began to dart blue fire.

"Calm down! Calm down!" said Panos.

Panos crossed his toes inside his shoes and prayed his plan would work. "I haven't fixed your motorbike yet because it needs spare parts that are not available in Greece. The agency has ordered these parts from abroad, but they will take months to arrive."

"Months!" **bellowed** Yannis. "And how am I going to get around without my motorbike?"

"You could walk," suggested Panos.

"Walk! I've got a tight schedule. How am I going to give all my lessons if I have to walk?" Yannis looked ready to explode.

"Or you could ride a bike."

"A bike you pedal?"

Panos nodded. "Just temporarily of course, until the spare parts come for your motorbike."

So that is how Yannis Daskalos took to riding around on a bicycle. He bought one of those mountain bikes with bright metalwork and eighteen speeds. He also bought himself a blue-and-yellow cycling outfit and a safety helmet, and a friend of his in Texas sent him an enormous cowboy hat that he wore *over* the safety helmet.

When Yannis Daskalos rode from house to house to give his lessons, people thought, How stately! How colorful! How grand!

And because the people in the town admired the big teacher, they all wanted to have mountain bikes, too, and ride around in colorful outfits.

Panos sold hundreds of mountain bikes and road-racing bikes, and the old bicycles came out of the backyards and sheds and Panos fixed them up again. Pretty soon motorbikes were being used only for long trips while everyone who was fit enough was riding a bicycle. And occasionally, just occasionally, there was nothing to be heard in the narrow streets but the sound of people's voices and the whir of bikes.

"How modern and up-to-date we are!" said the people. "Just like Yannis Daskalos! How modern and up-to-date our town is! It's quieter and cleaner and not nearly as smelly as the big city!"

Pretty soon Panos had so many bicycles to look after that he was obliged to send the motorbike owners across the road to where a motorbike mechanic had set up shop.

And sometimes, when he wasn't busy, Panos would stand in the door of his workshop and watch the bikes whir by, swift as birds in flight, quiet as squares of silk pulled through a ring. "Sweet machines," he'd say to himself. If you'd asked him now, "Panos, are you a happy man?" he'd have smiled under his silky mustache. "I'm all right. Things are much better now than they used to be." ●

Strategy Follow-up

Now complete the problem-solution frame with information from the second part of this story. Some of the frame has been filled in for you.

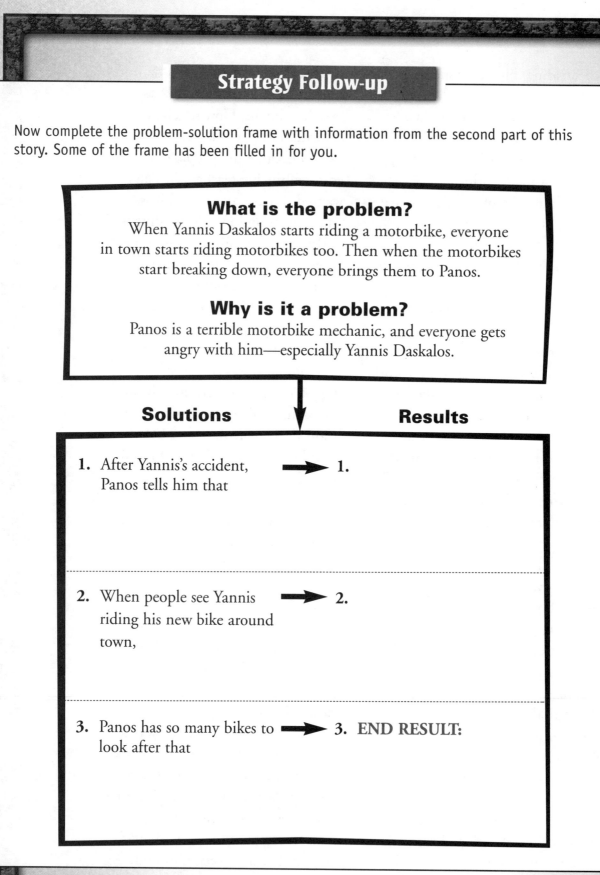

What is the problem?

When Yannis Daskalos starts riding a motorbike, everyone in town starts riding motorbikes too. Then when the motorbikes start breaking down, everyone brings them to Panos.

Why is it a problem?

Panos is a terrible motorbike mechanic, and everyone gets angry with him—especially Yannis Daskalos.

Solutions   **Results**

1. After Yannis's accident, Panos tells him that   1.

2. When people see Yannis riding his new bike around town,   2.

3. Panos has so many bikes to look after that   3. **END RESULT:**

✓Personal Checklist

Read each question and put a check (✓) in the correct box.

1. How closely do the advantages and disadvantages discussed in "Sweet Machines" match the ones that you listed in Building Background for those modes of transportation?
   - ☐ 3 (extremely well)
   - ☐ 2 (fairly well)
   - ☐ 1 (not well)

2. In the Vocabulary Builder, how well were you able to list each word on the appropriate clipboard?
   - ☐ 3 (extremely well)
   - ☐ 2 (fairly well)
   - ☐ 1 (not well)

3. How well were you able to complete the problem-solution frame in the Strategy Follow-up?
   - ☐ 3 (extremely well)
   - ☐ 2 (fairly well)
   - ☐ 1 (not well)

4. How well do you understand why Panos tells Yannis that the spare parts for his motorbike will take months to arrive?
   - ☐ 3 (extremely well)
   - ☐ 2 (fairly well)
   - ☐ 1 (not well)

5. How well do you understand why everyone in the town switched from motorbikes to mountain bikes?
   - ☐ 3 (extremely well)
   - ☐ 2 (fairly well)
   - ☐ 1 (not well)

Vocabulary Check

Look back at the work you did in the Vocabulary Builder. Then answer each question by circling the correct letter.

1. The story says that Yannis has a deep, booming voice. How do you think it sounds?
   - a. as quiet as a whisper
   - b. very loud and deep
   - c. high and screechy

2. Which part of a bicycle is likely to get a puncture?
   - a. a tire
   - b. a chain
   - c. a ball bearing

3. When a bee flies by you, what might you hear its wings do?
   - a. scream
   - b. whir
   - c. chatter

4. Which meaning of the word *chatter* best fits this story?
   - a. vibrate or rattle while in use
   - b. talk without stopping
   - c. move uncontrollably

5. Which of these people is most likely to bellow?
   - a. someone telling a secret
   - b. someone visiting a library
   - c. someone talking at a football game

Add the numbers that you just checked to get your Personal Checklist score. Fill in your score here. Then turn to page 219 and transfer your score onto Graph 1.

Personal	
Vocabulary	
Strategy	
Comprehension	
TOTAL SCORE	✓ T

Check your answers with your teacher. Give yourself 1 point for each correct answer, and fill in your Vocabulary score here. Then turn to page 219 and transfer your score onto Graph 1.

Personal	
Vocabulary	
Strategy	
Comprehension	
TOTAL SCORE	✓ T

Strategy Check

Review the problem-solution frame that you completed in the Strategy Follow-up. Then answer these questions:

1. When Panos tells Yannis that his motorbike parts will take months to arrive, what is the result?

    a. Yannis buys another motorbike.

    b. Everyone in town starts riding motorbikes.

    c. Yannis must go back to riding a bicycle.

2. Why does everyone in town start riding mountain bikes?

    a. because they admire Yannis and want to be like him

    b. because they dislike Yannis and want to be better than he is

    c. because they can't get spare parts for their motorbikes

3. What is the result of Panos's having so many bikes to look after?

    a. Everyone gets mad at him, and he loses his business.

    b. Everyone starts riding motorbikes again.

    c. He sends motorbike owners to the mechanic across the street.

4. What is the end result of Panos's problem?

    a. He is still waiting for Yannis's spare motorbike parts to arrive.

    b. He is happier, and things are much better than they used to be.

    c. He is miserable because the motorbike mechanic takes all his business.

5. Why might Panos be a happier man at the end of the story?

    a. He doesn't have to fix motorbikes anymore.

    b. His town is cleaner now that people are riding bikes.

    c. Both of the above reasons are correct.

Comprehension Check

Review the story if necessary. Then answer these questions:

1. Why does Yannis Daskalos need to get around town quickly?

    a. He needs to get to his students.

    b. He needs to travel the world.

    c. He needs to train for a race.

2. How does the town change when everyone starts riding motorbikes?

    a. It becomes more sensible.

    b. It becomes noisy and smelly.

    c. It becomes quieter and cleaner.

3. What event causes Yannis to stop riding his motorbike for a while?

    a. He runs into a mule and ends up in the hospital.

    b. He gets a job as an English tutor in the school.

    c. He realizes that his motorbike is too noisy.

4. After reading this story, what can you conclude about the people of Panos's town?

    a. They are independent thinkers who don't follow the crowd.

    b. They are easily influenced by what other people do.

    c. They are resistant to change and to trying new things.

5. Why is riding a bicycle better for the environment than riding a motorbike?

    a. Bicycles are better looking than motorbikes.

    b. Bicycles are slower moving than motorbikes.

    c. Bicycles are cleaner and quieter than motorbikes.

Check your answers with your teacher. Give yourself 1 point for each correct answer, and fill in your Strategy score here. Then turn to page 219 and transfer your score onto Graph 1.

Personal	
Vocabulary	
Strategy	
Comprehension	
TOTAL SCORE	✓ T

Check your answers with your teacher. Give yourself 1 point for each correct answer, and fill in your Comprehension score here. Then turn to page 219 and transfer your score onto Graph 1.

Personal	
Vocabulary	
Strategy	
Comprehension	
TOTAL SCORE	✓ T

Extending

Choose one or both of these activities:

MAKE A BICYCLE-SAFETY VIDEO

With more people riding bicycles every day, it's a good idea to know how to stay safe on one. With two or three other students, make a video that covers some or all of the following information:

- choosing the right bike
- choosing the right safety equipment for your bike (bell, horn, reflectors, etc.)
- choosing protective gear (helmet, reflective clothing, etc.)
- rules of the road

To get started, use some of the resources listed on this page, or talk to a local bike-shop owner. Share your completed video with the rest of your class or school.

RESEARCH GREECE

The little town in Greece where this story takes place is probably quite different from your hometown. Find some photographs of modern Greece, particularly photos of small towns where using a bicycle makes good sense. Check sources such as an encyclopedia, travel brochures, and Internet sites to find out what you would see and experience if you visited or lived in Greece.

Resources

Books

Allard, Denise. *Greece*. Postcards From. Raintree/Steck-Vaughn, 1997.

Bellingham, David. *Greece*. Travel Bug Guide. Sun Tree, 1994.

Francis, John. *Bicycling*. How to Play the All-Star Way. Raintree/Steck-Vaughn, 1998.

Web Sites

http://homepage.ntlworld.com/anthony.campbell1/cycling/greece/
This site offers maps, photos, and other information related to bicycling in Greece.

http://kidshealth.org/kid/watch/out/bike_safety.html
This Web site explains the importance of bike safety and provides a bike-safety checklist.

Supergrandpa

Building Background

"Supergrandpa" is a story based on a real person named Gustaf Håkansson. In 1951, when Håkansson was 66 years old, he entered the Tour of Sweden, the longest bicycle race in that country's history. A little girl who saw Håkansson ride by during the race called him *Stålfarfar*, which in English means "Steel Grandfather." Author David M. Schwartz translated *Stålfarfar* as "Supergrandpa" because the Swedish name for the comic hero Superman is *Stålman*.

Schwartz based "Supergrandpa" on Håkansson's actual experiences during the race, but he invented most of the dialogue and other small details. The outcome of the race, however, was not one of Schwartz's inventions.

banner

collapsed

official

sprinted

struggling

victory

Vocabulary Builder

1. The words in the margin are all from "Supergrandpa." Find those words in the sentences below. If the boldfaced word in a sentence is used correctly, write a **C** on the line next to it. If the boldfaced word is used incorrectly, write an **I**.

2. Save your work. You will refer to it again in the Vocabulary Check.

   _____ a. The manager hung a **banner** in the widow to advertise the store's grand opening.

   _____ b. The rickety old chair **collapsed** when Mick piled too many books on it.

   _____ c. We knew Malik's letter was a fake when we saw the **official** seal at the top.

   _____ d. The Tortoise **sprinted** to the finish line by taking slow, steady steps.

   _____ e. **Struggling** with this math problem was the easiest thing I've done.

   _____ f. Jason led his team to **victory** as he scored the winning touchdown.

Strategy Builder

Following the Sequence of a Story

- When you read a story, you are reading a series of events. Those events happen in chronological order, or **sequence**. Paying attention to the sequence of events will help you (1) follow what is happening, (2) predict what might happen next, and (3) make sense of the story.

- To make the sequence of events as clear as possible, authors often use **signal words**. Some examples of signal words are *first, next, before dinner,* and *early the next morning.*

- As you read the following paragraphs, use the underlined signal words to help you follow the sequence of events.

<u>Early last spring</u>, the Anderson family decided to visit Sweden. <u>First</u>, they read all they could about the country. They checked travel magazines, encyclopedia articles, and the Internet for information. <u>After they had found enough</u>, they contacted a travel agent. <u>When she heard what they wanted to see</u>, she made reservations for them.

The Andersons couldn't wait to get started. They set out on their journey <u>in June</u>. They stopped <u>for a while</u> in Stockholm and took in the sights of the capital. <u>After that</u>, they visited small towns such as Grantofta. The Andersons thoroughly enjoyed themselves. <u>By the end of their trip</u>, they had fallen in love with Sweden.

If you wanted to show the sequence of events in the paragraphs above, you could use a **sequence chain** like this one:

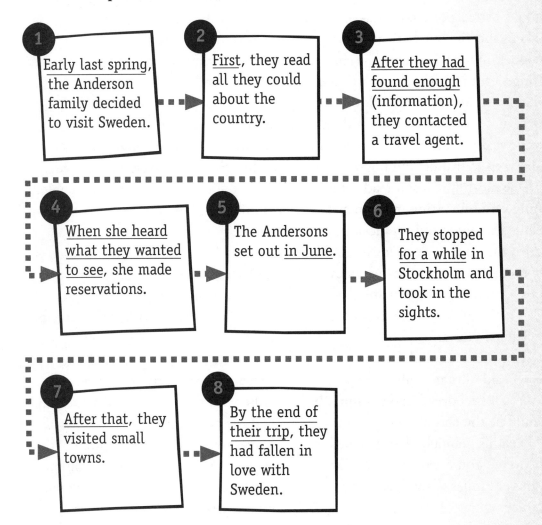

1. Early last spring, the Anderson family decided to visit Sweden.

2. <u>First</u>, they read all they could about the country.

3. <u>After they had found enough</u> (information), they contacted a travel agent.

4. <u>When she heard what they wanted to see</u>, she made reservations.

5. The Andersons set out <u>in June</u>.

6. They stopped <u>for a while</u> in Stockholm and took in the sights.

7. <u>After that</u>, they visited small towns.

8. <u>By the end of their trip</u>, they had fallen in love with Sweden.

Supergrandpa

by David M. Schwartz

As you read the first part of "Supergrandpa," apply the strategies that you just learned. Notice the underlined signal words. They will give you a more exact picture of the sequence of events.

Gustaf Håkansson was sixty-six years old. His hair was snow-white. His beard was a white bush. His face rippled with wrinkles whenever he smiled. Gustaf Håkansson looked like an old man, but he didn't feel old and he certainly didn't act old.

Everyone for miles around knew Gustaf. People saw him on his bicycle, rain or shine, riding through the crooked streets of Grantofta—past the baker's and the butcher's and the wooden-toy maker's, over the stone bridge leading out of town, up steep hills scattered with farms, down narrow lanes bordered by stones, then home again to his morning paper and a bowl of sour milk and lingonberries.

<u>One morning</u> Gustaf read something very interesting in the paper. There was going to be a bicycle race called the Tour of Sweden. It would be more than one thousand miles long, and it would last many days.

"This Tour of Sweden is for me!" exclaimed Gustaf.

"But you're too old for a bicycle race," said Gustaf's wife.

"You'll keel over," said his son. "It would be the end of you."

Even his grandchildren laughed at the idea. "You can't ride your bike a thousand miles, Grandpa," they scoffed.

"*Struntprat!*" Gustaf answered. "Silly talk!" And he hopped onto his bike and rode off to see the judges of the race. He would tell them that he planned to enter the Tour of Sweden.

"But this race is for young people," said the first judge. "You're too old, Gustaf."

"You would never make it to the finish," said the second judge.

"We can only admit racers who are strong and fit," said the third judge. "What if you **collapsed** in the middle of the race?"

"*Struntprat!*" protested Gustaf. "I have no intention of collapsing, because I *am* strong and fit!"

But the judges were not moved. "We're sorry, Gustaf," they grumbled. "Go home. Go home to your rocking chair."

Gustaf went home, but he did not go to his rocking chair. "They can keep me out of the race," he muttered, "but they can't keep me off the road."

<u>The next morning</u>, Gustaf began to prepare for the long ride ahead. He arose with the sun, packed some fruit and rye bread, and cycled far out of town—over rolling hills dotted with ancient castles, across valleys dimpled with lakes, through forests thick with birches and pines. <u>It was midafternoon</u>

before he returned. The next day he biked even farther. Each day he added more miles to his ride.

A few days before the race, all the young cyclists boarded a special train to Haparanda, in the far north of Sweden, where the race was to begin. But Gustaf was not an **official** racer. He had no train ticket.

There was only one way for Gustaf to ride in the Tour of Sweden. He would have to pedal six hundred miles to the starting line!

It took him several days to bike there. He arrived just as the Tour of Sweden was about to begin.

All the racers wore numbers, but of course there was no number for Gustaf. So he found a bright red scrap of fabric and made his own.

What number should he be? He had an idea. He wasn't supposed to be in the race at all, so he would be Number Zero!

He chuckled as he cut out a big red zero and pinned it to his shirt. Then he wheeled his bicycle to the starting line.

The starting gun went off and all the young cyclists took off in a spurt. Their legs pumped furiously and their bikes **sprinted** ahead. They soon left Gustaf far behind.

⬛ **Stop here for the Strategy Break.**

Strategy Break

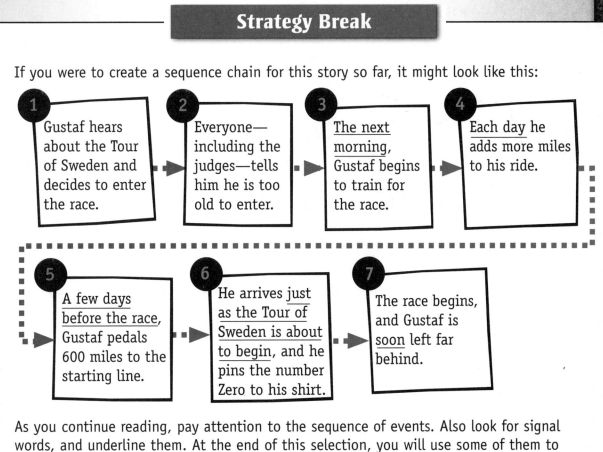

If you were to create a sequence chain for this story so far, it might look like this:

1. Gustaf hears about the Tour of Sweden and decides to enter the race.

2. Everyone—including the judges—tells him he is too old to enter.

3. The next morning, Gustaf begins to train for the race.

4. Each day he adds more miles to his ride.

5. A few days before the race, Gustaf pedals 600 miles to the starting line.

6. He arrives just as the Tour of Sweden is about to begin, and he pins the number Zero to his shirt.

7. The race begins, and Gustaf is soon left far behind.

As you continue reading, pay attention to the sequence of events. Also look for signal words, and underline them. At the end of this selection, you will use some of them to complete a sequence chain of your own.

➡️ **Go on reading to see what happens.**

That night, the racers stopped at an inn. They were treated to dinner and a bed.

Hours later, Gustaf reached the inn, too. But there was no bed for him, so he just kept riding. While the others snoozed the night away, Gustaf pedaled into the dawn.

Early the next day, the other cyclists passed Gustaf. But he kept up his steady pace, and late that evening he again overtook the young racers as they rested. In the middle of the night, he napped for three hours on a park bench.

On the third morning, Gustaf was the first to arrive in the little town of Lulea. A small crowd of people waited, hoping to catch a glimpse of the racers zooming by. Instead they saw Gustaf. His white beard fluttered in the breeze. His red cheeks were puffed out with breath. "Look!" cried a little girl. "Look! There goes Supergrandpa!"

"Supergrandpa?" Everyone craned to see.

"Yes, yes, he does look like a Supergrandpa!" A few clapped. Others shouted friendly greetings. Some of the children held out their hands and Gustaf brushed their palms as he rode by. "Thank you, Supergrandpa! Good luck to you."

A photographer snapped Gustaf's picture. It appeared the next day in the newspaper. The headline read: *Supergrandpa Takes a Ride.*

Now all of Sweden knew about Supergrandpa Gustaf Håkansson.

When he got hungry or thirsty, people gave him sour milk with lingonberries, tea and cake, fruit juice, rye bread, or any other snack he wanted.

Newspaper reporters rushed up to talk with him. Radio interviewers broadcast every word he spoke. Everyone wanted to know how he felt.

"I have never felt better in my whole life," he told them.

"But aren't you tired?" they asked.

"How can I be tired when I am surrounded by so much kindness?" And with a push on the pedal and a wave of his hand, Gustaf was rolling down the road again.

Once again Gustaf rode through the night, passing the other racers while they slept. When his muscles felt stiff, he remembered his cheering fans. He pedaled harder.

And so it went, day after night, night after day. By the light of the moon, Gustaf quietly passed the young racers in their beds, then slept outside, but only for a few hours. Under the long rays of the morning sun, they overtook him and left him **struggling** to keep up his spirits and his pace. But each day it took them a little longer to catch up with Gustaf.

On the sixth morning of the race, thousands lined the road. As Gustaf rode by, their joyful cheers traveled with him like a wave through the crowd.

"You're almost there, Supergrandpa!"

"A few more miles!"

"Don't look back."

"You're going to win!"

Win? Gustaf hadn't thought about winning. He had simply wanted to ride in the Tour of Sweden and reach the finish line. But win?

"You're out in front, Supergrandpa."

"A few more miles, Supergrandpa, and you'll be the winner!"

The winner? Gustaf glanced over his shoulder. The pack of racers was catching up. Their heads and shoulders were hunched low over their handlebars. Their backs were raised high above their seats.

Gustaf decided not to think about them. Instead he thought about his many fans. He thought about how they wanted him to win. And suddenly, he wanted to win too!

Gustaf looked ahead. In the distance he could see a bright **banner** stretched all the way across the road. The finish line!

Gustaf lowered his head. He raised his back. He whipped his legs around with all their might and all their motion.

The next time he looked up he was bursting through the banner and rolling over the finish line—just before another racer thundered past.

The crowd roared. People lifted Gustaf onto their shoulders. They showered him with flowers. They sang **victory** songs. The police played patriotic marches.

The three judges, however, said that Gustaf could *not* be the winner, because he was never actually in the race. Besides, it was against the rules to ride at night. No, the big gold trophy would go to another racer, not to Gustaf.

But no one seemed to care what the judges said. Even the king stepped up to hug Gustaf and invite him to the palace. And to nearly everyone in Sweden, Gustaf Håkansson—sixty-six years old, his hair as white as snow, his beard a great white bush, his smiling face an orb of wrinkles—to them, Supergrandpa Gustaf Håkansson had won the Tour of Sweden. ●

Strategy Follow-up

Now create a sequence chain for the second part of "Supergrandpa." Use a separate sheet of paper if you need more room. Don't forget to use (and underline) as many signal words as possible.

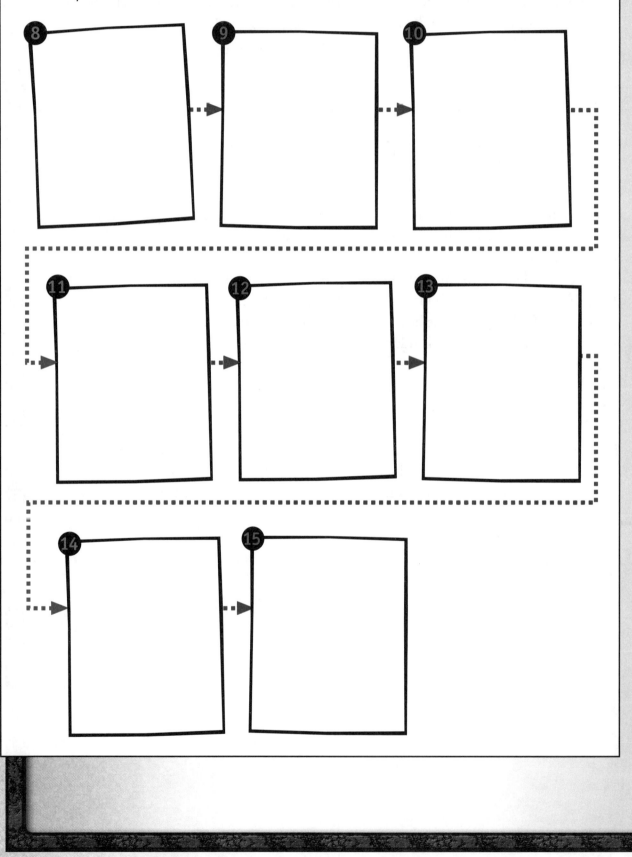

✓Personal Checklist

Read each question and put a check (✓) in the correct box.

1. How well do you understand what happens in "Supergrandpa"?
   - ☐ 3 (extremely well)
   - ☐ 2 (fairly well)
   - ☐ 1 (not well)

2. How well do you understand why participating in the Tour of Sweden was so important to Gustaf Håkansson?
   - ☐ 3 (extremely well)
   - ☐ 2 (fairly well)
   - ☐ 1 (not well)

3. In the Vocabulary Builder, how well were you able to decide if the vocabulary words were used correctly or incorrectly?
   - ☐ 3 (extremely well)
   - ☐ 2 (fairly well)
   - ☐ 1 (not well)

4. How well were you able to follow the sequence of events leading up to Gustaf's victory?
   - ☐ 3 (extremely well)
   - ☐ 2 (fairly well)
   - ☐ 1 (not well)

5. How well were you able to complete the sequence chain in the Strategy Follow-up?
   - ☐ 3 (extremely well)
   - ☐ 2 (fairly well)
   - ☐ 1 (not well)

Vocabulary Check

Look back at the work you did in the Vocabulary Builder. Then answer each question by circling the correct letter.

1. Which word is an antonym of *victory*?
   - a. defeat
   - b. triumph
   - c. success

2. Which word or phrase does this story use to mean the same thing as *collapse*?
   - a. admit
   - b. keel over
   - c. sprint

3. Which of the following is an example of an official document?
   - a. a greeting card
   - b. a name tag at a party
   - c. a birth certificate

4. Which meaning of the word *banner* fits this selection?
   - a. a type of flag or pennant
   - b. outstanding or superior
   - c. a heading on a newspaper

5. At the beginning of the race, the young racers sprinted. Why did they do that?
   - a. because they were tired and needed a push
   - b. because they wanted to set the race's pace
   - c. because they wanted to get a quick lead

Add the numbers that you just checked to get your Personal Checklist score. Fill in your score here. Then turn to page 219 and transfer your score onto Graph 1.

Personal

Vocabulary

Strategy

Comprehension

TOTAL SCORE

✓ T

Check your answers with your teacher. Give yourself 1 point for each correct answer, and fill in your Vocabulary score here. Then turn to page 219 and transfer your score onto Graph 1.

Personal

Vocabulary

Strategy

Comprehension

TOTAL SCORE

✓ T

Strategy Check

Review the sequence chain that you completed in the Strategy Follow-up. Then answer these questions:

1. Which sentence could you have written for Event 8?
    a. That night, the racers stop at the inn.
    b. Hours later, Gustaf reaches the inn but keeps on riding.
    c. Day after night, night after day, Gustaf passes the racers.

2. Which phrase is *not* an example of signal words?
    a. in the middle of the night
    b. the trophy goes to someone else
    c. on the sixth morning of the race

3. How long after the racers stop at the inn does Gustaf get there?
    a. hours later
    b. days later
    c. weeks later

4. On what day of the race does a little girl call Gustaf Supergrandpa?
    a. on the first day
    b. on the third day
    c. on the sixth day

5. Which sentence could be the last event on your sequence chain?
    a. In the middle of the night, Gustaf naps for three hours.
    b. Hours later, Gustaf reaches the inn but keeps on riding.
    c. On the sixth morning of the race, Gustaf wins the Tour of Sweden.

Comprehension Check

Review the selection if necessary. Then answer these questions:

1. Why is Gustaf not allowed to enter the Tour of Sweden?
    a. He doesn't have energy for a long race.
    b. There are too many people entered already.
    c. The judges tell him that he is too old.

2. How does Gustaf get to the place where the race begins?
    a. He takes the train there.
    b. He rides his bike there.
    c. He takes a car there.

3. Why are people so interested in Gustaf?
    a. because he is so unusual and inspiring
    b. because he is from a very small town
    c. because he is the fastest cyclist in the race

4. What does Gustaf do each night of the race?
    a. He collapses from weariness.
    b. He sleeps at the inns, as the others do.
    c. He rides for hours to get ahead.

5. What lesson do you think Gustaf would want people to learn from this story?
    a. Bicycle racing is only for young people.
    b. You're never too old to do what you enjoy.
    c. Judges are always against old people.

Check your answers with your teacher. Give yourself 1 point for each correct answer, and fill in your Strategy score here. Then turn to page 219 and transfer your score onto Graph 1.

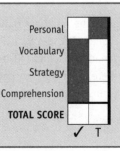

Check your answers with your teacher. Give yourself 1 point for each correct answer, and fill in your Comprehension score here. Then turn to page 219 and transfer your score onto Graph 1.

Extending

Choose one or both of these activities:

CREATE A CYCLIST'S DIARY

Suppose you were a participant in one of the many bicycle tours that take place around the world each year. What experiences might you encounter during a several-day bike ride? What would be your feelings and thoughts during that time? Write diary entries for a six-day bicycle tour from the standpoint of a participant. Before you begin, you might use some of the resources listed on this page to research a popular bike tour to learn about the experiences of some of its participants.

LEARN THE BASICS OF BICYCLE TOURING

Is just any bicycle appropriate if you want to take up touring? To find out, use some of the resources on this page, or visit a bike store and ask a salesperson to show you what makes a good touring bike. What should you look for in a touring bike that sets it apart from other kinds? Bring a large photo of a touring bike to class—or a real bike, if possible—and give a short demonstration. Point out what to look for in a good touring bike.

Resources

Books

Butterman, Steve. *Bicycle Touring: How to Prepare for Long Rides.* Wilderness Press, 1994.

Gutman, Bill. *Bicycling.* Action Sports. Capstone Press, 1996.

Hamlin, Charlotte. *Ride with the Wind: The Adventures of a Grandmother Who Bicycled Around the World.* Review & Herald Publishing, 1997.

Web Sites

http://home5.swipnet.se/~w-51766/scf.html
This is the Web site of the Swedish Cycling Federation.

http://www.cyclingtouristresources.net/touringbikes.htm
This Web site explains what makes a good touring bike.

The Challenge

aerial acrobatics

altitude

aviation

aviatrix

celebrity

confidence

determination

inspired

Building Background

The stunt flyers of the early 20th century were real daredevils. Many of them had been trained as pilots during World War I. After the war, they bought their own planes and traveled around the United States, entertaining crowds with air shows known as flying circuses. At night, they would park their planes in nearby barns, and so they were called barnstormers.

These pilots did amazing tricks. For example, Lincoln Beachey was able to pick up a handkerchief from the ground with his wing tip. He also flew under the bridge at Niagara Falls. Many pilots did loop-the-loops, figure eights, and death-defying dives.

Sometimes daredevils walked on the wings of the planes in flight. Gladys Roy, for example, danced the Charleston on a plane's wing. Mabel Cody, hanging by her teeth from a cord attached to a wing, spun hundreds of feet above the ground. Unfortunately, these trick often ended in disaster. Many stunt pilots and wing walkers fell to their death. Eventually, stricter rules were put into place, and flying circuses became a thing of the past.

CLIPBOARD 1

Airplanes and Pilots

Vocabulary Builder

1. Before you begin reading "The Challenge," separate the words in the margin into two groups. (Use a dictionary for any words you don't know.) On the first clipboard, list the vocabulary words that are connected to airplanes and pilots.

2. On the second clipboard, list the vocabulary words that could be connected to people who face challenges.

3. As you read the article, look for other words that you could add to each clipboard. Save your work. You will refer to it again in the Vocabulary Check.

CLIPBOARD 2

Facing Challenges

Strategy Builder

How to Read a Biography

- In this lesson, you will read a biography of a stunt pilot named Bessie Coleman. A **biography** tells the story of a real person's life and is written by someone else. Since it is written by someone else, we say it is written from the **third-person point of view**.

- Since the events in most biographies are described in chronological order, the organizational pattern of a biography is **sequence**. To make the sequence as clear as possible, authors often use **signal words**. Some signal words—such as *then, next,* and *a short time later*—help you link one smaller event to the next in a biography. However, signal words such as *When she was twelve* or *in 1926* help you see the sequence of the major, or most important, events in a person's life.

- To show the major events in a person's life, you can use a **time line**. Study this time line of the life of pilot Amelia Earhart. Notice how the major events in her life are arranged from left to right.

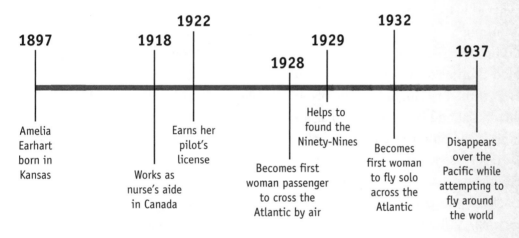

1897	1918	1922	1928	1929	1932	1937
Amelia Earhart born in Kansas	Works as nurse's aide in Canada	Earns her pilot's license	Becomes first woman passenger to cross the Atlantic by air	Helps to found the Ninety-Nines	Becomes first woman to fly solo across the Atlantic	Disappears over the Pacific while attempting to fly around the world

The Challenge

by Margaret Roberts

Now use what you've learned to track the events in this biography of Bessie Coleman. Notice the signal words. They will help make the sequence clearer. (The words signaling major events are underlined twice.)

As the little airplane soared higher and higher into the clear blue sky, every face in the crowd was turned upward, intently watching. The only sound was the plane's engine, growing fainter now as the pilot urged the craft still higher.

Suddenly the plane flipped upside down and began to fall, almost like a leaf, turning over and over as it lost **altitude**. The silence on the ground exploded into a great roaring cry—but the cry turned to laughter as the plane righted itself and began to climb again. In a flash the pilot leveled the aircraft and began a series of snap rolls around the horizontal axis, spinning like a top while flying straight ahead. The crowd went crazy, yelling and cheering.

The superb exhibition of **aerial acrobatics** ended ten minutes later as the plane came in for a perfect landing. The pilot, thirty-year-old Bessie Coleman, hopped down from the open cockpit, grinning happily as she took off her goggles and unbuttoned her heavy jacket.

The date was September 1922. Orville and Wilbur Wright had flown the first airplane less than twenty years earlier, but that flight had lasted only twelve seconds. Now who was this incredible woman and how had she arrived at this triumphant moment?

Bessie Coleman, the first black woman to fly an airplane, was born January 26, 1892, the tenth of George and Susan Coleman's thirteen children. When Bessie was nine years old, her father left the family home in Waxahachie, Texas, and never returned. To earn money for food and clothing, the children pitched in and picked cotton on a nearby plantation. Their mother, Susan, took in washing and did maid work for a white family in town.

Bessie was a good student and completed all eight grades at the little Waxahachie school for black children. She wanted to continue her education, but in those days white people and black people went to separate schools—from kindergarten all the way through college. Unfortunately, there was no black high school close enough for Bessie to attend.

As a young teenager, Bessie conceived her dream of becoming a famous pilot. It seemed an impossible goal. But Bessie was never one to shy away from challenges, for she had great **determination** and solid **confidence** in herself. Carefully, she developed a plan.

First she had to earn money for flying lessons. She began by taking in washing, walking four miles to town to pick up the laundry. After carrying it home, she scrubbed the garments on a washboard, starched them, wrung them out by hand, and hung them on a clothesline to dry. <u>Then</u> she pressed the clothes, using a heavy iron heated on the kitchen stove. It was hard, unpleasant, boring work, but Bessie never felt humbled by it—she was willing to work at anything that would bring her closer to her goal. Her self-confidence and ability to finish whatever she undertook kept her going. <u>By day</u> she worked like a trouper; <u>at night</u> she indulged in her only pleasure, reading the books she constantly borrowed from the town library.

<u>By the time she was nineteen</u>, Bessie had earned enough money to begin her next step. She withdrew her savings from the bank and took the train to Chicago, sitting on one of the hard wooden benches in the section assigned to African-Americans—far from the comfortable, upholstered seats reserved for white passengers.

In Chicago she stayed with her married brother, Walter, and enrolled in a beauty school for African-Americans. <u>Soon after</u>, she found a cheap apartment of her own. <u>Through the months of beauty-school training</u>, she walked the cold winter streets to classes, counting the days until graduation when she would find a professional, well-paying job. Her savings lasted <u>just long enough</u> for her to complete the course.

<u>For the next five years</u>, Bessie worked in the White Sox Barber Shop, manicuring the nails of customers while they had their shaves and haircuts. Between salary and tips at the barber shop, and a second job working at a chili parlor, Bessie was now saving money in earnest. <u>When at last satisfied with the size of her bank account</u>, she began to look for a flying school.

⬣ **Stop here for the Strategy Break.**

Strategy Break

If you were to show the major events described in this biography so far, your time line might look like this:

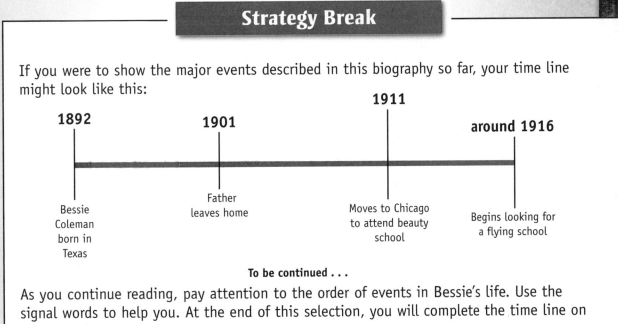

1892	1901	1911	around 1916
Bessie Coleman born in Texas	Father leaves home	Moves to Chicago to attend beauty school	Begins looking for a flying school

To be continued . . .

As you continue reading, pay attention to the order of events in Bessie's life. Use the signal words to help you. At the end of this selection, you will complete the time line on your own.

➡️ **Go on reading.**

She quickly learned that all doors to **aviation** were closed to her. A black woman wanting to fly airplanes? No way! Unthinkable! But Bessie Coleman was a person who refused to take no for an answer.

She introduced herself to Robert S. Abbott, African-American owner and publisher of the *Chicago Defender*, a respected newspaper in the city. She hoped he would have some ideas for her—and he did. A few women were flying in France, he said. He suggested she take an intensive language course, learn to speak at least some French, and then go to France to become a pilot. For the next few months Bessie studied French until her teacher felt that she could "get by"; then, with the encouragement and financial help of Abbott and some of his friends, she booked passage on a ship to France. Bessie was grateful to Mr. Abbott. She once told a newspaper reporter that "he is the man who gave me my chance. I will never forget him."

The first flight school Bessie applied to in France refused to accept her because two women students had recently been killed in crashes. That might have been enough to scare off the average person, but Bessie was far from average. She found another school and at long last began to learn to fly.

Shortly after she began her flight training, Bessie witnessed an accident in which one of the male student pilots was killed. "It was a terrible shock to my nerves," she wrote, "but I never lost them. I kept going."

After ten months of tough, exhausting training and after passing all the examinations, both written and in the air, Bessie stayed on for an extra month to polish her skills in aerial acrobatics. In September 1921 she sailed back to the United States—the world's first licensed black woman pilot.

Bessie had, of course, kept in touch with Robert Abbott during her absence. Upon her arrival in New York, he proudly arranged her first American appearance, sponsored and financed by the *Chicago Defender*. The announcement proclaimed: "CHICAGO **AVIATRIX** TO SHOW NEW YORKERS HOW SHE DOES HER STUFF! BESSIE COLEMAN WILL GIVE AN AERIAL ACRO-BATIC EXHIBITION ON AUGUST 27TH. THIS WILL BE HER FIRST FLIGHT IN AMERICA!"

Rain caused cancellation of the August 27 exhibition, but a few days later Bessie performed at Glenn Curtiss Field in Long Island, New York. Her aerial acrobatics were part of a program honoring veterans of World War I. An even greater triumph was her first performance at Checkerboard Field in her "home-town" of Chicago on October 15, 1922. Bessie gave a dazzling perfor-mance of loop-the-loops, slow rolls, snap rolls, tailspins, inverted flight, and her own distinctive rendition of the "falling leaf." The crowd went wild. After that, Bessie speedily

LESSON 10: THE CHALLENGE

became a **celebrity**, performing her marvelous acrobatic flights all over the country—sometimes alone and sometimes with small groups of ex-World War I pilots who organized air shows of their own.

Early in 1924 Bessie had an accident when her plane's engine failed. But not even several broken ribs, a broken leg, and assorted cuts and bruises could dampen her effervescent spirit. As she told a reporter who interviewed her in the hospital, "You just tell the world that I'm coming back!" And, of course, she did.

In 1925, as she toured the country, Bessie began giving lectures in schools, churches, and theaters, urging her African-American audiences to become involved in the fast-expanding aviation industry. There would soon be great career opportunities, she told them, and they must be a part of them. It was due in part to Bessie's influence that many young African-American men became military pilots during World War II, earning high honors as members of the famous 99th Squadron of fighters. Bessie's example also **inspired** countless others to make careers in various aspects of aviation.

On April 29, 1926, disaster struck again. Bessie and another pilot were in the air when a wrench someone had carelessly left in the open cockpit slipped into the space where the control stick emerged through the floor. It jammed the stick into the full-forward position, sending the plane into a vertical dive from which it could not recover. Both pilots were killed. Bessie was just thirty-four years old.

Bessie Coleman has by no means been forgotten. In 1990, sixty-four years after her death, the mayor of Chicago gave the honorary name "Bessie Coleman Drive" to a highway leading to that city's busy O'Hare International Airport. In 1992, the Chicago City Council passed a resolution that said, "Bessie Coleman continues to inspire untold thousands of young persons with her sense of adventure, her positive attitude, and her determination to succeed." In 1995 the U.S. Postal Service issued a thirty-two-cent postage stamp in her honor—depicting Bessie in her leather flying helmet and jacket, ready to climb into the cockpit and soar high above the earth. ●

Strategy Follow-up

Now complete the time line below with information from the second part of this biography. (Note that some of the events occur after Bessie's death.) Use another sheet of paper if you need more room.

✓Personal Checklist

Read each question and put a check (✓) in the correct box.

1. How well do you understand what kind of person Bessie Coleman was?
    - ☐ 3   (extremely well)
    - ☐ 2   (fairly well)
    - ☐ 1   (not well)

2. How well were you able to use the information in Building Background to help you understand her accomplishments?
    - ☐ 3   (extremely well)
    - ☐ 2   (fairly well)
    - ☐ 1   (not well)

3. In the Vocabulary Builder, how well were you able to put each word on the appropriate clipboard?
    - ☐ 3   (extremely well)
    - ☐ 2   (fairly well)
    - ☐ 1   (not well)

4. How well were you able to complete the time line in the Strategy Follow-up?
    - ☐ 3   (extremely well)
    - ☐ 2   (fairly well)
    - ☐ 1   (not well)

5. How well do you understand why Bessie Coleman had part of a Chicago highway named after her?
    - ☐ 3   (extremely well)
    - ☐ 2   (fairly well)
    - ☐ 1   (not well)

Vocabulary Check

Look back at the work you did in the Vocabulary Builder. Then answer each question by circling the correct letter.

1. Which word is most closely related to airplanes and pilots?
    - a. aviation
    - b. celebrity
    - c. inspire

2. Which word is most closely related to people who successfully face challenges?
    - a. altitude
    - b. aviation
    - c. determination

3. Which meaning of the word *confidence* best fits this selection?
    - a. faith in oneself
    - b. secret kept
    - c. credit given

4. Which phrase describes every aviatrix?
    - a. stunt flyer
    - b. female
    - c. African American

5. Which of the following is *not* an example of aerial acrobatics?
    - a. loop-the-loop
    - b. handspring
    - c. snap roll

Add the numbers that you just checked to get your Personal Checklist score. Fill in your score here. Then turn to page 219 and transfer your score onto Graph 1.

Check your answers with your teacher. Give yourself 1 point for each correct answer, and fill in your Vocabulary score here. Then turn to page 219 and transfer your score onto Graph 1.

Strategy Check

Review the time line that you completed in the Strategy Follow-up. Then answer these questions:

1. How old was Bessie Coleman when she became the world's first licensed black woman pilot?

    a. about 23 years old

    b. about 29 years old

    c. about 31 years old

2. In what year did she give her first American aerial acrobatic exhibition?

    a. 1922

    b. 1924

    c. 1926

3. What happened in 1926?

    a. Bessie became the world's first black woman pilot.

    b. Bessie had an accident when her plane's engine failed.

    c. Bessie was killed in a plane crash.

4. Which event occurred 64 years after Bessie's death?

    a. A Chicago highway was named after her.

    b. A resolution about Bessie was passed in Chicago.

    c. A U.S. postage stamp was issued in her honor.

5. In what year did the U.S. Postal Service issue a stamp in her honor?

    a. 1990

    b. 1992

    c. 1995

Comprehension Check

Review the selection if necessary. Then answer these questions:

1. What detail from Bessie's life suggests that she was not a quitter?

    a. She was the tenth of thirteen children in her family.

    b. She worked for years to save money for flying school.

    c. She read books whenever she got a chance.

2. Which event points out the difficult situation that African Americans faced in the early 20th century?

    a. Bessie was not allowed to attend the white high school in her hometown.

    b. Bessie's return to the States was announced in the newspaper.

    c. Bessie became a celebrity and performed all over the country.

3. Where did Bessie enroll in Chicago?

    a. flight school

    b. beauty school

    c. secretarial school

4. How did Robert Abbott help Bessie?

    a. He scheduled all of her appearances in U.S. air shows.

    b. He persuaded a school in France to accept her as a student.

    c. He provided financial support so that she could study in France.

5. According to this biography, what was the cause of Bessie's death?

    a. A wrench jammed the control stick and sent her plane into a dive.

    b. Bessie never recovered from her terrible plane accident in 1924.

    c. Bessie died during a fancy flying trick that failed.

Check your answers with your teacher. Give yourself 1 point for each correct answer, and fill in your Strategy score here. Then turn to page 219 and transfer your score onto Graph 1.

| Personal |
| Vocabulary |
| Strategy |
| Comprehension |
| **TOTAL SCORE** |

Check your answers with your teacher. Give yourself 1 point for each correct answer, and fill in your Comprehension score here. Then turn to page 219 and transfer your score onto Graph 1.

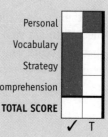

| Personal |
| Vocabulary |
| Strategy |
| Comprehension |
| **TOTAL SCORE** |

Extending

Choose one or both of these activities:

MAKE A COMIC BOOK

Make a comic book about Bessie Coleman's life. Use your time line and some of the resources listed on this page to help you list the events that you want to include. Draw a panel depicting each major event. Then cut out the panels and arrange them in chronological order on sheets of paper. Next, write simple captions to explain what is happening in each panel. Finally, bind the sheets together into a book.

CONDUCT A SURVEY

As an African American and a woman, Bessie Coleman faced many obstacles and limitations in her life. Conduct a survey among classmates, family, and friends about the limitations that women and African Americans still face in the United States today. Report your findings in the form of a chart or a written report.

Resources

Books

Hart, Philip S., and Barbara O'Connor. *Up in the Air: The Story of Bessie Coleman.* Trailblazers. Carolrhoda Books, 1996.

Johnson, Dolores. *She Dared to Fly: Bessie Coleman.* Benchmark Biographies. Benchmarks Books, 1997.

Rich, Doris L. *Amelia Earhart: A Biography.* Smithsonian Institution Press, 1996.

———. *Queen Bess: Daredevil Aviator.* Smithsonian Institution Press, 1993.

Web Sites

http://www.bessiecoleman.com/
This Web site is dedicated to Bessie Coleman.

http://www.ninety-nines.org
This is the Web page of the Ninety-Nines, an international organization of women pilots.

Videos/DVDs

Dreams of Flight. Smithsonian. Questar, 1998.

The New Heroes of the 20th Century. Questar, 1997.

Learning New Words

Compound Words

A compound word is made up of two words put together. In "The Tale of the Tiger's Paintbrush" you read about how Chen-cho paints landscapes with a paintbrush made from Lao-hu's tail hairs. *Landscapes* and *paintbrush* are compound words. A landscape is a picture or view of a land scene. A paintbrush is a brush used to paint landscapes and other things.

Fill in each blank with a compound word by combining a word from Row 1 with a word from Row 2.

Row 1:   tea   snow   silver   gem
Row 2:   ware   stone   pot   storm

1. utensils that you eat with = _____

2. container for brewing hot beverages = _____

3. blizzard = _____

4. precious jewels = _____

Suffix

A *suffix* is a word part that is added to the end of a root word. When you add a suffix, you often change the root word's meaning and function. For example, the suffix *-ful* means "full of," so the root word *pain* changes from a noun to an adjective meaning "full of pain."

-ist

The suffix *-ist* turns a word into a noun that means "a person who _____." For example, Chen-cho is an artist. The word *artist* can be defined as "a person who creates or performs art."

Write the word that describes each person below.

1. a person who styles people's hair   _____

2. a person who manicures nails   _____

3. a person who terrorizes others   _____

4. a person who's an expert in chemistry   _____

5. a person who has specialized skills or knowledge   _____

Multiple-Meaning Words

A single word can have more than one meaning. For example, the word *banner* can mean "flag or pennant" or "headline across the top of a newspaper." To figure out which meaning of *banner* an author is using, you have to use context. Context is the information surrounding a word or situation that helps you understand it. When you read "Supergrandpa" in Lesson 9, you used context to figure out that *banner* meant "flag or pennant."

Now use context to figure out the meaning of each underlined word. Circle the letter of the correct meaning.

1. Jackson and I arrived at the New Year's Eve party at the <u>stroke</u> of midnight.

   a. sound made by striking a bell or other object

   b. movement made over and over while swimming

2. Beneath the <u>surface</u>, Mr. Niedermaier is a very sensitive person.

   a. top or side of something

   b. outward appearance

3. The <u>chains</u> around the gate kept people from getting into the parking lot after 10:00 P.M.

   a. individual businesses owned by a single company

   b. metal links joined together

4. The audience <u>roared</u> as the comedian told one joke after another.

   a. laughed loudly

   b. made a loud, deep sound

5. The neon colors in Jacquie's dress <u>screamed</u> for our attention.

   a. produced a startling effect

   b. made a high, piercing sound

VOCABULARY

From Lesson 6
- strokes
- surface

From Lesson 8
- chains
- chatter
- roar
- scream

From Lesson 9
- banner

Amusement- Park Rides

Building Background

Almost everyone has been to an amusement park at one time or another. When you were little, you probably enjoyed rides that are different from the ones you like now. If you went to an amusement park today, which rides would you gladly stand in line for, and why?

Think of the five amusement-park rides that you enjoy riding most, and list them below. Then predict which rides the kids in this article will say they like best.

Favorite: _____

Second Favorite: _____

Third Favorite: _____

Fourth Favorite: _____

Fifth Favorite: _____

adrenaline

airtime

horseplay

inertia

misdemeanor

overwhelmed

Vocabulary Builder

1. The vocabulary words in this article are all explained in context. That means that the surrounding words and sentences contain examples or definitions that help explain the words.

2. Read the following sentences, which are taken from the article. The vocabulary word in each sentence is boldfaced. Underline the context clues that help you understand the word.

   a. Your body responds to terror by releasing chemicals such as **adrenaline**.

   b. Backseat riders also enjoy the most **airtime**—the flying-out-of-your-seat feeling you get as the car goes over the top of a hill.

   c. Airtime is caused by **inertia** (the tendency of moving objects to keep moving in the same direction) and makes you feel nearly weightless—if only for a moment.

   d. But when it gets so many signals, your brain can get **overwhelmed**.

   e. **Horseplay** like rocking a Ferris-wheel car or standing up on a roller coaster can put you and other riders in danger.

   f. In some states it's a crime (a **misdemeanor**) to act reckless on a ride!

3. Save your work. You will refer to it again in the Vocabulary Check.

Strategy Builder

Identifying Causes and Effects in Nonfiction

- As you know, every piece of nonfiction follows a particular pattern of organization. Although this article is written in a question-and-answer format, its organizational pattern is **cause and effect**. To find the cause-and-effect relationships while you read, keep asking yourself, "What happened?" and "Why did it happen?"

- To highlight the cause-and-effect relationships in this article, you can use **cause and effect links**. For example, the links below are from an article that explains what happens when you don't brush your teeth.

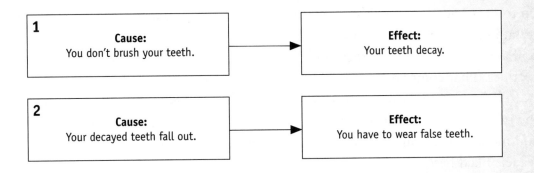

Amusement-Park Rides

from ZILLIONS magazine

As you read this article, apply what you just learned about identifying causes and effects.

Ah, a day at the amusement park! Wouldn't it be great if you could go on every ride 100 times? Better stop dreaming and look at the *lines* leading up to those rides! Some kids we spoke to said that, after all the waiting, their $30 admission fee bought them only *six* rides. That comes to $5 a ride!

To help make your next trip—and the rides you pick—worth your time and money, check out which rides our readers liked best.

What rides do kids like best?

Kids rode roller coasters more than any other kind of ride. The reason? Frightening fun! Coasters that are "fast and scary make you want to go on them over and over," said Pelton, 14. Sam, 9, said his dream coaster would go "8,000 miles an hour." The kids we surveyed gave the highest fun score to coasters that go upside down.

Free-falling rides got the next-highest fun score. "I wasn't afraid until we were going up," said Eddie, 13. "All of a sudden, I wanted there to be a button to press so I could get off. Then, as soon as we started falling, it was fun."

Getting scared is part of the fun, said Emily, 11, summing up how lots of kids felt about their favorite rides. Tamer rides, like Ferris wheels and carousels, got much lower marks. Hillary, 14, says those slower rides usually aren't worth the wait.

But what if you're not tall enough to go on scary rides—or if you just don't *want* to? Try water rides or motion-simulator rides. Our survey kids gave both good marks. These rides usually have lower height limits—and jostle you less—than the scarier rides.

Matt, 10, enjoyed the excitement of a motion-simulator ride based on the movie "Back to the Future." The seats move in conjunction with the images on the screen, so you feel like you're in the movie, he said. "The ride becomes your world." And as Rebecca, 9, pointed out, "you're jerking around but [otherwise] you're not actually moving, so it feels safer than a roller coaster."

Blair, 8, enjoyed a white-water-rapids ride because it was the only non-kiddie ride she was tall enough to go on. Rebecca recommends water rides that have lots of jumps and bumps—and last a long time.

⬤ **Stop here for the Strategy Break.**

Strategy Break

If you were to create cause-and-effect links to show why kids liked certain rides better than others, your links might look like this:

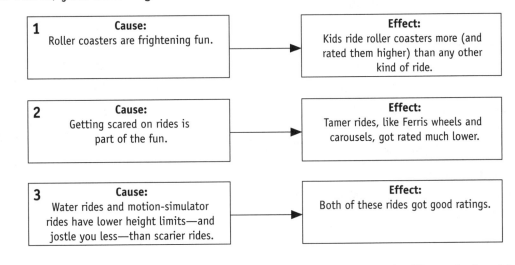

1 **Cause:**
Roller coasters are frightening fun.

→ **Effect:**
Kids ride roller coasters more (and rated them higher) than any other kind of ride.

2 **Cause:**
Getting scared on rides is part of the fun.

→ **Effect:**
Tamer rides, like Ferris wheels and carousels, got rated much lower.

3 **Cause:**
Water rides and motion-simulator rides have lower height limits—and jostle you less—than scarier rides.

→ **Effect:**
Both of these rides got good ratings.

As you continue reading, keep paying attention to the cause-and-effect relationships. At the end of this article, you will complete some cause-and-effect links of your own.

 **Go on reading.**

Why do some rides have height rules?

Standard-sized seat belts, lap bars, and shoulder harnesses may not keep small riders snugly in their seats. You could be injured if you slip, slide, or get bumped extra hard when the car goes upside down or around sharp turns.

Even some kids who were tall enough had trouble on these rides. Pelton, for example, won't go back on a looping coaster. "Unless you are very tall," he said, "your head will bounce from side to side too much."

Why do we like rides that scare us?

Leave it to a scientist to know the answers. According to Dr. Jaimeson Walker of Edinburgh University, your body responds to terror by releasing chemicals such as **adrenaline**. These chemicals make you ready to deal with danger by boosting your energy and making your heart beat faster, among other things.

But if the danger is just a three-minute roller-coaster ride, the leftover chemicals put you in a good mood and give you the feeling that you've conquered the danger. So the scary ride ends up making you feel good.

Still, you may have to psych yourself up to go on a scary ride. Miguel, 14, got over his fear of rides by riding a roller coaster with his eyes open,

Kids Rate the Rides	
Type of ride	Fun score*
Roller coaster that goes upside down	94
Free-falling ride	90
Virtual-reality ride	85
Water flume	85
Spinning ride where floor falls out	83
Spinning ride that tips on its side	82
Regular roller coaster	80
Motion-simulator ride	79
Swinging-ship ride	71
Spinning-car ride (with many arms)	69
Haunted house	63
Bumper cars	47
Cable-car ride	45
Ferris wheel	40
Carousel	21

*Number of kids out of every 100 who thought this ride was "awesome" or "very good." Source: ZILLIONS survey. Only kids who rode these rides rated them.

saying to himself, "It's nothing, it's nothing." "Ever since then, I go on every ride," he says.

If you want the scariest ride on a roller coaster, sit in the front car. That way you'll see each hill and turn as you approach it.

To feel the most speed, sit in the last seat. It tops each hill just as the coaster is going fastest.

Backseat riders also enjoy the most **airtime**—the flying-out-of-your-seat feeling you get as the car goes over the top of a hill. It's caused by **inertia** (the tendency of moving objects to keep moving in the same direction) and makes you feel nearly weightless—if only for a moment. When the coaster bottoms out, inertia will make you feel very heavy—up to 3-1/2 times your normal weight!

Why do some rides make us sick?
On rides that spin or swing like the infamous swinging ship, you may feel nauseated. That's because your brain is receiving loads of messages from your eyes and inner ears. These messages normally tell your brain whether you're moving or standing still—and which way is down. But when it gets so many signals, your brain can get **overwhelmed**. That sensation may give some people a

thrill—but cause others to spill their lunch.

If you feel dizzy on a ride, closing your eyes to block out some signals may help. Afterward, sit still and wait a while before going on the next ride.

How safe are the rides?

If you've ever heard about a horrible amusement-park accident, you've probably wondered whether the rides are really safe. But as it turns out, relatively few accidents on amusement-park and carnival rides are due to ride operators or mechanical problems with the rides.

In fact, most accidents on rides are caused by riders themselves. **Horseplay** like rocking a Ferris-wheel car or standing up on a roller coaster can put you and other riders in danger.

If your friends try stuff like that, don't go along with it. Even if they make fun of you, you're better off not doing something that can get you all hurt. (If you're looking for a "cool" way out, just tell them you're going to barf. Then they'll leave you alone—fast!)

To make sure you don't get hurt, obey the height limits, health restrictions, and other posted safety rules; listen to the ride operators; and skip a ride if it looks rickety. You can even ask ride operators to show you the ride's most recent inspection certificate. Many carnival and park owners inspect their rides every day.

One more reason to stay seated and follow the rules: Some states are now considering laws that would fine "disorderly" riders up to $1,000. In some states it's a crime (a **misdemeanor**) to act reckless on a ride! ●

Strategy Follow-up

Now complete the cause–and–effect links for the second part of this article. Some of the information has been provided for you.

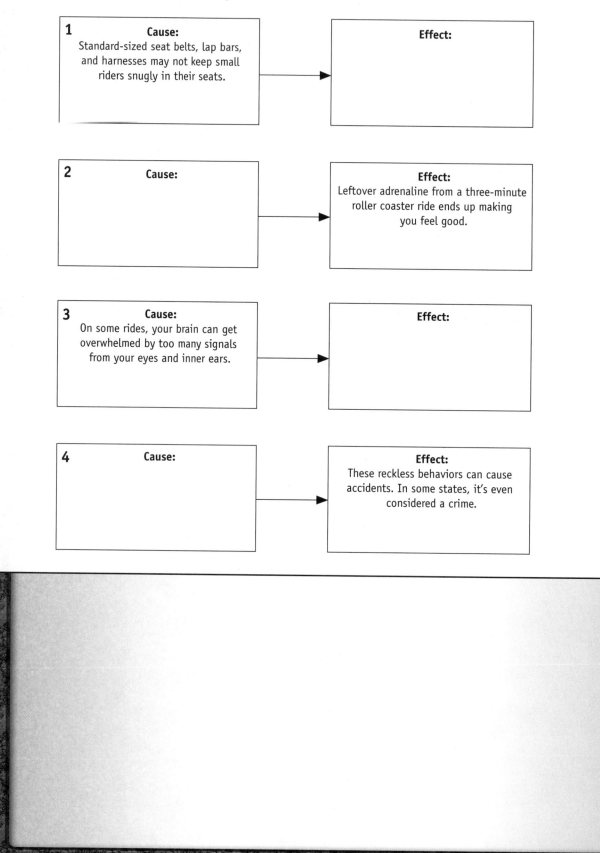

1 **Cause:**
Standard-sized seat belts, lap bars, and harnesses may not keep small riders snugly in their seats.

Effect:

---

2 **Cause:**

Effect:
Leftover adrenaline from a three-minute roller coaster ride ends up making you feel good.

---

3 **Cause:**
On some rides, your brain can get overwhelmed by too many signals from your eyes and inner ears.

Effect:

---

4 **Cause:**

Effect:
These reckless behaviors can cause accidents. In some states, it's even considered a crime.

✓Personal Checklist

Read each question and put a check (✓) in the correct box.

1. How well do you understand the information presented in this article?
   - ☐ 3 (extremely well)
   - ☐ 2 (fairly well)
   - ☐ 1 (not well)

2. In Building Background, how well were you able to predict which rides the kids in this article would like best?
   - ☐ 3 (extremely well)
   - ☐ 2 (fairly well)
   - ☐ 1 (not well)

3. In the Vocabulary Builder, how well were you able to underline the context clues that helped you understand each vocabulary word?
   - ☐ 3 (extremely well)
   - ☐ 2 (fairly well)
   - ☐ 1 (not well)

4. In the Strategy Follow-up, how well were you able to complete the cause and effect links?
   - ☐ 3 (extremely well)
   - ☐ 2 (fairly well)
   - ☐ 1 (not well)

5. After reading this article, how well would you be able to explain the cause of the good feeling you get after a scary ride?
   - ☐ 3 (extremely well)
   - ☐ 2 (fairly well)
   - ☐ 1 (not well)

Vocabulary Check

Look back at the work you did in the Vocabulary Builder. Then answer each question by circling the correct letter.

1. Which word best describes adrenaline?
   - a. an electric shock
   - b. a chemical
   - c. a strong wind

2. Standing up in a moving roller coaster is an example of which vocabulary word?
   - a. inertia
   - b. airtime
   - c. horseplay

3. Which word describes what causes the momentary weightlessness you feel on some amusement-park rides?
   - a. adrenaline
   - b. inertia
   - c. overwhelmed

4. Some people get nauseated on certain rides when their brains become overwhelmed with signals. What is another word for *overwhelmed*?
   - a. confused
   - b. relieved
   - c. thrilled

5. Which word is a synonym of *misdemeanor*?
   - a. joke
   - b. crime
   - c. reward

Add the numbers that you just checked to get your Personal Checklist score. Fill in your score here. Then turn to page 219 and transfer your score onto Graph 1.

Personal	
Vocabulary	
Strategy	
Comprehension	
TOTAL SCORE	
	✓ T

Check your answers with your teacher. Give yourself 1 point for each correct answer, and fill in your Vocabulary score here. Then turn to page 219 and transfer your score onto Graph 1.

Personal	
Vocabulary	
Strategy	
Comprehension	
TOTAL SCORE	
	✓ T

Strategy Check

Review the cause-and-effect links that you completed in the Strategy Follow-up. Also review the rest of the article. Then answer the following questions.

1. Why do some rides have height rules?
    a. because taller riders might hit their heads or hurt their necks
    b. because smaller riders might not stay in their seats well enough
    c. because some riders might be too tall to fit in the seats

2. Which of these is *not* an effect of the body's release of adrenaline?
    a. You become nauseated.
    b. Your heart beats faster.
    c. Your energy level is boosted.

3. When you are on some rides, what is the effect of receiving too many signals from your eyes and inner ears?
    a. Those rides can make you feel sick.
    b. Those rides end up making you feel good.
    c. Those rides can make you feel terrified.

4. According to this article, who or what causes most of the accidents on amusement-park rides?
    a. mechanical problems
    b. the ride operators
    c. the riders themselves

5. What are some states thinking of doing to prevent reckless behavior on amusement-park rides?
    a. having height rules for some rides
    b. shutting down some amusement parks
    c. fining disorderly riders up to $1,000

Comprehension Check

Review the article if necessary. Then answer these questions:

1. According to the chart, which ride got the highest fun score?
    a. spinning-car ride (with many arms)
    b. roller coaster that goes upside down
    c. spinning ride where floor falls out

2. Which ride got the lowest score?
    a. carousel
    b. water flume
    c. bumper cars

3. What happens in a motion-simulator ride?
    a. The seats move in conjunction with the images on the screen.
    b. The bottom drops out as the ride spins.
    c. You get all wet as you ride through the rapids.

4. If you want the scariest ride on a roller coaster, where should you sit?
    a. in the last car of the coaster
    b. in the middle of the coaster
    c. in the front car of the coaster

5. According to the article, what do backseat riders experience?
    a. the most airtime
    b. the least fun
    c. the most danger

Check your answers with your teacher. Give yourself 1 point for each correct answer, and fill in your Strategy score here. Then turn to page 219 and transfer your score onto Graph 1.

Personal	
Vocabulary	
Strategy	
Comprehension	
TOTAL SCORE	

✓ T

Check your answers with your teacher. Give yourself 1 point for each correct answer, and fill in your Comprehension score here. Then turn to page 219 and transfer your score onto Graph 1.

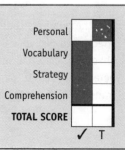

Personal	
Vocabulary	
Strategy	
Comprehension	
TOTAL SCORE	

✓ T

Extending

Choose one or both of these activities:

SURVEY YOUR SCHOOLMATES

Would the kids in your school rate amusement-park rides in the same order that the kids in this article did? To find out, survey your schoolmates. Ask them to rate the rides listed on the chart in this article as excellent, good, or just okay. If you'd like, you can ask a few other questions, such as what their favorite amusement park is, and why. If possible, publish the results in your school newspaper so everyone can read them.

BUILD A MODEL AMUSEMENT PARK

Using craft sticks, pipe cleaners, toothpicks, or other materials of your choosing, build your own amusement park. (The resources listed on this page might help you get started.) Include all your favorite rides and attractions, as well as the people who work at the park and ride the rides. Give your amusement park a name that will attract fun seekers.

Resources

Book

Adams, Judith A. *The American Amusement Park Industry: A History of Technology and Thrills.* Twayne's Evolution of American Business. Twayne Publishers, 1991.

Web Sites

http://www.joyrides.com/
Links on this Web site take you to photos of roller coasters and other rides at amusement parks around the United States.

http://www.rcdb.com/
This roller coaster database gives you facts about roller coasters around the world.

Video/DVD

Awesome Rides. Pinnacle Video Productions, 1994.

centripetal force

dangerous

friction

gravity

kinetic energy

megacoaster

monstrous

potential energy

smooshed

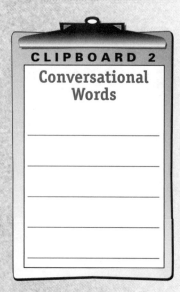

CLIPBOARD 1

Scientific Terms

CLIPBOARD 2

Conversational
Words

Building Background

You just read an article in Lesson 11 that describes why kids enjoy roller coasters so much. But how much do you know about how roller coasters work? Before you begin reading "Scream, Too!" get together with a partner and list several things that you already know about roller coasters and how they work. Then list some questions about roller coasters that you hope this article will answer. Save your work. You will use it again later in this lesson.

Vocabulary Builder

1. The words in the margin can all be used to describe roller coasters and how they work. Some of the words are scientific terms, and some are words that you might hear in everyday conversations.

2. Before you begin reading "Scream, Too!" separate the vocabulary words into two groups. (Use a dictionary for any words you don't know.) On the first clipboard, list the vocabulary words that describe roller coasters in scientific terms.

3. On the second clipboard, list the vocabulary words that people use in everyday conversations about roller coasters.

4. As you read the article, look for other words to add to each clipboard. Save your work. You will refer to it again in the Vocabulary Check.

Strategy Builder

Outlining Main Ideas and Supporting Details

- As you learned in Lesson 4, an **informational article** gives facts and details about a particular topic. The **topic** of "Scream, Too!" is roller coasters.

- Even though some of the events in this article are told in sequence, the main organizational pattern of "Scream, Too!" is description. **Descriptions** tell what things are or how they work. They usually are organized according to **main ideas** and **supporting details**.

- There are many ways to keep track of main ideas and details as you read. One way is to use a concept map. Another way is to use an outline. Some outlines use a system of Roman numerals (I, II, III, and so on), capital letters, and Arabic numerals (1, 2, 3, and so on).

• Read the following paragraphs from an article on camping. Then read how one student outlined the main ideas and details.

Before you go on a camping trip, be sure to prepare carefully. First, think about where you want to go. You might want to go to a family campground that has plenty of activities for all ages. Or you might prefer a more remote and primitive spot that has very few amenities.

   Once you've chosen a campsite, it's important to choose the proper equipment. Equipment ranges from fancy RVs to simple nylon tents. If you go camping with tents, don't forget to pack sleeping bags and a camp stove.

   Select your camping clothes carefully. Nights can be chilly almost anywhere, so pack enough clothes for layering. Be sure one of those layers is waterproof to keep you dry in the rain. And remember that having comfortable footwear can make a big difference in your vacation fun. Consider packing shoes or boots that are lightweight yet rugged. Also make sure they are waterproof.

How to Prepare for a Camping Trip

I. Decide where to go.
   A. Might choose a family campground.
   B. Might choose a more remote and primitive spot.
II. Choose the proper equipment.
   A. Might choose an RV.
   B. Might choose tents.
III. Choose the right clothing.
   A. Pack enough for layering.
     1. Be sure one layer is waterproof.
   B. Pack comfortable shoes.
     1. Should be lightweight yet rugged.
     2. Should be waterproof.

Scream, Too!
How Roller Coasters Dish Out Thrills and Chills

by John Kontakis

As you read the first part of this article, apply some of the strategies that you just learned. Look for the main ideas and supporting details in this description, and think about how you might outline them.

Just looking at one can make some people sick. And when riders actually get on, they usually end up screaming their lungs out. Even so, the first thing most people do at an amusement park is head for the biggest roller coaster in sight. You know the one—it's usually called Viper Skull or Screaming Mountain or Rip-Your-Guts-Out Shocker, or something like that.

But what happens on a roller coaster isn't as scary as the name makes it sound. "Roller coasters aren't really **dangerous**," says physics expert David Wright. He works with coasters at Busch Gardens Williamsburg in Virginia. Wright thinks you can take the fear out of coaster rides by knowing how the ride works.

Gravity Control

Monstrous coasters may look high-tech. But it's energy, not computers or machines, that makes them go up, down, and around.

The only time a motor is used is to get the coaster up the steep hill at the beginning of the ride. At the top of the hill, the coaster is full of **potential energy**. That's the energy a motionless object has when it's above the ground.

When **gravity** takes over and the coaster shoots down the track, the potential energy begins to change into **kinetic energy**. Kinetic energy is the energy an object has because it's moving.

As kinetic energy increases, so does the coaster's speed. "Coasters hit maximum speed when they reach the bottom of the first hill," Wright explains. That kinetic energy gets the coaster up the next hill or around a loop.

Each time the coaster tackles a hill or curve, it loses energy to **friction**, air resistance, and other elements. That slows the coaster down. It also explains why the first hill or loop in a ride is always the tallest: If a bigger hill came later, the coaster wouldn't have enough energy to go up and over it. When the coaster has lost most of its energy, it slows to a stop—and the ride is over!

 Stop here for the Strategy Break.

Strategy Break

If you were to create an outline for this article so far, it might look something like this:

I. How Roller Coasters Work
 A. Energy makes roller coasters go.
 B. At the top of the hill, the coaster is full of potential energy.
 C. When the coaster goes down the hill, the potential energy turns to kinetic energy.
  1. As kinetic energy increases, so does the coaster's speed.
  2. Coasters hit maximum speed at the bottom of the first hill.
  3. That kinetic energy moves the coaster to the next hill or loop.
 D. Each time the coaster hits a hill or curve, it loses energy and slows down.
 E. When the coaster has lost most of its energy, it slows to a stop—and the ride is over.

As you continue reading, pay attention to the main ideas and supporting details.
At the end of this article, you will use some of them to complete an outline of your own.

 Go on reading.

Steep Turn Ahead

"One of the parts of a good coaster is a smooth ride with little jerking motions," says roller coaster designer Steve Okamoto. The jerking motions in a coaster are caused by quick, sharp curves in the track.

If you've ever ridden a coaster, you know what it feels like to get **smooshed** up against the car as it whips around a curve. That's caused by something called inertia. "Your body always wants to go in a straight line," Wright explains. "But suddenly, the roller coaster goes around a sharp turn. So the side of the car gets jerked into your body."

What keeps you—and the car— from flying off the track as you round the curve? **Centripetal force** helps. That's the force that pushed an object traveling in a circle toward the center of the circle. Centripetal force helps the car turn the corner.

Coaster designers also keep the car on track by "banking" the curves. Instead of laying flat, the track is tilted to the side. When you speed around a banked curve, you feel less like you're being thrown sideways and more like you're being pushed down.

Staying on Track

A coaster ride lasts for only a few minutes. But it takes tons of time to get the coaster right. Designers can spend more than a year working on a typical **megacoaster**.

Before beginning a coaster design, Okamoto digs up information on the park where the coaster will end up. He visits the park to get a better idea of how the ride will fit in. Then he creates a rough layout of the new coaster. Once he's done that, engineers and designers make the parts and put the coaster together. "It sounds easy," Okamoto says. "But in reality, it involves months of work with my assistant."

Okamoto's "assistant" is a powerful computer. Computers give designers a chance to "try out" the coaster before construction even begins. That lets designers create a complex, fun coaster—and make sure it's ultra-safe. "We now have the capability to go higher and faster than anyone 100 years ago would have thought possible," Okamoto says. That's good news for the millions of thrill-seekers who conquer coasters each year. ●

Name of Coaster	Riddler's Revenge	Alpengeist	Cyclone	Desperado	Batman the Ride	Magnum 200
Type	Stand-up steel coaster	Inverted steel coaster	Wooden coaster	Steel Inverted looping hypercoaster	Out-and-back steel coaster	steel coaster
Location	Six Flags Magic Mountain, Valencia, CA	Busch Gardens Williamsburg, Williamsburg, VA	Astroland/ Coney Island, Brooklyn, NY	Buffalo Bill's Hotel and Casino, Stateline, NV	Six Flags Great Adventure, Jackson, NJ	Cedar Point, Sandusky, OH
Year Built	1998	1997	1927	1993	1993	1989
Ride Time	3 minutes	3 minutes, 10 seconds	1 minute, 40 seconds	2 minutes, 45 seconds	2 minutes	2 minutes
Top Speed	65 mph	67 mph	60 mph	78 mph	50 mph	72 mph
Claim to Fame	At 156 feet, it's the world's tallest and fastest stand-up coaster	The world's tallest (195 feet), fastest, and most twisted inverted coaster	The granddaddy of wooden coasters has a steep 59-degree drop	Tallest (224 feet), fastest coaster in the U.S.	You're sent head-over-heels five times	A steep 60-degree first drop, three tunnels

Strategy Follow-up

First, get together with your partner again and list at least three things that you learned while reading this article.

Next, work alone or with your partner to complete the outline for the second part of this article. Some of the information has been provided for you.

II. What Makes a Good Roller Coaster
    A. Part of a good coaster is
    B. Inertia
    C. Centripetal force
    D. Designers also keep the car on the track by

III. Planning a Coaster
    A. Designers can spend more than a year working on a coaster.
      1.

      2.
      3.
    B. Computers assist designers in building coasters.
      1.
      2.
      3.

✓Personal Checklist

Read each question and put a check (✓) in the correct box.

1. After reading this article, how well could you tell someone what makes a roller coaster work?
   - ☐ 3 (extremely well)
   - ☐ 2 (fairly well)
   - ☐ 1 (not well)

2. In Building Background, how well were you able to list some questions about roller coasters that you hoped this article will answer?
   - ☐ 3 (extremely well)
   - ☐ 2 (fairly well)
   - ☐ 1 (not well)

3. In the Vocabulary Builder, how well were you able to write the vocabulary words on the appropriate clipboards?
   - ☐ 3 (extremely well)
   - ☐ 2 (fairly well)
   - ☐ 1 (not well)

4. How well were you able to understand the information presented on the chart in this article?
   - ☐ 3 (extremely well)
   - ☐ 2 (fairly well)
   - ☐ 1 (not well)

5. In the Strategy Follow-up, how well were you able to complete the outline for the second part of this article?
   - ☐ 3 (extremely well)
   - ☐ 2 (fairly well)
   - ☐ 1 (not well)

Vocabulary Check

Look back at the work you did in the Vocabulary Builder. Then answer each question by circling the correct letter.

1. What is the opposite of potential energy?
   - a. kinetic energy
   - b. centripetal force
   - c. friction

2. Which of the following has kinetic energy?
   - a. a book that is sitting on a bookshelf
   - b. a vase filled with flowers on a table
   - c. a bowling ball rolling down a lane

3. When you start a fire by rubbing two sticks together, what are you using?
   - a. centripetal force
   - b. friction
   - c. gravity

4. Which of these words is an antonym of *monstrous*?
   - a. massive
   - b. tiny
   - c. gigantic

5. Which word means the same thing as *smashed* or *squashed*?
   - a. smooshed
   - b. spaced
   - c. spread

Add the numbers that you just checked to get your Personal Checklist score. Fill in your score here. Then turn to page 219 and transfer your score onto Graph 1.

	Personal	
	Vocabulary	
	Strategy	
	Comprehension	
	TOTAL SCORE	

✓ T

Check your answers with your teacher. Give yourself 1 point for each correct answer, and fill in your Vocabulary score here. Then turn to page 219 and transfer your score onto Graph 1.

	Personal	
	Vocabulary	
	Strategy	
	Comprehension	
	TOTAL SCORE	

✓ T

Strategy Check

Review the outline that you completed in the Strategy Follow-up. Then answer these questions:

1. Which of these could be a supporting detail under "What Makes a Good Roller Coaster"?
   a. Engineers and designers make the parts and put them together.
   b. Designers keep the car on the track by "banking" the curves.
   c. Computers allow designers to make sure a coaster will be safe.

2. Which of these would *not* be a supporting detail under "What Makes a Good Roller Coaster"?
   a. Inertia causes you to get smooshed against the car as it goes around a curve.
   b. Centripetal force keeps the car from flying off the track as it goes around curves.
   c. Computers give designers a chance to "try out" their coasters before they're constructed.

3. What causes jerking motions on a coaster?
   a. quick, sharp curves in the track
   b. the friction of cars rubbing together
   c. the coaster's motor pulling the cars

4. What is the first thing that Steve Okamato does when he designs a new coaster?
   a. He creates a rough layout of the roller coaster.
   b. He learns about the park where the coaster will end up.
   c. He makes the coaster's parts and puts them together.

5. What is one way in which computers help designers plan roller coasters?
   a. They help designers build higher and faster coasters than anyone thought possible.
   b. They help designers construct the motors.
   c. They help designers electronically create the quick, jerking motions that riders feel.

Comprehension Check

Review the article if necessary. Then answer these questions:

1. For what is a roller coaster's motor used?
   a. to get the coaster up to the top of the first hill
   b. to get the coaster up to the top of every hill
   c. to shoot the coaster down the hills at top speed

2. According to the article, what finally slows a roller coaster to a stop?
   a. kinetic energy
   b. centripetal force
   c. friction and air resistance

3. According to the chart, which roller coaster ride reaches the highest speed?
   a. Desperado
   b. Batman
   c. Magnum 200

4. Which coaster on the chart is the oldest?
   a. Alpengeist
   b. Cyclone
   c. Riddler's Revenge

5. According to the article, why is it good to know how a roller coaster works?
   a. Knowing how coasters works helps you choose the best one.
   b. Knowing how a coaster works helps you know how to ride it.
   c. Knowing how a coaster works can take the fear out of riding them.

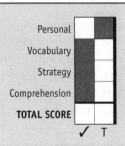

Check your answers with your teacher. Give yourself 1 point for each correct answer, and fill in your Strategy score here. Then turn to page 219 and transfer your score onto Graph 1.

Personal
Vocabulary
Strategy
Comprehension
TOTAL SCORE
✓ T

Check your answers with your teacher. Give yourself 1 point for each correct answer, and fill in your Comprehension score here. Then turn to page 219 and transfer your score onto Graph 1.

Personal
Vocabulary
Strategy
Comprehension
TOTAL SCORE
✓ T

Extending

Choose one or both of these activities:

DESIGN YOUR OWN ROLLER COASTER

If you could design your own roller coaster, what features would it include? Would people sit or stand while riding it? Would it loop around once, twice, or more than that? Would riders travel with a companion, or would they travel alone? What would it be called, and why? Answer these questions and others as you plan your roller coaster. Then make a sketch of your coaster. Be sure to label and briefly describe your coaster's special features. Use the resources listed on this page if you need help getting started.

PLAN A ROLLER COASTER TOUR

Plan a tour around the United States that would take you to all the roller coasters you'd like to try. Choose the coasters you are interested in from the resources on this page or the chart in this article. Then map out your trip on a U. S. map, using a felt-tipped marker to show your route. Put a star and any important information on each roller coaster's location.

Resources

Book

Alter, Judy. *Amusement Parks: Roller Coasters, Ferris Wheels, and Cotton Candy.* First Book. Franklin Watts, 1997.

Web Sites

http://dsc.discovery.com/convergence/coasters/interactive/interactive.html
You can build your own roller coaster on this interactive Web site.

http://www.rollercoasterworld.com/SearchParks/ParkMap.asp
To learn about amusement parks and roller coasters in the United States, click on the map on this Web site.

Videos/DVDs

America Screams. Rhino Video, 1990.

Here Comes a Roller Coaster, and Other Fun-Filled Rides. A Vision, 1995.

The Clever Thief

abandoned

afraid

bright

dull

empty

frightened

grin

large

roared

small

smile

whispered

Building Background

When you were young, you probably read fairy tales and other stories about thieves. For example, you might have read about pirates who robbed other ships of their cargo. Or you might have read about gangs of thieves who robbed train or stagecoach passengers of their valuables.

Think about the title "The Clever Thief," Using what you know about thieves in other stories, what do you predict the thief in this story will do in order to be called clever?

Vocabulary Builder

1. Study the vocabulary words in the margin. Each word is half of a pair of antonyms (words with opposite meanings) or synonyms (words with similar meanings).

2. Write the antonym pairs on the first clipboard and the synonym pairs on the second clipboard.

3. As you read "The Clever Thief," look for at least one more antonym and synonym pair each, and write them on the clipboards.

4. Save your work. You will refer to it again in the Vocabulary Check.

CLIPBOARD 1

Antonym Pairs

1. _____

_____

2. _____

_____

3. _____

_____

4. _____

_____

CLIPBOARD 2

Synonym Pairs

1. _____

_____

2. _____

_____

3. _____

_____

4. _____

_____

Strategy Builder

Making Predictions While Reading a Story

- When you read a story, you continually make predictions about what will happen next. As you know, a **prediction** is a guess that you make based on information or clues that the author provides. Those clues help "set the scene" and help you understand what's happening. They also help you predict what might be coming next.

- As you read "The Clever Thief," you will pause twice to make predictions. At Strategy Break #1, you will write down your predictions. You also will write which clues helped you make your predictions.

- At Strategy Break #2, you will check your earlier predictions. Then you will make more predictions, and you will tell which clues helped you make them.

- After you finish reading, you will see if any of your predictions match what actually happened in the story.

The Clever Thief

by Sophie Masson

See if you can use clues that the author provides to help you make predictions while you read.

There once was a boy who was captured by robbers. Now, these robbers were the most feared in the whole country. They held up travelers and robbed coaches, and their cave was full of stolen gold and silver and precious stones.

It was the custom of the robbers to make all their captives steal as well. In this way, the robbers kept adding new members to their gang, because no one ever dared to refuse. And once you'd stolen, you were in for good, because you were marked as a member of the gang and would go to prison if you were caught.

Now, the boy I am telling you about was as **bright** as a dewdrop and twice as fast as the breeze. But in the robbers' case, he pretended to be **dull** and stupid while he tried to think of a way out of his predicament.

One night, the robber chief said to him, "Boy, tonight you will join our gang. I want you to go down to the highroad and relieve all the travelers of their purses." And he smiled, his broken yellow teeth giving him a wolfish look. The boy, though very much **frightened**, nodded vacantly and grinned a silly **grin**. The robber chief felt a little uneasy at that grin—was the boy too stupid to understand?—but he sent him out nevertheless and waited in the cave for his return.

The boy went out to the highroad, and he saw all the travelers passing by. As he had been told to do, he stepped out into the road, shouting, "Your purse or your life!" He was a tall, thin, gangling boy, with eyes that shone like ice, and the travelers were frightened by his strangeness. So they stopped, pulled out their purses, heavy with gold and silver and copper coins, and gave them to him, trembling.

⬢ **Stop here for Strategy Break #1.**

Strategy Break #1

1. What do you predict will happen next? _____

_____

2. Why do you think so? _____

_____

3. What clues from the story helped you make your prediction(s)? _____

_____

_____

➡ **Go on reading to see what happens.**

He opened the purses, tipped out all the money into the travelers' palms, and took the **empty** bags, saying, "My chief has told me he wants your purses." Then he gave a grin as empty as an **abandoned** house. The travelers didn't wait to hear more; they bolted, taking their money with them, full of their good fortune.

So the boy went back to the cave, loaded with silk and leather and cotton purses, some new, some old, some **large**, some **small**. And he said to the robber chief, "Master, here are the purses you wanted," while he grinned his silly grin.

"Fool!" The robber chief called out, pale with rage. "Fool! I didn't just

want their purses; I wanted their money as well!"

"Oh," the boy said, and his face drooped at the corners, as if he were sorry for what had happened. Inside his bright, quick heart, though, a **smile** danced and sparkled.

The robber chief contained himself with difficulty. Then he said, "Tomorrow night, you will go out again. And this time, this time, boy, I want you to get all their change! Do you hear, *all their change*, boy!"

The boy nodded eagerly, his eyes seeming as dull as dirty water. Again the robber chief felt uneasy, but he thought that surely no one could be as stupid as that a second time.

So the next night, the boy went out again to the highroad. Again he stepped into the road, calling out,

"Your change or your life! Your change or your life!" And his tall, thin shape, ghostly in the moonlight, made travelers uneasy and frightened, so they stopped and pulled out their purses, heavy with gold and silver and copper coins. The boy carefully emptied the purses, counted out all the copper coins, and put them in his large pockets. Then, just as carefully, he returned all the gold and silver coins to the travelers' purses and handed them back. He smiled at them with a smile that did not seem quite as dull and vacant and told them to go on their way.

After a hard night's work, the boy went back to the robbers' cave, his pockets filled with copper coins. He emptied them out in front of the robber chief, grinning like a jack-o'-lantern.

The robber chief couldn't believe his eyes. "Copper?" he **roared**. "Where is the gold, where is the silver?"

"But you said change," the boy **whispered**, as if he were **afraid**. "Change is copper, isn't it?"

"Boy!" the robber chief screamed. "You will go out one more time and bring back *everything*. Everything, you hear! And if you don't . . ." His broken teeth glittered, his wicked eyes flashed, his hand drew slowly across the boy's throat.

The boy gulped a little, as if he were afraid. And indeed he was, a bit, but his bright, quick mind was working like a windmill, spinning out ideas. "Yes, master," he whispered, and bent his head.

 Stop here for Strategy Break #2.

Strategy Break #2

1. Do your earlier predictions match what happened? _____
   Why or why not? _____
   _____

2. What do you predict will happen next? _____
   _____

3. Why do you think so? _____
   _____

4. What clues from the story helped you make your prediction(s)?
   _____
   _____

**Go on reading to see
what happens.**

So the next night, the boy went out for the third and final time. He stepped into the highroad in the moonlight, his figure tall and straight, his eyes shining, and he stopped the travelers and talked to them. As he spoke, their eyes would begin to shine, their mouths to smile.

At the end of the night, there were many travelers assembled there, with the boy in the middle of them. As the sun began to edge over the corner of the world, they were all climbing up the hill toward the robbers' cave, where they found the thieves snoring, fast asleep. Working quickly and quietly, the travelers and the boy gathered up all the robbers' weapons and put them in a huge sack.

Wasn't the robber chief surprised when he opened his eyes to the great assembly in his cave! He sprang to his feet, as did the other members of his gang, but it was too late. Every sword, every dagger, every knife and bow and arrow had gone into the sack the boy held. Weaponless, helpless, the robbers and their chief looked at the boy and heard him say, "You told me to bring everything. Everything I brought, and everyone."

Now it was the turn of the robber chief to bend his head as he and his men were led out of the cave, down the hill, and toward the town. Now and then, he lifted his eyes and looked at the boy, so thin and gangling, and felt his smile, as bright and fleeting as the dew on the grass. ●

Strategy Follow-up

Go back and look at the predictions that you wrote in this lesson. Do any of them match what actually happened in this story? Why or why not?

_____

_____

_____

_____

_____

_____

_____

✓Personal Checklist

Read each question and put a check (✓) in the correct box.

1. How well do you understand what happens in "The Clever Thief"?
   - ☐ 3 (extremely well)
   - ☐ 2 (fairly well)
   - ☐ 1 (not well)

2. In Building Background, how well were you able to predict what the thief would do in order to be called clever?
   - ☐ 3 (extremely well)
   - ☐ 2 (fairly well)
   - ☐ 1 (not well)

3. How well were you able to list synonym pairs and antonym pairs in the Vocabulary Builder?
   - ☐ 3 (extremely well)
   - ☐ 2 (fairly well)
   - ☐ 1 (not well)

4. How well were you able to use context clues to predict what would happen next in this story?
   - ☐ 3 (extremely well)
   - ☐ 2 (fairly well)
   - ☐ 1 (not well)

5. How well do you understand the boy's actions in this story?
   - ☐ 3 (extremely well)
   - ☐ 2 (fairly well)
   - ☐ 1 (not well)

Vocabulary Check

Look back at the work you did in the Vocabulary Builder. Then answer each question by circling the correct letter.

1. What is the meaning of the word *bright* as it is used in this story?
   a. beaming
   b. clever
   c. glistening

2. Which word is an antonym of *whispered*?
   a. abandoned
   b. frightened
   c. roared

3. Which vocabulary word is a synonym of *empty*?
   a. full
   b. occupied
   c. abandoned

4. Which meaning of *empty* best fits the context of this story?
   a. not lived in
   b. foolish
   c. without meaning

5. Which pair of words can be used to describe sizes?
   a. large/small
   b. bright/dull
   c. empty/abandoned

Add the numbers that you just checked to get your Personal Checklist score. Fill in your score here. Then turn to page 219 and transfer your score onto Graph 1.

Personal
Vocabulary
Strategy
Comprehension
TOTAL SCORE
✓ T

Check your answers with your teacher. Give yourself 1 point for each correct answer, and fill in your Vocabulary score here. Then turn to page 219 and transfer your score onto Graph 1.

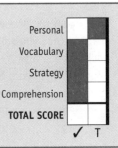

Personal
Vocabulary
Strategy
Comprehension
TOTAL SCORE
✓ T

Strategy Check

Look back at what you wrote at each Strategy Break. Then answer these questions:

1. Which detail supports the prediction that the boy would take the purses but not the money?

    a. The robbers made all their captives steal as well.

    b. The robbers kept adding new members to the gang, because no one ever dared to refuse.

    c. As he had been told to do, he stepped out into the road, shouting, "Your purse or your life!"

2. Which clue let you know the boy was not really stupid but was trying to outsmart the robber?

    a. He was a tall, thin, gangling boy, with eyes that shone like ice.

    b. The boy . . . was as bright as a dewdrop and twice as fast as the breeze.

    c. The boy nodded vacantly.

3. Which clue might have helped you predict that the boy would disobey the robber chief again?

    a. "You will go out one more time and bring back *everything*. Everything, you hear!"

    b. His bright, quick mind was working like a windmill, spinning out ideas.

    c. "Yes, master," he whispered, and bent his head.

4. What does the writer mean when she says that even though the boy looked sorry, "Inside . . . a smile danced and sparkled"?

    a. The boy was secretly happy that he had disobeyed the robber chief.

    b. The boy could not understand why the robber chief was angry.

    c. His heart beat rapidly because he was afraid.

5. What clue suggests that the boy would face a terrible fate if he failed the chief a third time?

    a. The boy gulped a little, as if he were afraid.

    b. "Yes, master," he whispered.

    c. His hand drew slowly across the boy's throat.

Comprehension Check

Review the story if necessary. Then answer these questions:

1. How do the robbers make sure that their captives will never leave them?

    a. They make their captives steal too.

    b. They guard their captives carefully.

    c. They treat their captives as friends.

2. When the robber chief tells the boy to relieve all the travelers of their purses, what does he want the boy to do?

    a. Take the travelers' purses only.

    b. Take the travelers' change only.

    c. Take the travelers' money and valuables.

3. Why does the boy pretend to be stupid?

    a. He doesn't want to have to steal from people.

    b. He is trying to find a way out of his predicament.

    c. Both of the above reasons are correct.

4. Why do the travelers give the boy what he asks for every time he stops them?

    a. because they like him

    b. because they fear him

    c. because they pity him

5. Why don't the robbers fight back when the boy brings the travelers to the robbers' cave?

    a. They feel that they deserve to be punished.

    b. All their weapons have been gathered up.

    c. They decide they want to become honest citizens.

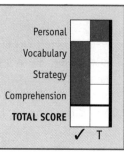

Check your answers with your teacher. Give yourself 1 point for each correct answer, and fill in your Strategy score here. Then turn to page 219 and transfer your score onto Graph 1.

Personal
Vocabulary
Strategy
Comprehension
TOTAL SCORE   ✓ T

Check your answers with your teacher. Give yourself 1 point for each correct answer, and fill in your Comprehension score here. Then turn to page 219 and transfer your score onto Graph 1.

Personal
Vocabulary
Strategy
Comprehension
TOTAL SCORE   ✓ T

Extending

Choose one or both of the following activities:

MAKE A "WANTED" POSTER
Design and produce a wanted poster for the robber gang in this story. Using words and pictures, describe the robber chief and his followers, their crimes, and the reward that is being offered for their capture and arrest. Try to make the poster as eye catching as possible.

STAGE A READERS THEATER PERFORMANCE
In readers theater, the characters' words are read by a group of actors sitting in a circle. Transform "The Clever Thief" into a readers theater play. Write parts for several characters, including the boy, the robber chief, and a narrator to tell the story. You also may want to add parts for the travelers and members of the robber gang. After the play is written, assemble several readers to practice and present it to an audience.

Resources

Books
Holub, Josef. *The Robber and Me.* Holt, 1997.

Kimmel, Eric A. *A Tale of Ali Baba and the Forty Thieves: A Story from the Arabian Nights.* Holiday House, 1996.

Kronberg, Ruthilde M. *Clever Folk: Tales of Wisdom, Wit, and Wonder.* Libraries Unlimited, 1993.

What Exercise Can Do for You

cardiovascular

endurance

energy

flexible

metabolism

moderate (adj.)

strength

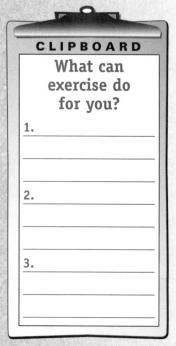

CLIPBOARD

What can exercise do for you?

1. _____

_____

2. _____

_____

3. _____

_____

CLIPBOARD

4. _____

_____

5. _____

_____

6. _____

_____

7. _____

_____

Building Background

Everywhere you look, you can find information about exercise. What do *you* do for exercise? How much do you know about its benefits? Before you begin reading, fill in the first column of the chart below with at least five things that you know—or think you know—about what exercise can do for you. Then fill in the second column with five questions that you hope the article will answer about what exercise can do for you. At the end of this lesson, you will fill in the last column of the chart.

What Exercise Can Do for You		
K (What I **K**now)	**W** (What I **W**ant to Know)	**L** (What I **L**earned)
1.		
2.		
3.		
4.		
5.		

Vocabulary Builder

1. The words in the margin are all found in the following article. Turn the title of the article into a question: What can exercise do for you? Then predict how the article will answer the question by writing seven answers. Include at least one vocabulary word in each answer. Also include enough context to explain the meaning of each vocabulary word.

2. As you read the article, find the sentences that contain the seven vocabulary words. Do your sentences use the words similarly to the ways the article uses them? Why or why not?

3. Go back and revise your sentences if necessary. Then save your work. You will refer to it again in the Vocabulary Check.

Strategy Builder

How to Read an Informational Article

- As you know, an **informational article** gives readers information about a particular topic. The **topic** of the article you are about to read is exercise— or, more specifically, what exercise can do for you.

- Like all other nonfiction, this article follows a particular pattern of organization. The pattern of "What Exercise Can Do for You" is description. **Descriptions** usually tell what things are, what they do, or how and why they work.

- Descriptions are usually organized according to **main ideas** and **supporting details.** Read the following excerpt and try to locate its topic, main ideas, and supporting details.

> Ants are insects that live in communities called colonies. Some colonies are in underground tunnels, while others are in hills above the ground or in trees. There are three main kinds of ants: queens, workers, and males. These ants have different jobs. Queens lay eggs. Workers build and take care of the colony, search for food, and take care of the queen's eggs. Male ants mate with queen ants. That is their only job. Soon after mating, male ants die.

- If you wanted to arrange the main ideas and supporting details of this paragraph on a graphic organizer, you could use a **concept map**, or web. It might look like this:

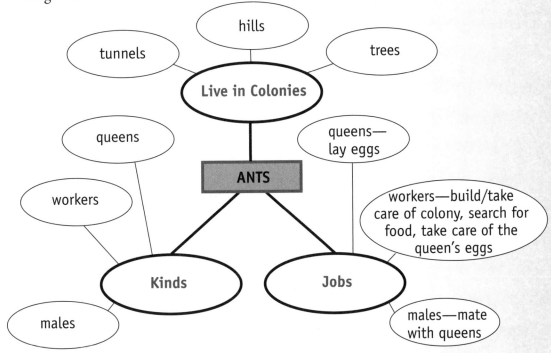

- Informational articles often contain graphics, such as lists, tables, diagrams, and graphs. Read all the graphics in an article. They give extra information about the topic. The article you are about to read contains a **table**, which explains how many calories you could burn while doing several different exercises. To find information on a table, remember to read both *across* and *down*.

What Exercise Can Do for You

by Sheila Globus

As you read the introduction to this article, apply the strategies that you just learned. Look for details that support the main idea "What's so great about exercise?"

What's so great about exercise? "It gives me **energy**," says Brinley, a member of the Junior Olympic Diving Team. "Instead of always being tired, I'm more awake and can focus on my schoolwork better."

Albee, a 15-year-old football player who lifts weights in the off-season, admits that pregame workouts and scrimmages tire him out. But, he says, "I feel a lot stronger and I'm a better player, especially since I started weight lifting."

Beth, a ninth grader, plays field hockey and lacrosse. She says that exercise helps her look and feel better and gives her a chance to be on a team with her friends. "It gives us a chance to work toward a common goal," she says.

 Stop here for the Strategy Break.

Strategy Break

If you were to create a concept map for this article's introduction, it might look like this:

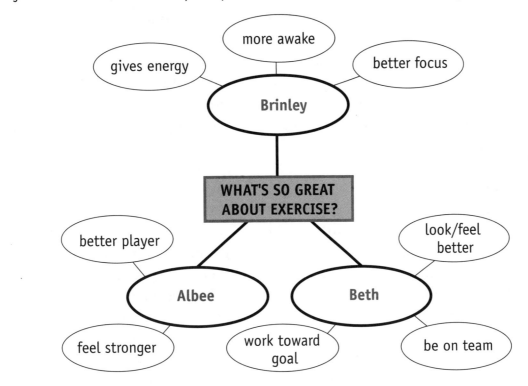

As you continue reading, pay attention to the main ideas and supporting details that describe what exercise can do for you. At the end of this article, you will use some of them to create a concept map of your own.

 Go on reading.

Shaping Up

We all know we should exercise: It's good for the heart, can help keep your weight under control, and might even help you live longer. Studies show, however, that as teenagers get older, they exercise less. Few can run a mile in under 10 minutes. Fewer still get the recommended 30 minutes of **moderate** exercise three or more times a week. In fact, as the use of computers and technology continues to grow, many teenagers are exercising little more than their fingers, tapping away at the keyboard.

It takes effort to make exercise a habit, but those who invest the time and energy are seldom disappointed. "Our coach makes us do a half-hour workout before we get into the pool," says Brinley, a high school sophomore. We do sit-ups, run stairs, do crunches, and stretch. That's what helped me get stronger, build more **endurance**, and stay loose and limber. I think it's also made me a better diver."

Brinley has the right idea. Just participating in a sport doesn't automatically get you into shape. To really get fit, you have to develop each component of fitness—**cardiovascular** endurance, muscle **strength**, and flexibility. For that, a combination of aerobics, stretching, and strengthening exercises works best.

Reducing Risk

Fitness experts say that nearly half of all young people ages 12 to 21 aren't active enough. That can lead to problems later in life, including heart disease, high blood pressure, diabetes, osteoporosis (thin, brittle bones that break easily), and even early death. What's more, a couch-potato lifestyle is harder to change the older you get.

Besides reducing your risk of these diseases, regular exercise can help you in smaller ways, too, such as helping you bounce back quicker from a cold and boosting your **metabolism** so that you burn more calories. A healthy heart, stronger bones, and a trim and toned body, however, are just the *physical* benefits of exercise. Even more important is what it does for your mood and your mind.

Exercise makes me feel better about myself and about the way I look," says Brinley. "I can even see my muscles. I always feel better after diving practice. I'm more confident, too—not just about diving, but about everything."

Finding an exercise that's fun is the key to getting something out of it. If lessons or team sports aren't your thing, try other activities that you think you might enjoy more. "Five

Going for the "Caloric Burn"
You may burn more or fewer calories per hour, depending on how vigorously you do the following activities.

Activity	Calories Burned per 30 Minutes	
	(Your Weight in Pounds)	
	120 pounds	150 pounds
swimming	209	261
walking	130	162
running (9 min/mile)	314	393
tennis	179	224
skiing	194	243
cycling (10 mph)	163	204
racquetball	217	272
hiking (vigorous)	191	239

years of karate made me a lot more **flexible**," says Rachel, "but it was boring. What I really like is step aerobics. I always leave the class feeling energized and stronger."

Fitting Exercise In

Even if you're not into sports, you can still find ways to sneak in a little extra physical activity wherever you can. Walk the dog, take the stairs instead of escalators, ride your bike to school. You won't be sorry. Here are some other ideas:

- Plan some fun into your schedule— a couple sets of tennis, a game of volleyball, a leisurely jog or hike along a trail.
- Shovel snow for a great heart-strengthening activity. (Builds your biceps, too, if you lift and toss it.)
- Vacuum, sweep, and scrub around the house (preferably with the stereo playing in the background).
- Help out in the yard raking leaves, or weeding and planting, depending on the season.

Exercise that's fun is exercise you'll stick with. In addition to possibly concentrating on developing a single skill, like sinking baskets or executing a perfect dive, think about all the things exercise can do for you—and go for it. You'll condition your heart and lungs, build strong muscles, make your tendons and ligaments supple, and maintain a healthy weight. What's more, you'll feel great. Take it from Brinley: "Even if I never make it to the Olympics, I won't ever stop doing exercise," she says. "It feels too good." ●

Strategy Follow-up

First, go back and fill in the last column of the K-W-L chart on page 144 with at least five new things that you learned while reading this article.

Then, on a separate sheet of paper, create a concept map for the section of this article called "Shaping Up." Work with a partner if you'd like.

✓Personal Checklist

Read each question and put a check (✓) in the correct box.

1. How well do you understand the information presented in this article?
   - ☐ 3 (extremely well)
   - ☐ 2 (fairly well)
   - ☐ 1 (not well)

2. After reading this article, how well would you be able to tell others what exercise can do for them?
   - ☐ 3 (extremely well)
   - ☐ 2 (fairly well)
   - ☐ 1 (not well)

3. On the K-W-L chart, how well were you able to list at least five new things that you learned from reading this article?
   - ☐ 3 (extremely well)
   - ☐ 2 (fairly well)
   - ☐ 1 (not well)

4. In the Vocabulary Builder, how many words were you able to use correctly to explain what exercise can do for you?
   - ☐ 3 (6–7 words)
   - ☐ 2 (3–5 words)
   - ☐ 1 (0–2 words)

5. How well were you able to complete the concept map in the Strategy Follow-up?
   - ☐ 3 (extremely well)
   - ☐ 2 (fairly well)
   - ☐ 1 (not well)

Vocabulary Check

Look back at the work you did in the Vocabulary Builder. Then answer each question by circling the correct letter.

1. Five years of karate made Rachel flexible. What other word from the article has the same meaning as *flexible*?
   a. older
   b. brittle
   c. limber

2. In the context of this article, what would be an example of someone using a lot of energy?
   a. turning on a light
   b. doing a half-hour aerobic workout
   c. working at a computer

3. What do cardiovascular exercises help strengthen besides your blood vessels?
   a. your arms
   b. your legs
   c. your heart

4. Which meaning of the word *moderate* fits this selection?
   a. within the proper amount or limit
   b. not very large or good
   c. person who holds opinions that are not extreme

5. According to the article, exercise can speed up your metabolism. Why is this beneficial?
   a. It helps you burn more calories.
   b. It helps you keep your weight down.
   c. Both of the above answers are correct.

Add the numbers that you just checked to get your Personal Checklist score. Fill in your score here. Then turn to page 219 and transfer your score onto Graph 1.

Personal
Vocabulary
Strategy
Comprehension
TOTAL SCORE
✓ T

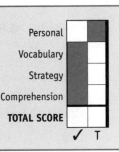

Check your answers with your teacher. Give yourself 1 point for each correct answer, and fill in your Vocabulary score here. Then turn to page 219 and transfer your score onto Graph 1.

Personal
Vocabulary
Strategy
Comprehension
TOTAL SCORE
✓ T

Strategy Check

Review the concept map that you completed for "Shaping Up." Also review the rest of the article. Then answer these questions:

1. Which supporting detail from the first paragraph under "Shaping Up" does *not* describe what exercise can do for you?

   a. It takes effort to make exercise a habit.

   b. It's good for the heart.

   c. It can help keep your weight under control.

2. According to the supporting details in the second and third paragraphs under "Shaping Up," what does Brinley's coach's workout help her do?

   a. It helps her do sit-ups, run stairs, do crunches, and stretch.

   b. It helps her do aerobics and stretch.

   c. It helps her get stronger, build endurance, stay loose and limber, and be a better diver.

3. If you were to create a concept map for "Reducing Risk," you would include the main idea "Reduces Risk of Certain Diseases." Which disease would you not include as a supporting detail?

   a. heart disease

   b. low blood pressure

   c. osteoporosis

4. In your concept map for "Reducing Risk," which detail would you include under the main idea "Mental Benefits"?

   a. boosts your strength

   b. boosts your metabolism

   c. boosts your confidence

5. If you were to create a concept map for "Fitting Exercise In," what might you call the main idea under which you would list the bulleted activities?

   a. Boring Ways to Exercise

   b. Chores as Exercise

   c. Ways to Get in Extra Exercise

Comprehension Check

Review the article if necessary. Then answer these questions:

1. According to the article, what is the recommended amount of exercise a person should have per week?

   a. 30 minutes, three or more times per week

   b. 20 minutes, five times per week

   c. 60 minutes, two or more times per week

2. The article says that to get really fit, you have to develop all three components of physical fitness. What are they?

   a. aerobic exercise, stretching, toning

   b. improved self-esteem, energy, appearance

   c. cardiovascular endurance, muscle strength, flexibility

3. According to the table, if you weighed 120 pounds, which activity would you be doing if you burned 209 calories in 30 minutes?

   a. swimming

   b. cycling

   c. racquetball

4. If you weighed 150 pounds and played tennis for 30 minutes, how many calories would you burn?

   a. 179

   b. 224

   c. 243

5. Why does the article say it is important to do exercise that is fun?

   a. You'll laugh more while you exercise.

   b. You'll stick with exercise if it's fun.

   c. You'll develop a new game.

Check your answers with your teacher. Give yourself 1 point for each correct answer, and fill in your Strategy score here. Then turn to page 219 and transfer your score onto Graph 1.

Personal
Vocabulary
Strategy
Comprehension
TOTAL SCORE
✓ T

Check your answers with your teacher. Give yourself 1 point for each correct answer, and fill in your Comprehension score here. Then turn to page 219 and transfer your score onto Graph 1.

Personal
Vocabulary
Strategy
Comprehension
TOTAL SCORE
✓ T

Extending

Choose one or both of these activities:

DESIGN A PERSONAL FITNESS PROGRAM

Do you need to get more exercise? If so, design a personal fitness program that you can do for 30 minutes, three or more times a week. Be sure to vary your activities so you don't become bored with them. Refer to the table or the list in this article, as well as the resources listed on this page, for some activities to include.

MAKE A DEMONSTRATION VIDEO

If you already play a sport, lift weights, dance, or perform some other activity for exercise, make a video to inform others about it. Before you demonstrate the activity, give a brief introduction to explain it. Your introduction can include such information as the origin of the sport or activity, an explanation of its rules or procedures, a description of any special equipment or clothing needed, and the health benefits involved.

Resources

Books

Anderson, Bob, Ed Burke, and Bill Pearl. *Getting in Shape: Workout Programs for Men and Women.* Shelter Publications, 1994.

Greene, Bob, and Oprah Winfrey. *Make the Connection: Ten Steps to a Better Body and a Better Life.* Hyperion Books, 1996.

Web Sites

http://www.apta.org/Consumer/ptandyourbody/fitness
On this Web site of the American Physical Therapy Association, you can find information about fitness, exercise, and physical therapy.

http://www.cyberparent.com/fitness
Learn about exercise and physical fitness on this Web site.

Brochure

Better Health and Fitness Through Physical Activity
Send a stamped, self-addressed business-size envelope to American Academy of Pediatrics, Department C—Better Health and Fitness Through Physical Activity, 141 Northwest Point Boulevard, Elk Grove Village, IL 60007-1098.

backboards

bases

baskets

catcher

footwork

hoops

innings

pitcher

punching

thrusts

It Wasn't Always Called Baseball

CLIPBOARD
Baseball

CLIPBOARD
Boxing

Building Background

Sports are a big part of many people's lives. If we don't play sports ourselves, we watch others play them. Fortunately, every sport is a little different. This variety gives us all choices. Decide which sport is your favorite. Then fill out the chart below with information about that sport.

Name of sport: _____

Where it is played: _____

Number of players: _____

Equipment used: _____

Clothing/gear worn: _____

How points are scored: _____

Vocabulary Builder

1. The words in the margin are all related to sports. Before you begin reading the article, decide which of the words are related to baseball, which are related to boxing, and which are related to basketball. List each word on the appropriate clipboard.

2. As you read the article, look for the words and decide if you wrote them on the right clipboards. Also, notice other words that are related to these sports. If you can, add them to the clipboards.

3. Save your work. You will refer to it again in the Vocabulary Check.

Strategy Builder

Comparing and Contrasting While You Read

- You already know that nonfictional writing follows certain patterns of organization. The article you are about to read follows the pattern of compare-contrast. **Comparing** means looking at how two or more people, things, or ideas are alike. **Contrasting** means looking at how two or more people, things, or ideas are different.

- Read the following paragraph, which compares and contrasts the writer's town today with the way it was years ago.

> My town has changed a great deal since the year 1900. Back then, many of the town's streets were unpaved. When it rained, they would turn to mud. Now, of course, every street in town is paved. Long ago, the downtown area had just a few buildings, and most of them were only one story. Now there are dozens of buildings with five to ten stories. One thing that has stayed the same in my town is the spirit of cooperation. It's what the town was founded on, and it's what helps us continue to grow.

CLIPBOARD

Basketball

- If you wanted to show the information in this paragraph on a **comparison chart**, it might look like this:

My Town Then	My Town Now
dirt roads	paved roads
just a few buildings	dozens of buildings
one-story buildings	five- to ten-story buildings
strong cooperation	strong cooperation

It Wasn't Always Called Baseball

by Vicki McClure

As you begin reading this article, apply the strategies that you just learned. Ask yourself how the original game of baseball compares and contrasts with the game of baseball today.

Did you know that baseball, one of the most popular games in the United States and Japan, was originally called "rounders"? That may sound strange, but it was so named because posts were used instead of **bases**, and the runners ran *around* them. Batters weren't called batters, either. They were called "strikers." Runs were called "aces," and whichever team made twenty-one aces won the game. **Innings** didn't exist then—quite a difference from how things are today!

Sports have been a big part of people's entertainment for thousands of years. Many popular games have changed dramatically from the way they were played when they first started.

Baseball was played by the Egyptians, the Greeks, and the Romans many centuries ago, but the game didn't start looking like the baseball we know until about a hundred years ago in England. Even as it was then, you probably wouldn't recognize the game. Twelve people were on the field instead of the nine to which we're accustomed. The **pitcher** was called the "thrower," and the opposing team would actually throw the ball at the runner and try to hit him! Instead of one **catcher**, there were two, one behind the other.

The playing field was strange, too. There were no regulations for the distance between bases, and all sorts of shapes were used. In fact, five bases were used instead of four.

A man named Alexander Cartwright finally came up with the field design we know. He also devised the diamond-shaped running area. Posts were replaced by flat bases because posts had proved to be too dangerous. Because of the bases, the game's name was changed to baseball.

⬣ **Stop here for the Strategy Break.**

Strategy Break

If you were to use a comparison chart to compare and contrast baseball, your chart might look like this:

Baseball Then	Baseball Now
was called rounders	is called baseball
players ran around posts	players run bases
strikers hit the ball	batters hit the ball
scored aces	score runs
played until a team made 21 aces	play 9 innings
12 players	9 players
thrower	pitcher
throw ball at runners	throw ball to the bases
two catchers	one catcher
five bases	four bases

As you continue reading, pay attention to the ways in which sports in the past and sports today are alike and different. At the end of this article, you will use some of the information to create a comparison chart of your own.

➡ Go on reading.

Bowling is another sport that has gone through many changes. Did you know that bowling was once a religious ceremony in ancient Germany? Church people rolled a large, round stone at a pin called a *Heide*, or heathen. If the thrower knocked down the pin, it was believed that he had overpowered the heathen and was leading a good, clean life. Afterward, a huge party would take place to honor the successful *kegelspielers*, or bowlers.

The popularity of the game spread to England, and people started to play it all the time. To play, you had to bring your own pin! The number of pins changed with the number of people playing. Eventually, the rule was made that only nine pins would be used in a game. Bowling was then called "ninepins."

The king of England was concerned that the new game was taking up the people's time and that they wouldn't practice archery. Bows and arrows were the country's main defense. Also, since gambling was popular at the games, all sorts of dreadful people began to mingle there. So, the king outlawed ninepins.

To bypass the new law, a game called "tenpins" was invented. The people added a pin and rearranged the pins' positions. After all, the law was only for *nine*pins—not *ten*pins!

Bowling wasn't the only sport to be outlawed. Boxing had been, too, but for different reasons.

Boxing used to be a "fight-to-the-death" game, although the only people who were allowed to watch it at first were the rulers of ancient Greece and Rome. To entertain these people of royalty, gladiators were matched against each other, fighting and **punching** with their hands encased in leather. The game was over when one of them was killed. As time passed, the leather hand coverings had fancy metal spikes attached to them. Without doubt, the "game" was bloody and horrid.

Over and over again, boxing was banned, but popular demand kept bringing it back. Finally, a man named James Figg decided to clean up the image of boxing.

He was the bareknuckle champion in England. He introduced **footwork**, **thrusts**, and defense into the game, and eliminated all the kicking and gouging that had been a part of the sport. He proved that boxing could be entertaining without being so violent. Other boxers began to imitate him. The sport became less dangerous. James Figg started the first school for boxers.

Unlike many other games, basketball is a very young sport. It was created in 1891 in the United States by a physical education teacher at the YMCA. Dr. James Naismith needed a sport that could be played indoors during the cold, snowy months in Massachusetts. All the indoor games around at the time were dull. He wanted one that would be competitive and fun.

Dr. Naismith hung two peach **baskets**, one at each end of the gym's balcony. He divided the athletes into two teams and instructed them to try to throw a ball into one of the baskets. As they played, different rules were formed. Many of the rules today are still the same.

Basketball was an immediate success. People liked to go and watch the competitions because the gyms were warm and comfortable. The bottoms of the peach baskets were cut away to speed up the game.

The game spread across the United States in just a few years. The peach baskets were replaced with metal **hoops**. **Backboards** had to be installed because the spectators often interfered with shots the players were making.

Volleyball was born four years after basketball. William Morgan decided that a second indoor game would be good for the YMCA. He strung a tennis net across the gym and lined up six players on each side. He tossed a "bladder" from a soccer ball to the players and told them to bat it back and forth. Later, standard rules were made. Mr. Morgan called his new game "mintonette," but the officials at the YMCA exhibitions didn't like the name. Mr. Morgan renamed it "volleyball."

Sports are fun to play and to watch. People have enjoyed them for centuries. But nobody knows *everything* about how they started. For instance, did you know that golf balls were once called "featheries"? That's because the first golf balls were made of leather and they were stuffed with goose feathers! ●

Strategy Follow-up

Now create a comparison chart for one of the sports described in the second part of this article (bowling, boxing, basketball, or volleyball). If you need more room, use a separate sheet of paper.

_____ Then	_____ Now

✓Personal Checklist

Read each question and put a check (✓) in the correct box.

1. How well do you understand the information presented in this article?
   ☐ 3 (extremely well)
   ☐ 2 (fairly well)
   ☐ 1 (not well)

2. After reading this article, how well would you be able to explain how one or more of the sports described have changed?
   ☐ 3 (extremely well)
   ☐ 2 (fairly well)
   ☐ 1 (not well)

3. How well were you able to complete the chart in Building Background?
   ☐ 3 (extremely well)
   ☐ 2 (fairly well)
   ☐ 1 (not well)

4. In the Vocabulary Builder, how many words were you able to write on the appropriate clipboards?
   ☐ 3 (7–10 words)
   ☐ 2 (4–7 words)
   ☐ 1 (0–3 words)

5. In the Strategy Follow-up, how well were you able to create a comparison chart for your chosen sport?
   ☐ 3 (extremely well)
   ☐ 2 (fairly well)
   ☐ 1 (not well)

Vocabulary Check

Look back at the work you did in the Vocabulary Builder. Then answer each question by circling the correct letter.

1. Which of these terms is related to baseball?
   a. tenpins
   b. hoops
   c. innings

2. Which meaning of the word *pitcher* fits the context of this article?
   a. a player who throws the baseball
   b. a container for holding liquid
   c. the amount that a container will hold

3. For what reason does the article say that backboards were installed on basketball nets?
   a. to keep the ball from hitting the walls
   b. to help the ball go into the basket
   c. to prevent interference by spectators

4. According to the article, which sport is most concerned with footwork?
   a. baseball
   b. boxing
   c. volleyball

5. Which meaning of the word *base* fits the context of this selection?
   a. a number that is raised to a power
   b. the foundation of a building
   c. a station at the corner of a baseball diamond

Add the numbers that you just checked to get your Personal Checklist score. Fill in your score here. Then turn to page 219 and transfer your score onto Graph 1.

	Personal	
	Vocabulary	
	Strategy	
	Comprehension	
	TOTAL SCORE	
	✓	T

Check your answers with your teacher. Give yourself 1 point for each correct answer, and fill in your Vocabulary score here. Then turn to page 219 and transfer your score onto Graph 1.

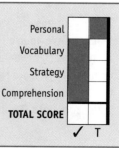

	Personal	
	Vocabulary	
	Strategy	
	Comprehension	
	TOTAL SCORE	
	✓	T

Strategy Check

Review the comparison chart you created for the Strategy Follow-up. Also review the rest of the article. Then answer these questions:

1. When bowling was first invented, how many pins did it have?
   a. one
   b. nine
   c. ten

2. Why was early boxing much more dangerous than boxing today?
   a. It used to have many more rounds.
   b. It used to be a "fight-to-the-death" game.
   c. It used to have lots of fancy footwork.

3. In the sport of basketball, how were the first baskets different from today's metal ones?
   a. The first baskets were peach baskets.
   b. The first baskets didn't have bottoms.
   c. The first baskets had backboards.

4. What is one way in which volleyball has changed since its creation?
   a. It uses a net.
   b. It is often played indoors.
   c. It has a different name.

5. In which sport were "featheries" first used?
   a. volleyball
   b. golf
   c. bowling

Comprehension Check

Review the article if necessary. Then answer these questions:

1. What was baseball's original name?
   a. aces
   b. rounders
   c. strikers

2. Why did Alexander Cartwright replace the posts in baseball with flat bases?
   a. The posts blocked the fans' view.
   b. The posts were too expensive.
   c. The posts were too dangerous.

3. Why did the king of England outlaw ninepins?
   a. He wasn't good at ninepins himself.
   b. Ninepins was a dangerous sport.
   c. It was taking people away from archery.

4. How did James Figg clean up boxing's image?
   a. He introduced strategy and eliminated kicking.
   b. He introduced kicking and gouging.
   c. He introduced leather gloves with metal spikes.

5. What is one main idea that you can learn from this article?
   a. Sports weren't much fun in years past.
   b. Sports are more fun to watch than to play.
   c. Sports have changed over the years.

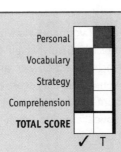

Check your answers with your teacher. Give yourself 1 point for each correct answer, and fill in your Strategy score here. Then turn to page 219 and transfer your score onto Graph 1.

Personal
Vocabulary
Strategy
Comprehension
TOTAL SCORE
✓ T

Check your answers with your teacher. Give yourself 1 point for each correct answer, and fill in your Comprehension score here. Then turn to page 219 and transfer your score onto Graph 1.

Personal
Vocabulary
Strategy
Comprehension
TOTAL SCORE
✓ T

Extending

Choose one or more of the following activities:

CREATE YOUR OWN SPORT

Would you like to be remembered as the creator of a new, exciting sport? Then design a brand-new one. Decide what the object of the game will be. Also decide what kind of equipment will be used. What kind of clothing will the players wear? Where will the sport be played? Make up a rule book and scoring procedures for your new sport. And don't forget to give it a name. If possible, ask for some volunteers to give a demonstration of your new sport.

INTERVIEW VETERAN SPORTS FANS

Interview a few people who have enjoyed participating in, observing, or coaching sports for many years. Ask them how their favorite sports have changed over the years. Then write an article that summarizes what you learned from your interviews.

RESEARCH THE HISTORY OF YOUR FAVORITE SPORT

Using resources listed on this page or ones you find yourself, research the history of the sport that you wrote about in Building Background. (If a classmate wrote about the same sport, you might want to work together.) Find out how the sport has changed over the years, and then create a comparison chart to show those changes. Share your chart with your classmates.

Resources

Book

McComb, David G. *Sports: An Illustrated History.* Illustrated Histories. Oxford University Children's Press, 1999.

Web Sites

http://mlb.mlb.com/NASApp/mlb/mlb/history/index.jsp
This Web site provides information on baseball history.

http://now2000.com/kids/sports.shtml
Find links on this page to Web sites about various sports.

http://www.bowlingmuseum.com/history.asp
This is the history page of the International Bowling Museum.

http://www.nba.com/history/thegame_index.html
On this site, learn about the origins of basketball and changes in the game over the years.

http://www.ussoccer.com/about/content.sps?iType=3998&icustompageid=6353
Read a time line of soccer in the United States on this site.

http://www.volleyball.org
This site offers information on volleyball.

Learning New Words

VOCABULARY

From Lesson 13
- abandoned/ empty
- afraid/ frightened
- grin/smile

From Lesson 13
- bright/dull
- large/small
- roared/ whispered

Synonyms

A synonym is a word that has the same meaning as another word. Author Sophie Masson uses several synonyms in "The Clever Thief." For example, she uses the synonyms *bright, fast, quick,* and *clever* to describe the boy and his actions.

Draw a line from each word in Column 1 to its synonym in Column 2.

COLUMN 1	COLUMN 2
silly	optimistic
hopeful	lively
energetic	sugary
transparent	stupid
sweet	clear

Antonyms

An antonym is a word that means the opposite of another word. "The Clever Thief" contains antonym pairs such as *bright/dull, large/small,* and *roared/whispered.*

Draw a line from each word in Column 1 to its antonym in Column 2.

COLUMN 1	COLUMN 2
quickly	happy
furious	full
empty	tiny
dark	light
gigantic	slowly

Prefixes

A prefix is a word part that is added to the beginning of a word. When you add a prefix, you often change the word's meaning and function. For example, the suffix *pre-* means "before." So adding *pre-* to the word *game* changes the noun to an adjective meaning "before the game."

mis-

The prefix *mis-* means "wrong or wrongly." In "Amusement-Park Rides" you learned that behaving recklessly on a ride is considered a misdemeanor in some states. A *misdemeanor* is a crime, or a wrongdoing.

Write the word that each definition describes.

1. put in the wrong place   _____

2. make a mistake in printing   _____

3. pronounce the wrong way   _____

4. spell the wrong way   _____

5. understand wrongly   _____

over-

The prefix *over-* has several meanings. For example, it can mean "above" or "across" or "above average." It also can mean "too much or too many." When a person feels *overwhelmed* on an amusement-park ride, he or she is receiving too many signals to the eyes and inner ears at once.

Write the word that each definition describes.

1. having too much enthusiasm   _____

2. coat worn over regular clothes _____

3. above one's head   _____

4. across the seas   _____

5. to charge too much money   _____

VOCABULARY

From Lesson 11
• misdemeanor

From Lesson 11
• overwhelmed

LESSON 16 Turkey Girl

Building Background

"Turkey Girl" is a Chippewa Indian legend. A **legend** is a traditional tale that has been passed down from generation to generation. As you were growing up, you probably read or heard many traditional tales. These tales probably featured some sort of magical element, such as animals or objects that could talk, or characters that could change themselves into different forms.

Sometimes a particular legend was passed from culture to culture. As the story was retold, certain details were changed to better fit that culture. For this reason, you might hear or read several different versions of the same basic tale. Think about the title "Turkey Girl." Given what you know about traditional tales—fairy tales, folk tales, legends, and myths—can you predict which popular tale this Chippewa legend will most resemble?

captive

discarded

eerie

finery

hardship

reunion

Vocabulary Builder

1. The boldfaced words in the questions below can all be found in "Turkey Girl." Use your knowledge of those words to answer the questions. Underline your answers.

   a. Whom would you expect to be dressed in **finery**—a queen or a beggar?

   b. If you were being held **captive**, would you come and go as you pleased, or would your freedom be taken away?

   c. Is a life of **hardship** easy or difficult?

   d. What would most people rather receive—something **discarded** by someone else or something that has never been used?

   e. When you have an **eerie** feeling, are you contented or uneasy?

   f. During a **reunion**, do people come together or do they separate?

2. Save your work. You will refer to it again in the Vocabulary Check.

Strategy Builder

Identifying Causes and Effects in Fiction

- In Lesson 11 you learned to identify causes and effects in an informational article. As you saw, not every cause-and-effect relationship is linked to another one.

- In fiction, however, the **cause-and-effect relationships** are often linked. Like the falling dominoes on this page, a single cause can start a chain reaction of other effects and causes.

- To find cause-and-effect relationships while you read, keep asking yourself, "What happened?" and "Why did it happen?" Doing this will help you understand what has happened so far. It also will help you predict what might happen next.

- As you read the following paragraph, look for the chain of causes and effects.

> Jackson was ravenously hungry after his football game, so he made himself a sandwich with everything on it. Just as Jackson was sitting down to eat, his dog Angel walked up and gave Jackson her paw. Jackson shook Angel's hand and gave her a corner of his sandwich. Angel gobbled it down and howled as if she were singing Jackson a song. Jackson applauded and gave Angel another piece of his sandwich. Angel ate that piece and rolled over twice. Jackson gave Angel another piece of his sandwich. Suddenly Jackson realized that he had given Angel almost all of his sandwich! He gave Angel the rest of his sandwich and got up and made himself another one.

- If you wanted to highlight the causes and effects in this paragraph, you could use a **cause-and-effect chain** like this one:

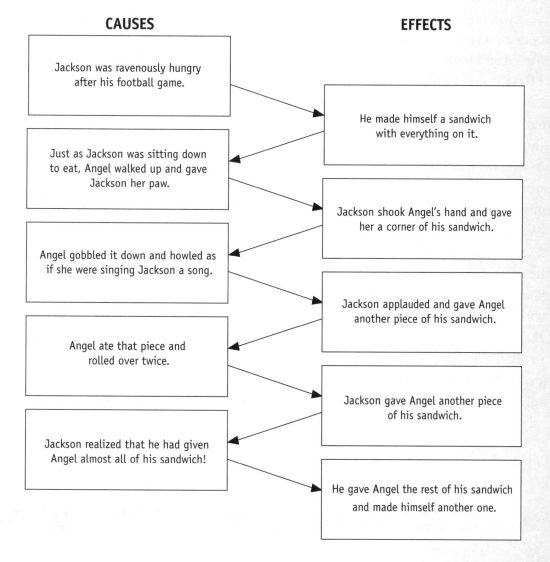

Turkey Girl

a Chippewa Indian legend retold by Patricia Isaacs

As you read the first part of this legend, apply the strategies that you just learned. To find the causes and effects, keep asking yourself, "What happened?" and "Why did it happen?"

Many years ago when the prairie lands were wild, there lived a Sioux Indian girl called White Moon. Her village went to war with the Chippewa, and suddenly fighting and bloodshed were all around her. The peaceful world she knew came to an end.

White Moon, the daughter of a powerful Sioux chief, was taken **captive**. She rode many weary days and nights northward with the war party. A few Chippewa women were along to cook and see to the warriors' needs, and White Moon was given to them. Tossed about among the women, she was scorned and beaten and thrown scraps of food as though she were a dog.

"Why don't we just kill her?" cried out one vengeful woman. "She is only a burden to us."

"No! We must let her be," said another. "Chief Red Eagle says we must bargain with her for horses and weapons."

"Yes, that is right, Old One," said the chief, overhearing. "The Sioux will pay much for her return. Put her to work if she burdens you. When we reach our village, she will tend our turkey flock. Tell her that if she fails and we lose even one turkey to the wolves, she will also die."

From then on White Moon was known as "Turkey Girl," and a new life of **hardship** and loneliness began for her in the Chippewa village. She hauled heavy buckets of water for all the camp, sometimes chipping away ice from the river's edge with rocks, leaving her hands raw and bleeding. She spent many hours tending to the turkey flock, leading the birds to the forest to eat and drink. Each night she enclosed them in a pen to protect them from wolves and other wild creatures.

Many months passed, and one of the older women, Yellow Buffalo Woman, began to feel sorry for the girl. She gave her fresh tobacco to chew to keep the hunger away. "Be careful," she warned. "Do not swallow the juice or you will become very sick." She also gave her one of her most prized possessions, a white man's handkerchief. "To spit the juice into," she explained, smiling at White Moon.

A lowly captive, Turkey Girl was unwelcome at any tepee or fire. She was forced to curl up among her flock for warmth. The winters were harsh, and she nearly froze when the snows swirled and drifted. Yellow Buffalo Woman found an old, **discarded** bearskin robe and gave it to Turkey Girl to protect her from the cold. The old woman crushed dried flowers and mixed the petals with sweet pine needles to freshen the girl's bedding. And so Turkey Girl survived.

⬢ **Stop here for the Strategy Break.**

Strategy Break

If you were to create a cause-and-effect chain for this story so far, it might look like this:

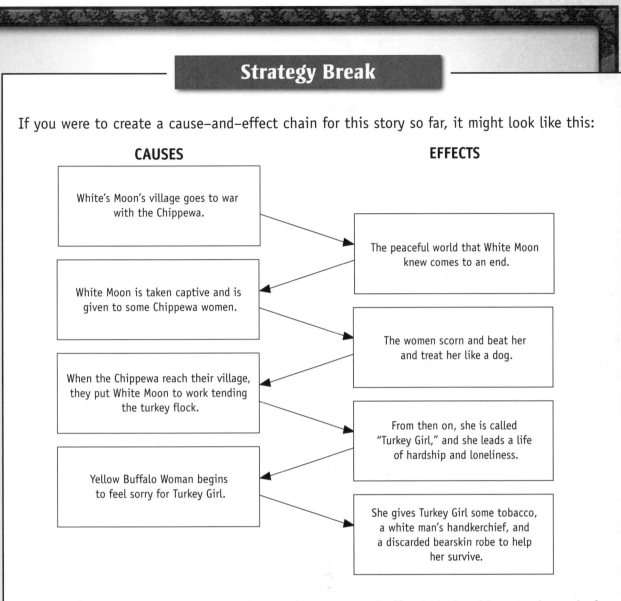

CAUSES

EFFECTS

White's Moon's village goes to war with the Chippewa.

White Moon is taken captive and is given to some Chippewa women.

When the Chippewa reach their village, they put White Moon to work tending the turkey flock.

Yellow Buffalo Woman begins to feel sorry for Turkey Girl.

The peaceful world that White Moon knew comes to an end.

The women scorn and beat her and treat her like a dog.

From then on, she is called "Turkey Girl," and she leads a life of hardship and loneliness.

She gives Turkey Girl some tobacco, a white man's handkerchief, and a discarded bearskin robe to help her survive.

As you continue reading, pay attention to the cause-and-effect relationships. At the end of this story, you will complete a cause-and-effect chain of your own.

⇒ Go on reading to see what happens.

When spring came, Turkey Girl took her digging stick to the river's edge to look for new turnips. She noticed a reflection in the water and went closer. "This can't be me!" she cried. "I look so ugly . . . like an evil spirit. How can this be?" She ran her fingers through her tangled hair and wept bitterly.

Finally, drying her face on her sleeve, she watched the image change. In the water appeared the kind and gentle face of her mother, and as if by magic, she heard her mother call to her. Turkey Girl held her breath and listened.

"Oh, White Moon, my beloved daughter, are you well and safe? Oh, child, we have not forgotten you. The wars are ending now, and we will come for you. Do not give up hope. . . ." The words and face faded away.

Turkey Girl stood and smoothed her ragged dress and held her head high. Yes, she was White Moon and she would be strong. She gathered into her skirt what few turnips she had found and hurried back to the village, her heart beating with new hope.

Upon her return, she found the entire camp preparing for the spring festival that was to begin that day. Chippewa from near and far would gather to visit and dance well into the night, and tomorrow there would be a great feast. But Turkey Girl knew that she would not be allowed to go. Feeling lonely and in the way, she fled to the turkey pen and her bed, hoping to dream of home. Her flock gathered around her, and she fell into a deep sleep.

As she slept, an **eerie** light appeared over the pen, and an old turkey gobbler began to speak. "Come, friends, and listen to me," he whispered. "We must help Turkey Girl. She has seen to all our needs and protected us for a long time. As you know, I am a maker of magic. My powers have grown weaker with age, but with your help, I think I have enough magic left to create a day that Turkey Girl will never forget. Let us begin."

When Turkey Girl awoke, she noticed neat piles of feathers gathered about the pen. She stood up, puzzled, and was startled when the old turkey spoke to her. Startled, but not afraid. Indian ways had taught her to accept such things on faith alone.

"Dear child," he began, "you have been our trusted friend. Let us help you now. Today you *shall* go to the celebration with the rest."

The turkeys laid feathers across her bare feet, and the feathers turned into decorated deerskin moccasins. Then the gobbler asked Turkey Girl to lie down, and when she did, the birds placed feathers across her dress of rags, changing it into velvet-soft white skins trimmed with fringe, beads, and tiny shells.

Turkey Girl's eyes sparkled with tears of wonder and happiness. "These are the most beautiful clothes I have ever seen. I must be dreaming," she laughed. As she twirled about the pen, her hair became shiny and silky again; her rough hands soft and smooth. The turkeys sighed and ruffled their feathers in delight.

Again the strange light appeared, and the gate swung open. The gobbler beckoned her forward. "Be happy and enjoy the dancing. We will go out and feed ourselves, but you must come for us before dark," he warned. "This you must do, or the wolves will surely find us."

Turkey Girl, in all her **finery**, mingled easily with the people, as many were strangers to the village. She sang and danced and had such a wonderful time that when darkness came, she forgot all about the turkeys. She stayed late into the night, and the next day she enjoyed the feast and ate more food than she had eaten in almost two years.

Only when it was too late did she remember the old gobbler's warning.

One of the women came running to tell of the disaster. Almost all of the turkeys had been found dead, killed by wolves. The rest had run far off into the forest and were now lost to the tribe.

Tears streaming down her cheeks, Turkey Girl stumbled off into the forest. "Oh, what have I done? What have I done?" she sobbed. As she ran, the moccasins on her feet changed back into feathers and blew away. Her dress became rags again, her hair a tangle of snarls and dirt, her hands weathered and rough.

She ran all the way to the stream where she had seen her mother's reflection, and there she fell to the ground. "Oh, Mother," she sobbed, "my heart is breaking. I have brought my friends to their deaths. I am not even worthy to be called Turkey Girl."

As she wept, gentle hands touched her shoulders, and Yellow Buffalo Woman spoke. "Come, you must leave this place. There is no forgiveness for you here. I have brought a robe and moccasins, dried meat and corn. Dry your tears and go quickly, for they are searching for you."

She laid a gnarled old hand against Turkey Girl's cheek. "Child, you have a long and dangerous journey ahead.

Follow the sun to the south and west, and at night let the moon and great star guide you. They will lead you safely to your own people. Trust me. Now . . . go!"

And so Turkey Girl did as she was told. Many, many days passed, and often, exhausted and weak, she felt she could no longer go on. But at last she came upon a Sioux village and there she fell to her knees.

White Moon was later returned to her own village and had a happy **reunion** with her family. She grew up and married a handsome Sioux chief and had strong, fine sons and daughters and many grandchildren. She was wise and kind and greatly honored by her people. They called her "Old Woman" then, a gesture of respect.

And when she was very old and even in the last days of her life, she could be found tending the tribe's turkey flock, as she had every day for over eighty years. She took the birds into the forest to eat and drink each day and penned them up safely each night. She alone stood guard over them each winter, protecting them from wolves and other wild creatures. Yes, even then, and perhaps for all time . . . somewhere. ●

Strategy Follow-up

Now complete the cause–and–effect chain for the second part of "Turkey Girl." Use a separate sheet of paper if you need more room to write.

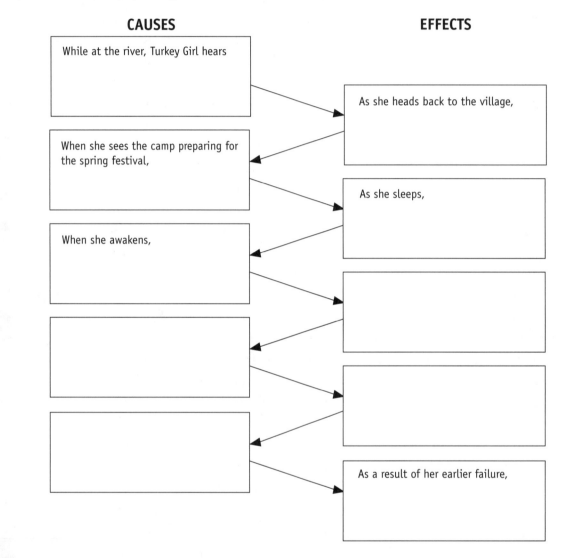

CAUSES

While at the river, Turkey Girl hears

When she sees the camp preparing for the spring festival,

When she awakens,

EFFECTS

As she heads back to the village,

As she sleeps,

As a result of her earlier failure,

✓Personal Checklist

Read each question and put a check (✓) in the correct box.

1. How well do you understand what happens in this legend?
   - ☐ 3 (extremely well)
   - ☐ 2 (fairly well)
   - ☐ 1 (not well)

2. How well do you understand why White Moon continues to guard turkeys for the rest of her life?
   - ☐ 3 (extremely well)
   - ☐ 2 (fairly well)
   - ☐ 1 (not well)

3. In Building Background, how well were you able to predict which traditional tale "Turkey Girl" would most resemble?
   - ☐ 3 (extremely well)
   - ☐ 2 (fairly well)
   - ☐ 1 (not well)

4. How well were you able to answer the questions in the Vocabulary Builder?
   - ☐ 3 (extremely well)
   - ☐ 2 (fairly well)
   - ☐ 1 (not well)

5. How well were you able to complete the cause-and-effect chain in the Strategy Follow-up?
   - ☐ 3 (extremely well)
   - ☐ 2 (fairly well)
   - ☐ 1 (not well)

Vocabulary Check

Look back at the work you did in the Vocabulary Builder. Then answer each question by circling the correct letter.

1. What does the word *reunion* mean?
   a. a splitting apart again
   b. a telling over again
   c. a coming together again

2. Which of these is an example of a captive?
   a. a bug in a sealed jar
   b. a butterfly on a flower
   c. a firefly in the woods

3. Which word is an antonym of *finery*?
   a. rags
   b. costume
   c. Sunday best

4. Which phrase best describes what you probably did after you decided that something was useless?
   a. captured it
   b. beckoned to it
   c. discarded it

5. Which word describes something that is spooky?
   a. beloved
   b. eerie
   c. captive

Add the numbers that you just checked to get your Personal Checklist score. Fill in your score here. Then turn to page 219 and transfer your score onto Graph 1.

Check your answers with your teacher. Give yourself 1 point for each correct answer, and fill in your Vocabulary score here. Then turn to page 219 and transfer your score onto Graph 1.

Strategy Check

Review the cause-and-effect chain that you created for the second part of "Turkey Girl." Then answer the following questions.

1. What is the effect when Turkey Girl hears her mother at the river?
   a. Turkey Girl becomes hopeful and decides to be strong.
   b. Turkey Girl becomes afraid and runs away.
   c. Turkey Girl becomes sad and thinks her mother has died.

2. Why do the turkeys help Turkey Girl?
   a. They want to trick her and get her into trouble.
   b. They want to repay her for taking care of them.
   c. They want to help her escape the Chippewa village.

3. Turkey Girl has such a wonderful time at the festival that she forgets to return before dark. What result do her actions cause?
   a. The turkeys starve to death while they wait for her to return.
   b. Turkey Girl changes back to her old self before the entire festival.
   c. Almost all the turkeys are killed, and the rest have run away.

4. If the old woman had not helped Turkey Girl escape, what probably would have been the effect?
   a. Turkey Girl would have been rewarded.
   b. Turkey Girl would have been killed.
   c. Turkey Girl would have been set free.

5. Why do you think White Moon continues to take care of turkeys for the rest of her life?
   a. She feels guilty and wants to repay them for their kindness.
   b. She must do what her captors demand.
   c. She is forced to guard the turkeys by her own tribe.

Comprehension Check

Review the legend if necessary. Then answer these questions:

1. To what tribe does White Moon belong?
   a. Chippewa
   b. Sioux
   c. Iroquois

2. What does the chief say will happen to White Moon if even one turkey dies?
   a. She will be killed.
   b. She will be given a new job.
   c. She will be traded away.

3. How do the turkeys help White Moon?
   a. They give her a package of food and help her escape.
   b. They take care of themselves while she sleeps.
   c. They give her beautiful clothes so she can go to the festival.

4. Which well-known fairy tale does "Turkey Girl" most resemble?
   a. "Cinderella"
   b. "Little Red Riding Hood"
   c. "Sleeping Beauty"

5. Which fairy-tale character does Yellow Buffalo Woman most resemble?
   a. a wicked witch
   b. a grandmother
   c. a fairy godmother

Check your answers with your teacher. Give yourself 1 point for each correct answer, and fill in your Strategy score here. Then turn to page 219 and transfer your score onto Graph 1.

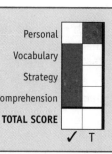

Personal
Vocabulary
Strategy
Comprehension
TOTAL SCORE

Check your answers with your teacher. Give yourself 1 point for each correct answer, and fill in your Comprehension score here. Then turn to page 219 and transfer your score onto Graph 1.

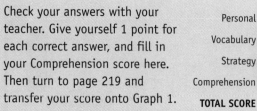

Personal
Vocabulary
Strategy
Comprehension
TOTAL SCORE

Extending

Choose one or both of the following activities:

PRODUCE A COLLECTION OF NATIVE AMERICAN FOLKLORE

Work with a group of classmates to create an anthology, or collection, of Native American folklore. Have each member of the group research and choose at least one story to include. Some of the resources on this page can help you get started. Ask some members of the group to illustrate the stories with pictures that imitate a Native American style. Then collect the stories and bind them into a book that others can use to study Native American literature.

COMPARE "TURKEY GIRL" AND "CINDERELLA"

In a paragraph or on a comparison chart, compare and contrast the Chippewa legend "Turkey Girl" with the European fairy tale "Cinderella." Point out ways in which the tales are both alike and different. Pay special attention to the characters, the settings, and the stories' outcomes. Then tell which story you prefer, and explain why you chose it.

Resources

Books

Ardagh, Philip. *North American Myths and Legends.* Dillon Press. 1998.

Bruchac, Joseph. *Flying with the Eagle, Racing the Great Bear: Stories from Native North America.* Troll, 1998.

Goble, Paul. *Adopted by the Eagles: A Plains Indian Story of Friendship.* Aladdin, 1998.

Rubalcaba, Jill. *Uncegila's Seventh Spot: A Lakota Legend.* Clarion, 1995.

Web Site

http://www.ilhawaii.net/~stony/loreindx.html
This Web site has a collection of 150 traditional Native American stories.

Audio Recording

Ortiz, Alfonso, and Richard Erdoes, narr. *American Indian Myths and Legends,* vol. 2. Sunset Productions, 1991.

Another Cinderella

Building Background

To get the most out of "Another Cinderella," it will help to review the classic fairy tale "Cinderella." Since it probably has been a long time since you've read or heard the tale, get together with a partner and summarize it. Be sure to discuss the main characters, the setting, and the important events in your summary. Then as you read "Another Cinderella," think about why the author decided to write this version of the story.

achievement

celebration

challenge

Vocabulary Builder

1. The words in the margin are from "Another Cinderella." For each word, create a word map like the example below. (Use a separate sheet of paper for each map.)

2. Predict how each vocabulary word might be used in "Another Cinderella." Then, as you read the story, find the boldfaced words. See if your predictions match the way the words are actually used.

3. Save your work. You will use it again in the Vocabulary Check.

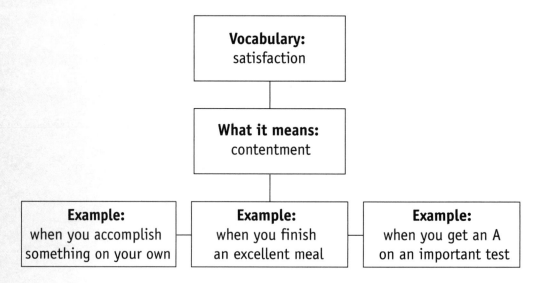

Vocabulary:
satisfaction

What it means:
contentment

Example:
when you accomplish something on your own

Example:
when you finish an excellent meal

Example:
when you get an A on an important test

Strategy Builder

Drawing Conclusions About Characters

- A **conclusion** is a decision that you reach after thinking about certain facts or information. When you read a story, you often draw conclusions based on information that the author gives you about the characters, setting, or events.

- You can draw conclusions about the **characters** in a story by paying attention to what they say, do, think, and feel.

- In many stories, the characters change in some way. These characters are called **dynamic characters**. Other characters stay the same throughout a story. They are called **static characters**. As you read the paragraphs below, see if you can draw any conclusions about Ben based on what he says, does, thinks, and feels. Is he a static or dynamic character? Why?

> When the new kid moved in next door, Ben knew that he wasn't going to like him. After all, Jake dressed in odd clothes and didn't talk much. He never looked anyone in the eye and never joined the neighborhood baseball games. Even though Ben's mother became friendly with Jake's mom, Ben decided to avoid Jake.
>
> One day Ben forgot his house key and was locked out. He remembered that his mom had given a key to Jake's mother, so he knocked on Jake's door. Jake answered the door and let Ben in. He offered Ben a soda, and they began to talk. Jake was interested in model trains, and he showed Ben his setup. Ben stayed at Jake's all afternoon, talking about trains.
>
> From then on, Ben stopped at Jake's house every morning, and they walked to school together.

- Did you decide that Ben is a dynamic character? If you wanted to track the changes in his attitude toward Jake, you could record them on a character wheel like the one below. The conclusions that one reader drew about Ben are in *italics*.

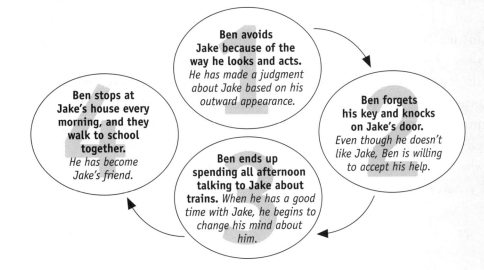

Another Cinderella

by Norman Stiles

As you read the first part of this story, notice what Cinderella says, does, thinks, and feels. What conclusions can you draw about her?

Once upon a time there lived a girl named Cinderella. Not *that* Cinderella. Another Cinderella.

This Cinderella lived with her really nice stepmother, really nice stepsister, and really nice stepbrother. She was the light of their lives. All they wanted was that Cinderella be as happy as a young girl could be.

From the day Cinderella became part of their family, they bent over backward to "give her space" and to "let her do her own thing." They freely and gladly worked their fingers to the bone to give her anything and everything she needed or wanted, and they never, ever made her do *any* chores.

That's right. No chores! Ever! Never!

Not only didn't she have to lift a finger, they would lift it for her.

She didn't have to clean up her room or put her stuff away or even put the cap back on the toothpaste if she didn't feel like it.

She didn't have to help wash the dishes or dry the dishes or bring her dish to the sink or even *use* a dish if she didn't feel like it.

She could do whatever she wanted to do whenever she wanted to do it and they never butted in.

If she didn't feel like it, she didn't have to go to school.

They did her homework for her.

She could eat whenever she was hungry and they would cook it for her no matter what time of day.

She could go to sleep whenever she wanted to go to sleep and get up whenever she wanted to get up.

She could eat in bed . . . even something with gravy!

Of course, she never, ever had to help clean the cinders out of the fireplace. She liked to watch *them* do that. (That's why they called her Cinderella.)

She had it made. What a life!

So how come she cried all the time?

"Who knows? Maybe it's a phase," her stepmother said. "She'll grow out of it . . . I hope."

Of course they tried to talk to her. "Why are you crying?" they would ask.

"I don't know," Cinderella would sob. "I don't know." And she didn't know why she cried. She just couldn't explain it.

"Hey, come on, stop crying," her stepmother would say. "Go out and have some fun! Here's some money. Buy yourself something."

"Eat something."

"Go see a funny play."

"Have your hair done."

"Have your nails done."

"Have a nice cup of tea."

"Have a nice day."

"Whatever it is, try not to think about it."

"Hold your breath and count to twenty. It works with hiccups, maybe it will work with crying."

"Take a trip."

"Take a ride."

"Take an aspirin."

"Take a hot bath."

"Take off a couple of pounds."

Some of these things worked for a little while, but soon, out of nowhere and for no apparent reason, Cinderella would burst into tears again.

Then, one Friday, Cinderella came home from school and said, "I have a book report to write. It's due on Monday."

"A book report? Over the weekend? Oh! You poor dear!" her stepmother said as she arrived home from work.

"Let me do it for you, Cinderella!" the stepbrother cried.

"No, let me!" the stepsister jumped in.

"No. Me!"

"No! Me!"

They argued back and forth.

"Now, now. No fighting, kids. You *both* can do it for her," said Cinderella's stepmother.

"Yay," they yelled as they jumped around happily.

Cinderella burst into tears.

But this time her stepmother offered something very, very special to soothe her. She showed Cinderella a beautiful designer gown that she had bought for her along with the most beautiful and perfect accessories, including an imported pair of hand-blown glass slippers.

Cinderella stopped crying when her stepmother took her outside to see a golden carriage pulled by two gorgeous horses and attended by two very impressive coachpersons.

"You bought all this for me?" Cinderella asked, blowing her nose.

"Well, I bought the gown and the accessories and the shoes. The coach and the horses and the coachpersons are a rental," her stepmother said proudly. "I did all this for you so you can go to the Prince's Ball at the palace on Sunday night. Maybe the Prince will fall in love with you and marry you and make you happy for ever and ever and then you won't cry all the time."

Cinderella burst into tears. At first everybody thought these were tears of joy. But tears of joy don't usually last from just before supper Friday night until breakfast Sunday morning with no sign of letting up.

While they worried that Cinderella might cry all day and not be able to go to the ball that night, a great wind began to blow outside their cottage. It blew louder and louder and stronger, shaking the cottage until finally it blew open the front door and then stopped blowing, all at once.

It was strangely calm and quiet, and they all stared at the open door, not knowing what to expect.

Then, from behind them, they heard, "Made you look! Made you look!"

It was Cinderella's Fairy Godmother. "Came in through the window! I love the unexpected," she said with a twinkle in her eye. "Hi! I'm your Fairy Godmother, and I'm here to help with this crying business."

Everyone was thrilled, including Cinderella. *Especially* Cinderella! It wasn't a lot of fun going through life crying all the time. "How are you going to do it? Wave your magic wand and my crying will stop?" Cinderella wondered.

"No, sweetheart," replied the Fairy Godmother patiently. "I'm good, but I'm not *that* good. And even if I could do that, I'm not sure it would be such a good idea."

"I know. You'll wave your magic wand and bring her a Prince who will make her happy and her crying will stop," offered the stepbrother.

"No. I could conjure up a Prince or two, but it wouldn't work anyway."

"Then you'll wave your wand and bring Cinderella riches beyond her dreams and that will make her crying stop," the stepsister said.

"No. That wouldn't work either."

"Then what *will* you do?" the stepmother demanded impatiently.

"Look," said the Fairy Godmother. "I think that what Cinderella needs is a sense of **achievement**, a feeling of accomplishment, and the satisfaction that comes from meeting a **challenge**."

"Oh, I see. You're going to wave your magic wand and give her all

that," said the stepmother. "Please hurry. We want the red in her eyes to clear up in time for the ball."

"No. She's going to get all that on her own . . . once she is given some reasonable guidelines and compassionate guidance," the Fairy Godmother said.

"Ah, ha! That must be where the wand comes in," said the stepmother.

"No. That's where *you* come in."

Everyone was very confused. Was she going to use that wand or wasn't she?

She was. And she did. First she waved it and turned the gown into overalls, the glass slippers into work boots, the coach into a pumpkin, and the coachpersons into mice. She left the horses as they were to graze peacefully in the yard.

Everyone except the horses was very upset. A Fairy Godmother wasn't supposed to take things away. What kind of Fairy Godmother was she anyway?

"Relax!" she said. "I'm not finished." And she waved her wand and out of thin air produced a piece of paper and a pencil. It was a very nice piece of paper and a good pencil with a sharp point, but what did a pencil and paper have to do with anything?"

The Fairy Godmother explained that she would help Cinderella's stepmother make a list of things Cinderella would have to accomplish before the gown and the other stuff would be restored. If she finished doing everything on the list before it was time to go to the ball, so be it. If not, no ball.

They didn't like it. It didn't sound fair or nice or kind or loving. The Fairy Godmother assured them that it was all of the above. She turned to Cinderella and said, "Just do your best, dear. It will work out. Trust me."

"Okay," Cinderella said in a surprisingly strong voice. "I'll try."

⬢ **Stop here for the Strategy Break.**

Strategy Break

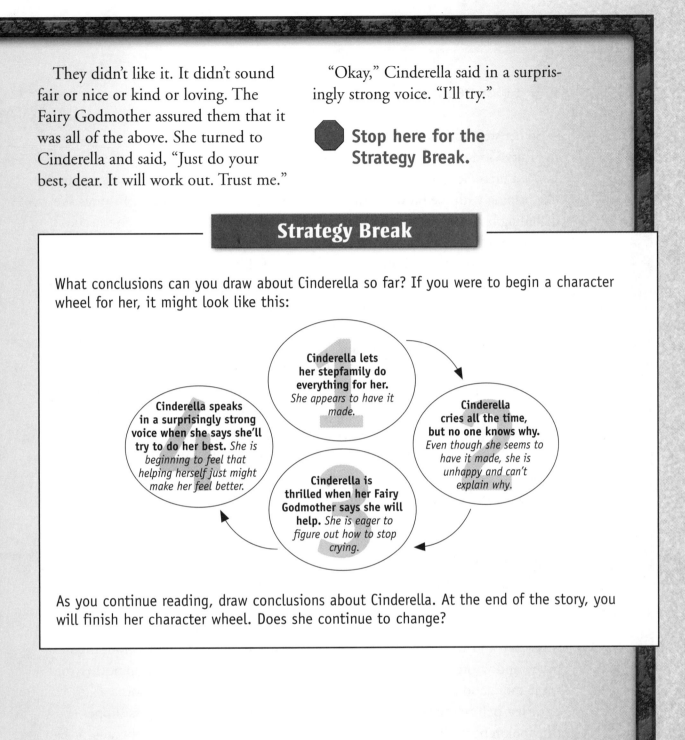

What conclusions can you draw about Cinderella so far? If you were to begin a character wheel for her, it might look like this:

Cinderella lets her stepfamily do everything for her. *She appears to have it made.*

Cinderella cries all the time, but no one knows why. *Even though she seems to have it made, she is unhappy and can't explain why.*

Cinderella is thrilled when her Fairy Godmother says she will help. *She is eager to figure out how to stop crying.*

Cinderella speaks in a surprisingly strong voice when she says she'll try to do her best. *She is beginning to feel that helping herself just might make her feel better.*

As you continue reading, draw conclusions about Cinderella. At the end of the story, you will finish her character wheel. Does she continue to change?

➡ Go on reading.

So her stepmother, with the help of the Fairy Godmother, made up the list. It was a pretty long list, too, with things like helping with the breakfast dishes, including bringing her dish to the sink; cleaning up her room by herself; helping with the laundry, etc. She even had to do her book report all by herself.

One by one Cinderella did the things on the list, and as she did, she began to feel and look happier and happier. As the day went by, she didn't cry once. It looked like her Fairy Godmother was right. But Cinderella still hadn't written the book report.

"Let us help her," the stepsister begged.

"No," said the stepmother firmly. "I think we should let her do it by herself."

Cinderella's Fairy Godmother smiled because she knew that Cinderella's stepmother was finally getting the picture.

Cinderella smiled, too, and then she wrote and wrote and paced and paced and wrote and erased and wrote some more and finally, with just one hour left before the ball, she finished the book report. She couldn't believe how good she felt. She had never felt that good in her entire life!

Everyone cheered as her Fairy Godmother waved her wand and restored the gown and the glass slippers and the accessories and the coach and the coachpersons.

Cinderella started to cry.

But this time she knew why. She didn't want to go to the ball if it meant she had to marry the Prince. She didn't feel she was ready to get married. She had a lot of things she wanted to do first, like go to school, learn things, grow, become a person, stuff like that.

Her stepmother agreed with her and promised that one thing she didn't have to do if she didn't feel like doing it was marry someone she didn't feel like marrying. The only thing she would be expected to do from now on were things like homework and chores and stuff like that.

"This calls for a **celebration**!" the Fairy Godmother said. "And what better place to celebrate than at a ball! Off you go!"

And off they went.

And they had a great time. Cinderella danced with the Prince and thought he was sort of cute and nice. She wanted to stay late, but she left early because she had school the next day and because her stepmother told her it was time to go home.

She did leave her glass slipper behind with the Prince because it had her name and address inside and she wanted to see him again. Besides, she knew where *he* lived so it was only fair.

Over the years Cinderella grew into a fine young woman who wrote book reports for a living. She and the Prince became very good friends, fell

in love, got married, and they had a
very nice life together.

Cinderella still cried once in a while
but, then, so does everybody. ●

Strategy Follow-up

Work with a partner to complete this activity. On a large sheet of paper, copy the character wheel below. Then fill in circles 5–8 with information from the second part of the story.

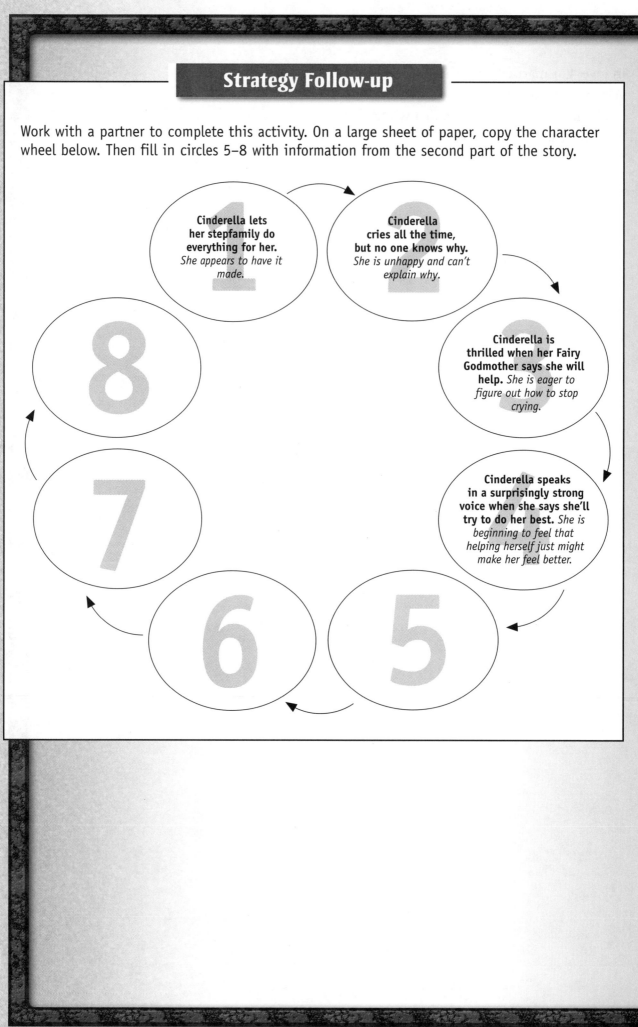

1 Cinderella lets her stepfamily do everything for her. *She appears to have it made.*

2 Cinderella cries all the time, but no one knows why. *She is unhappy and can't explain why.*

3 Cinderella is thrilled when her Fairy Godmother says she will help. *She is eager to figure out how to stop crying.*

4 Cinderella speaks in a surprisingly strong voice when she says she'll try to do her best. *She is beginning to feel that helping herself just might make her feel better.*

5

6

7

8

✓Personal Checklist

Read each question and put a check (✓) in the correct box.

1. Now that you've read this story, how well do you think you understand why the author decided to write this version of "Cinderella"?
    - ☐ 3 (extremely well)
    - ☐ 2 (fairly well)
    - ☐ 1 (not well)

2. How well were you able to complete the word maps in the Vocabulary Builder?
    - ☐ 3 (extremely well)
    - ☐ 2 (fairly well)
    - ☐ 1 (not well)

3. How well were you able to work with your partner to complete the character wheel in the Strategy Follow-up?
    - ☐ 3 (extremely well)
    - ☐ 2 (fairly well)
    - ☐ 1 (not well)

4. At the beginning of this story, how well do you understand why Cinderella cries all the time?
    - ☐ 3 (extremely well)
    - ☐ 2 (fairly well)
    - ☐ 1 (not well)

5. How well were you able to draw conclusions about the changes in Cinderella?
    - ☐ 3 (extremely well)
    - ☐ 2 (fairly well)
    - ☐ 1 (not well)

Vocabulary Check

Look back at the work you did in the Vocabulary Builder. Then answer each question by circling the correct letter.

1. What other word from this story has the same meaning as *achievement*?
    - a. celebration
    - b. challenge
    - c. accomplishment

2. What is *not* an example of an occasion for a celebration?
    - a. a birthday
    - b. losing a pet
    - c. a graduation

3. What does it mean when something is a challenge?
    - a. It is difficult to do.
    - b. It is easy to do.
    - c. It is embarrassing to do.

4. What is *not* an example of an accomplishment?
    - a. passing a driving test
    - b. having green eyes
    - c. winning a spelling bee

5. What does Cinderella's Fairy Godmother mean when she tells Cinderella that she needs a sense of achievement?
    - a. Cinderella needs to think she is special, even if she isn't.
    - b. Cinderella needs to be given special help to succeed.
    - c. Cinderella needs to feel that she can do things on her own.

Add the numbers that you just checked to get your Personal Checklist score. Fill in your score here. Then turn to page 219 and transfer your score onto Graph 1.

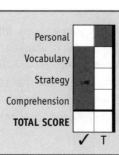

Check your answers with your teacher. Give yourself 1 point for each correct answer, and fill in your Vocabulary score here. Then turn to page 219 and transfer your score onto Graph 1.

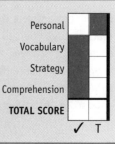

Strategy Check

Review the character wheel that you and your partner completed in the Strategy Follow-up. Also review the story if necessary. Then answer these questions:

1. At the beginning of the story, why does Cinderella's family do everything for her?
   a. They want her to stay useless and helpless.
   b. They love her and want her to be happy.
   c. They care more about their own happiness than hers.

2. Why does Cinderella always start crying again after she tries the activities that her family suggests?
   a. The activities are much too difficult for her.
   b. The activities don't solve her real problem.
   c. She never puts any effort into her attempts.

3. Why do you think Cinderella agrees so willingly to go along with her Fairy Godmother's plan?
   a. She realizes that doing things for herself might make her feel better.
   b. Being told what to do is easier than having to figure it out for herself.
   c. She feels she needs to be punished for not doing things all along.

4. Why does Cinderella begin to cry again when her Fairy Godmother restores the gown and slippers?
   a. She would rather stay home and do some more chores.
   b. She doesn't like the dress and slippers that she has to wear.
   c. She doesn't want to go to the ball if she has to marry the Prince.

5. How do you think Cinderella feels toward her Fairy Godmother at the end of the story?
   a. grateful
   b. jealous
   c. bitter

> Check your answers with your teacher. Give yourself 1 point for each correct answer, and fill in your Strategy score here. Then turn to page 219 and transfer your score onto Graph 1.
>
> Personal
> Vocabulary
> Strategy
> Comprehension
> **TOTAL SCORE**
> ✓ T

Comprehension Check

Review the story if necessary. Then answer these questions:

1. Where did the Cinderella in this story get her name?
   a. She likes to play in the cinders that are left in the fireplace.
   b. Her family always makes her clean the cinders out of the fireplace.
   c. She likes to watch her family clean the cinders out of the fireplace.

2. How does Cinderella feel after her Fairy Godmother tells her that she must do some hard work?
   a. disappointed
   b. hopeful
   c. angry

3. Why does Cinderella's stepmother tell her children to let Cinderella do her book report by herself?
   a. She realizes that doing things by herself is making Cinderella feel better.
   b. She is trying to punish Cinderella for not doing any chores before this.
   c. She is afraid of going against Cinderella's Fairy Godmother's wishes.

4. Why does Cinderella feel good after she completes her book report?
   a. She is proud of herself for completing a difficult task.
   b. She is sure she will get a good grade on the report.
   c. She has written a humorous book report.

5. Why does Cinderella leave the ball early?
   a. She wants to get away from the Prince.
   b. She isn't having a very good time.
   c. She has to get up for school the next day.

> Check your answers with your teacher. Give yourself 1 point for each correct answer, and fill in your Comprehension score here. Then turn to page 219 and transfer your score onto Graph 1.
>
> Personal
> Vocabulary
> Strategy
> Comprehension
> **TOTAL SCORE**
> ✓ T

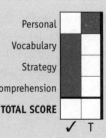

Extending

Choose one or more of the following activities:

WRITE YOUR OWN "CINDERELLA"
The author of this story changed the traditional story of "Cinderella" to make a point about the importance of independence. He took a few of the main ideas from the old story and combined them with his own new ideas. Following the author's lead, write your own variation on the "Cinderella" story. You can title your story "Still Another Cinderella" or any other title of your choosing. When you have finished your story, share it with your classmates. You might even ask a few of them to help you read it aloud.

COMPARE VERSIONS OF "CINDERELLA"
Find and read (or view) some of the versions of "Cinderella" that are listed on this page. Then make a large comparison chart on which you compare and contrast the characters, settings, and events in each version. If you started a comparison chart in Lesson 16 for "Turkey Girl" and the traditional European "Cinderella," you may want to expand on that chart.

RULES FOR RAISING AN INDEPENDENT PERSON
The family in "Another Cinderella" tries hard to raise Cinderella right. However, they make some mistakes along the way. Decide on the best way to raise an independent person, and write your own personal rules for good child raising. To get started, you might talk to a classmate about things that your parents do that you consider good ways of raising independent children. List your rules on a large sheet of paper, and, if possible, display them on a class bulletin board.

Resources

Books
Brooke, William J. "The Fitting of the Slipper." In *A Telling of the Tales: Five Stories.* HarperCollins Juvenile Books, 1990.

Philip, Neil. *The Cinderella Story.* Penguin, 1990.

Sierra, Judy. *Cinderella.* Oryx Press, 1992.

Zipes, Jack, ed. *Don't Bet on the Prince: Contemporary Feminist Fairy Tales in North America and England.* Routledge, 1989.

Web Site
http://www.usm.edu/english/fairytales/cinderella/cinderella.html Click on the "Archive Inventory" link on this Cinderella Project Web site for a dozen alternative versions of the Cinderella story.

Video/DVD
Ashpet: An American Cinderella. Tom Davenport, dir. Tom Davenport Films, 1990.

A Teenager in Combat: The Katyusha Mikhalova Story

Building Background

In August of 1939, Germany and Soviet Russia (the USSR) signed a 10-year nonaggression pact, each country pledging neutrality to the other in case of war. The agreement also prohibited either country from attacking the other or joining an association of powers aimed at the other. But the agreement didn't last. Within two years Hitler saw the Soviet Union as the only obstacle standing in his way of total control of the European continent.

Operation Barbarossa, the code word for Germany's invasion of the USSR, began in June 1941. Three million German soldiers pushed across the Russian border along a front line that extended more than 1,100 miles from the Arctic region to the Black Sea. The Nazi war machine crushed the ill-equipped and ill-prepared Soviet armies, and by late October, the Germans were positioned outside the capital city of Moscow.

But the Russians refused to give up. Despite incredibly high losses, the Soviet people rallied and fought back. With help from a bitterly cold winter, the Russians finally stopped the Nazi advance. And by early 1943, they counterattacked, defeating the German 6th Army at Stalingrad and forcing the Nazis to retreat. This was Hitler's first significant defeat and a turning point in the war.

Vocabulary Builder

amputate

comrades

elevated

flotilla

intact

ordeal

1. The words in Column 1 are from the selection you are about to read. Draw a line from each word in Column 1 to its definition in Column 2. If you're not sure of any of the words, guess for now. Then check or change your answers as you find the boldfaced words in the selection.

2. Save your work. You will refer to it again in the Vocabulary Check.

COLUMN 1	COLUMN 2
amputate	raised up
comrades	whole; uninjured
elevated	cut off from the body
flotilla	test or experience
intact	fellow members of a group; companions
ordeal	fleet of small ships

Strategy Builder

How to Read a Biographical Sketch

*   In Lesson 10 you learned that a **biography** is the story of a real person's life, written by someone else. A **biographical sketch** is the story of a part of a person's life.

*   As in biographies, the events in most biographical sketches are organized in chronological order, or **sequence**. There are times, however, when events are told out of sequence. In such cases, the author uses a **flashback** to tell about an important event that happened earlier in a person's life. Then the author goes back and relates the events that led up to that important event.

*   When you read a selection that contains a flashback, it is more important than ever to use **signal words** to help keep the sequence of events straight. Some signal words—such as *then, next,* and *a short time later*—help you link one smaller event to the next in a person's life. However, signal words such as *when she was fifteen* or *in 1942* help you see the sequence of the major events.

*   Even though the flashback in this selection is told out of sequence, you still can record the major events in Katyusha's life on a **time line**. To review how to use a time line, look back at the one you completed for Bessie Coleman's biography in Lesson 10.

A Teenager in Combat: The Katyusha Mikhalova Story

by Phyllis Raybin Emert

As you begin reading this selection, remember that it contains a flashback. Use the signal words to help you figure out the correct order of events. The words signaling major events are underlined twice.

When the **flotilla** of Soviet marines rushed onto the beach from their landing craft, the German defenders opened fire. The marines were forced to swim to shore while German machine gunners aimed at their foreheads. The continuous spray of enemy fire made the water bubble as if it were boiling. Most of the island's low-lying banks were flooded, and the Soviets kicked and thrashed through water above their heads.

It was December of 1944, and as the Russian armies moved west toward Berlin, the German capital, the marines were ordered to take part in an important battle in Yugoslavia. The strategically built fortress of Iluk was located on an island in the middle of the Danube River near the city of Vukovar, Yugoslavia. The marines' task was to land on a nearby island to divert German fire long enough for a Russian land force to take the fortress. The landing took place at night, but few had anticipated the treacherous flood.

Eighteen-year-old Katyusha Mikhalova, the only female member of the flotilla, swam for her life along with the rest of her **comrades**. Trained as a nurse, Katyusha carried a medical bag along with her grenades and machine gun. Katyusha would not abandon the wounded who were bleeding and drowning in the icy water around her. They were her friends and companions, and she was determined to rescue as many as she possibly could.

In the distance, Katyusha saw a small piece of **elevated** land and desperately began to pull the wounded men toward it. As reported by Shelley Saywell in her book *Women in War*, Katyusha described what happened in her own words. "I dragged each one up," she said, "and tied them with my bandages or their belts to the tree branches that were above water."

The Germans quickly surrounded the small piece of dry land. The wounded marines begged the Russian teenager to blow them up with one of her grenades. "Better to kill us now, Katyusha, than let us be slowly cut to pieces by the Germans," they pleaded.

"Never," declared the teenager. "I'll never give up as long as there's breath left in my body!"

Katyusha was true to her word. She continued to care for the wounded men even as dawn came, and the enemy could easily make out their positions. Suddenly a shot rang out, and a German bullet tore into the young girl's shoulder artery. Katyusha passed out from the loss of blood and pain.

"When I regained consciousness," she said many years later, "the Germans were very close—only ten feet away. I took an antitank grenade from my belt and threw it at them. . . . Our cook took several grenades and jumped toward them, dying instantly."

When Katyusha had no grenades left, she grabbed her machine gun and began shooting at the enemy. The Germans surrounded the Russian girl and her wounded companions and opened fire. Katyusha had no idea how long she continued to fight using her comrades' guns and ammunition.

The fortress at Iluk was finally conquered by Russian troops later that afternoon. Of the nearly one hundred members of the flotilla who took part in the landing, only the eighteen-year-old and twelve others were still alive. Katyusha had singlehandedly killed fifty-six German soldiers and was responsible for saving the lives of all of her surviving comrades.

After her **ordeal**, twenty-two shell fragments were removed from Katyusha's torn shoulder, and she then became ill with pneumonia. The courageous young woman recovered sufficiently to continue serving with the marines until the end of the war in May 1945.

According to the author Saywell, the teenage girl was recommended for the title of Hero of the Soviet Union by her commander after the battle of Iluk. But the generals in Moscow turned her down. Despite the commander's testimony, they simply could not believe that a young girl could have accomplished what was claimed.

Katyusha Mikhalova was a remarkable young woman. Like thousands of Russian women, she learned at an early age that when one's homeland is threatened, every able-bodied citizen, regardless of sex or age, is needed to fight. That was exactly the situation on June 22, 1941, a warm sunny morning, when war suddenly descended upon the unsuspecting Russian people.

Katyusha was a tiny fifteen-year-old girl on her way to visit her older brother for the summer. The pale blond teenager was the youngest of three parentless children who had spent most of their lives in an orphanage.

When the train that she was traveling on neared the Russian city of Smolensk, which is southwest of Moscow, the first German bombs began falling from the sky, effectively ending the nonaggression pact signed by Hitler and Stalin in 1939. Katyusha recalled those first moments of the war in Saywell's book. "There was chaos and screaming," she said. "I . . . saw bodies everywhere. I looked for the little girl who had been sitting with me. I found her body trembling, but her head had been blown off. . . ."

Along the two-thousand-mile Russian border, German troops were crushing the Russian army and advancing toward major cities such as Leningrad and Moscow. Katyusha was stranded in Smolensk and tried to enlist as a nurse, since she had Red Cross training. The recruiting officer turned her away. "You belong in kindergarten," he said.

Two weeks later, with the city of Smolensk under attack, the desperate commander of a rifle unit gave Katyusha a uniform and a weapon. In no time, Katyusha found herself on thirty-mile-a-day marches carrying a heavy pack, a gun, a shovel, and a medical bag. Her regiment was immediately sent north to help in the defense of Moscow.

In the first months of the war, the Russian forces retreated from the advancing Germans. But as the weather turned bitterly cold, the Russians dug in and took a stand against the invaders. But in early 1942, Katyusha was seriously wounded in the leg by an exploding shell. The doctor wanted to **amputate**, but the young girl refused. The doctor agreed reluctantly, and Katyusha recovered after several months away from the front lines—her leg **intact**.

In the summer of 1942, Katyusha was assigned to a naval medical ship and was involved in the battle of Stalingrad. Katyusha's ship traveled up the Volga River to evacuate the city's wounded. When the Germans bombed the medical ship, it sank in the icy waters of the Volga. Hundreds of the wounded drowned. ". . . I don't remember much," Katyusha recalled, "but they tell me I was rescued when I was near the bottom of the sea. When I was in the hospital, a nurse told me I was born lucky."

 Stop here for the Strategy Break.

Strategy Break

If you were to stop and arrange the main events in this biographical sketch so far, your time line might look like this:

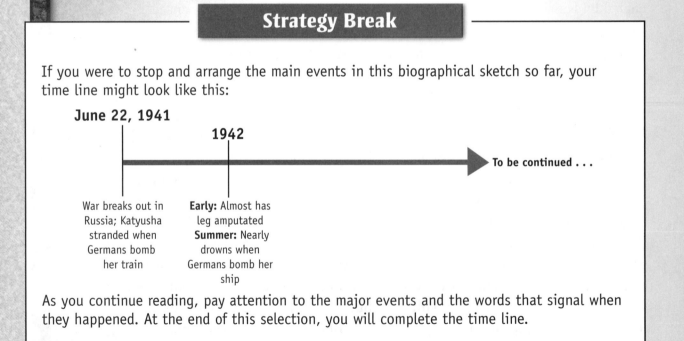

As you continue reading, pay attention to the major events and the words that signal when they happened. At the end of this selection, you will complete the time line.

Go on reading.

At the age of seventeen in late 1943, Katyusha received the Order of the Patriotic War during a night marine attack on Kerch'El'tigen, which took place during a terrible storm. The brave teenager rescued many of the wounded, carrying men who were more than twice her weight and size out of the water and onto land. There, she tended their wounds and engaged in hand-to-hand fighting when it was necessary.

After recovering from shoulder wounds she sustained in the Battle of Iluk in Yugoslavia, Katyusha was with her unit when the war finally ended on May 9, 1945. "I began to cry," she remembered. "I threw down my gun and said, 'I will never pick one up again'!"

The nineteen-year-old veteran returned to her home in Leningrad to discover that her brother and sister, the only remaining members of her family, had been killed in action.

Katyusha had survived major battles and suffered serious injuries during the war only to face more suffering when she returned home. One million people had starved to death in Leningrad while Katyusha was away. "The final battle that we faced together," she declared, "was hunger."

Each year since 1945, the Russian people have celebrated the end of World War II. The Russian women who participated in what is now called the "Great Patriotic War" turn out for the celebration bearing their medals pinned to the front of their dresses. Now they look like grandmothers, not battle-wise soldiers. They carry purses, not guns. They stand proudly, shedding tears for their fallen comrades and remembering the days when they valiantly fought for their homeland. ●

Strategy Follow-up

Now complete the time line for this biographical sketch. Be careful—one of the dates provided is the date of the flashback.

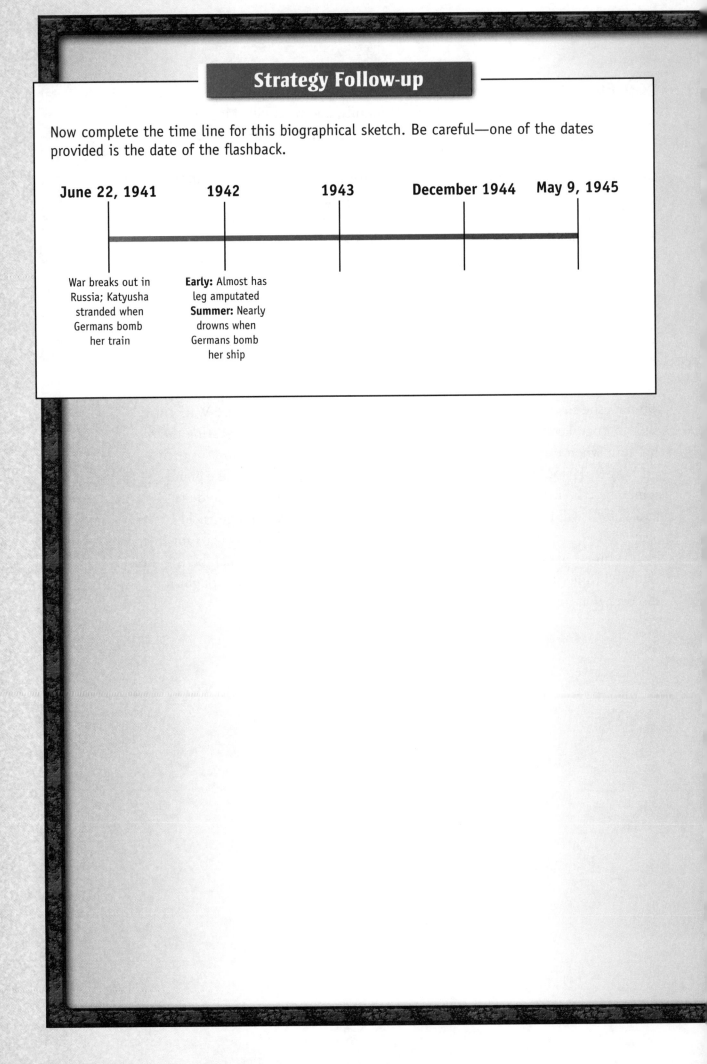

| June 22, 1941 | 1942 | 1943 | December 1944 | May 9, 1945 |

War breaks out in Russia; Katyusha stranded when Germans bomb her train

Early: Almost has leg amputated
Summer: Nearly drowns when Germans bomb her ship

✓Personal Checklist

Read each question and put a check (✓) in the correct box.

1. How well do you understand the information presented in this selection?
   - ☐ 3 (extremely well)
   - ☐ 2 (fairly well)
   - ☐ 1 (not well)

2. After reading this autobiographical sketch, how well do you think you could describe Katyusha Mikhalova's personality?
   - ☐ 3 (extremely well)
   - ☐ 2 (fairly well)
   - ☐ 1 (not well)

3. In the Vocabulary Builder, how well were you able to match the words and their definitions?
   - ☐ 3 (extremely well)
   - ☐ 2 (fairly well)
   - ☐ 1 (not well)

4. How well were you able to follow the sequence of events in this selection?
   - ☐ 3 (extremely well)
   - ☐ 2 (fairly well)
   - ☐ 1 (not well)

5. How well were you able to complete the time line in the Strategy Follow-up?
   - ☐ 3 (extremely well)
   - ☐ 2 (fairly well)
   - ☐ 1 (not well)

Vocabulary Check

Look back at the work you did in the Vocabulary Builder. Then answer each question by circling the correct letter.

1. Which word describes a group of ships?
   a. flotilla
   b. intact
   c. comrades

2. Which of these is an example of an ordeal?
   a. receiving a new sweater
   b. undergoing a painful operation
   c. going on a picnic on a beautiful day

3. If a doctor told you to keep your feet elevated after surgery, how would you do it?
   a. Fold them under you while you sit.
   b. Prop them up on some pillows.
   c. Dangle them in a tub of warm water.

4. What is the opposite of *intact*?
   a. charming
   b. perfect
   c. damaged

5. What would your comrade be most likely to do?
   a. Save your life during a battle.
   b. Attack you by surprise.
   c. Leave you alone and helpless.

Add the numbers that you just checked to get your Personal Checklist score. Fill in your score here. Then turn to page 219 and transfer your score onto Graph 1.

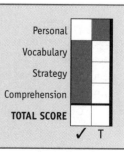

Check your answers with your teacher. Give yourself 1 point for each correct answer, and fill in your Vocabulary score here. Then turn to page 219 and transfer your score onto Graph 1.

Strategy Check

Review the time line that you completed in the Strategy Follow-up. Also review the selection if necessary. Then answer these questions:

1. How many years of Katyusha Mikhalova's life does this autobiographical sketch cover?

    a. about two years

    b. about four years

    c. about six years

2. Which of the following phrases signals a major event in this selection?

    a. on June 22, 1941

    b. two weeks later

    c. in the first months of the war

3. Why do you think the author begins this selection with a flashback?

    a. It is especially useful in proving Katyusha's courage.

    b. It happens before the other events in the selection.

    c. It is the only time that Katyusha shows courage.

4. Which date on the time line corresponds to the flashback?

    a. 1943

    b. December 1944

    c. May 9, 1945

5. What happened on May 9, 1945?

    a. Katyusha received the Order of the Patriotic War.

    b. Katyusha saved twelve lives at the Battle of Iluk.

    c. Katyusha threw down her gun at the end of the war.

Comprehension Check

Review the selection if necessary. Then answer these questions:

1. About how long did the nonaggression pact between Germany and the USSR last?

    a. two years

    b. five years

    c. ten years

2. How old was Katyusha when the war broke out in Russia?

    a. 15 years old

    b. 17 years old

    c. 19 years old

3. Where was the fortress of Iluk located?

    a. in Russia

    b. in Germany

    c. in Yugoslavia

4. Why didn't Katyusha receive an award for her bravery at Iluk?

    a. Katyusha didn't believe in awards.

    b. No one noticed Katyusha's bravery.

    c. Generals didn't believe her commander.

5. What suffering did Katyusha face when she returned home after the war?

    a. She was forgotten by the generals she worked for.

    b. She didn't receive any awards for bravery.

    c. Her family was dead, and everyone was starving.

Check your answers with your teacher. Give yourself 1 point for each correct answer, and fill in your Strategy score here. Then turn to page 219 and transfer your score onto Graph 1.

Personal
Vocabulary
Strategy
Comprehension
TOTAL SCORE
✓ T

Check your answers with your teacher. Give yourself 1 point for each correct answer, and fill in your Comprehension score here. Then turn to page 219 and transfer your score onto Graph 1.

Personal
Vocabulary
Strategy
Comprehension
TOTAL SCORE
✓ T

Extending

Choose one or more of these activities:

RESEARCH RUSSIA DURING WORLD WAR II
You just learned about one young woman's experiences during World War II. Now do some research to find out what life was like in Russia from the years 1941 to 1945. Make a time line showing the major events in Russia during those years. If you can, illustrate your time line with copies of photographs that depict some of the events.

RESEARCH OTHER WORLD WAR II HEROES
Using the resources on this page and ones you find yourself, learn about other men and women who served in World War II. Choose one person to report on, and make a time line of his or her life. Then use your time line to write a report that you can share with the rest of the class.

INTERVIEW A WORLD WAR II SURVIVOR
Most likely you know someone who lived through World War II. Interview that person to find out how the war affected him or her. Did that person serve in the armed forces? Did he or she have loved ones who served? How did the war affect daily life from 1941 to 1945? Prepare your questions before you begin your interview, and take notes on the answers. You might ask permission to tape the interview so you can share it with your classmates later.

Resources

Books
Emert, Phyllis Raybin. *True Valor: Stories of Brave Men and Women in the World War II.* Lowell House, 1996.

Saywell, Shelley. *Women in War.* Penguin, 1987.

Web Sites
http://www.pinn.net/~sunshine/essays/wwiivet.html
On this Web page, read about women who served in the U.S. military during World War II.

http://www.vor.ru/55/55_h/55.html
This Web site presents text and photographs related to the Great Patriotic War in Russia from 1941 to 1945.

http://www.worldwariihistory.info/Medal-of-Honor/
This Web site offers stories of soldiers who received the Congressional Medal of Honor in World War II.

LESSON 19 A Visit with Margaret Perry

Building Background

In history class, you have read about fascinating people from the past and the present. You may have heard about warriors who conquered armies, artists who painted masterpieces, or religious leaders who influenced the thinking of millions. If you could interview one of those people, who would it be? Why? What would you ask him or her?

Decide on the person you would like to interview. Then think of five questions that you would ask him or her. Write your questions on the lines below.

I would interview _____

because _____

Question 1: _____

Question 2: _____

Question 3: _____

Question 4: _____

Question 5: _____

culture

Harlem Renaissance

heritage

movement

unique

Vocabulary Builder

1. All of the words in the margin are related to the Harlem Renaissance. Use them to complete the word map on page 199.

2. If you don't know any of the words, look them up in a dictionary or an encyclopedia. Then, as you find them in the story, you can double-check your word map.

3. Save your work. You will use it again in the Vocabulary Check.

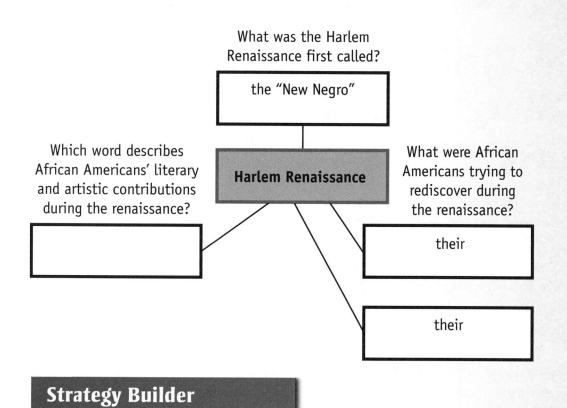

What was the Harlem Renaissance first called?

the "New Negro"

Harlem Renaissance

Which word describes African Americans' literary and artistic contributions during the renaissance?

What were African Americans trying to rediscover during the renaissance?

their

their

Strategy Builder

How to Read an Interview

- You know that all nonfiction writing follows particular patterns of organization. The selection you are about to read is an **interview**. Since an interview is like a conversation, it follows a **question-and-answer** pattern that is different from most other types of writing.

- The author's purpose in an interview is to **inform** the reader. The interviewer in this selection wants to inform readers about the Harlem Renaissance as it is viewed by historian Margaret Perry.

- Although the writer of this interview chose to record Margaret Perry's exact words, sometimes interviewers paraphrase the information they get. When you **paraphrase** information, you restate the gist, or main idea, in your own words.

- Read the following question and answer from an interview with a playwright.

> **Why did you move to New York after college?**
> I had dreamed of living in New York ever since my parents took me there on a family vacation when I was 12 years old. In the profession I had chosen, playwrighting, I knew that there was no better city for meeting people who could help my career. Basically, though, I just loved the hustle and bustle, the diversity, and the options that a city that size gives its residents.

- Here is how one student paraphrased the playwright's answer:

The playwright moved to New York for a variety of reasons. He had been introduced to the city as a child and had fallen in love with it then. As a playwright, he felt that he could make good professional connections there. And finally, he admitted that he just liked the opportunities that only a big city has to offer.

A Visit with Margaret Perry

by Harry Gardiner

*"The **Harlem Renaissance** was a fascinating time. Black people were creating literature, poetry, music, and art. Something really exciting and wonderful was happening. You could feel it!"*

*That is how Margaret Perry recently described the **movement** that became popular in the 1920s and that still serves as an inspiration for many African American artists. She knows the period well and has written several books about it, including* A Bio-Bibliography of Countee P. Cullen, Silence to the Drums, The Harlem Renaissance, *and* The Short Fiction of Rudolph Fisher. *In this interview, she talks about the renaissance from a historian's point of view.*

Why was this time called the Harlem Renaissance?

In 1925, Alain Locke edited a popular book called *The New Negro* consisting of drawings, paintings, and literature. For a long time, particularly while it was happening, the renaissance was called the "New Negro" movement. The name slowly evolved into the Negro Renaissance and eventually the Harlem Renaissance. In the 1970s, I talked with Arna Bontemps, and he said the term seemed to fit the spirit of the movement. Harlem was the cultural capital of black America, and it represented the spirit of rediscovery and cultural self-examination. That's where the heart of it was. It was a renaissance because it delved into the past to discover the **heritage** and patterns of a **culture** that had come out of Africa and the Caribbean to influence African Americans.

What years were represented by the Harlem Renaissance?

I tend to view it as covering the years 1919 to 1934. I like 1919 because that's when Claude McKay's poem "If We Must Die" appeared, following the race riots of that year. It pointed to a new spirit of assertiveness among African Americans and marked the beginning of a new period. The most important years were 1923 and 1929.

Why did the Harlem Renaissance happen?

A number of important events led up to it. One of the first was the publication of W.E.B. Du Bois's *Souls of Black Folk* in 1903. It was the first real examination of the inner workings of black people and became a cultural bible for African Americans growing up at that time. With the advent of the First World War, Du Bois urged African Americans to join the armed services, which many did.

They traveled to all parts of the world. Upon their return, they weren't willing to put up with previous conditions. Marcus Garvey's "back to Africa" movement encouraged African Americans to think about their heritage and regard themselves as having a past worth exploring.

Stop here for the Strategy Break.

Strategy Break

If you were to stop and paraphrase the last answer that you just read, your paraphrase might look like this:

Margaret Perry traces the beginning of the Harlem Renaissance back to a few important events and people. She says that a writer named W. E. B. Du Bois wrote an influential book called **Souls of Black Folk** in 1903. Then, after Du Bois urged African Americans to join the army during World War I, the soldiers came back with new ideas. They were ready to work to change their living conditions. Marcus Garvey began a "back to Africa" movement that put African Americans in touch with their roots.

As you continue reading, pay attention to the gist, or main idea, of each of Margaret Perry's answers. At the end of this selection, you will paraphrase one of them.

➡ Go on reading.

Were African American writers and artists living in other areas of the United States?

Indeed. Anne Spencer, who was well known at the time and wrote very nice poetry, never left Virginia. Quite a few others were in Washington, D.C. Arna Bontemps came from New Orleans, Langston Hughes from Kansas, and Claude McKay, who was from the West Indies, spent most of his time in Europe.

The movement had many widely known personalities. Can you tell us about some of the lesser known people?

One was Waring Cuney, whose poem "No Images" evokes sadness and reality while anticipating the recognition of real black beauty. Gwendolyn Bennett's poem "Heritage" is highly emotional and intense. Artist Aaron Douglas published some very moving sketches of African Americans being lynched.

Why are the literary and artistic achievements of the renaissance so important?

They helped instill a pride in one's heritage and showed that African Americans *did* come from somewhere and *did* have **unique** contributions to make—contributions that were colored by their past, spoke through their race, and were just as valid as anyone else's.

What do you see as the legacy of the Harlem Renaissance?

It helped to build a bridge stretching back to the past and forward to the future. One of its greatest contributions is a body of literature that one can still look at and study. These people made the effort to get in touch with their origins and to see themselves in a true light. The work of the renaissance continues to serve as an inspiration for today's writers. ●

Strategy Follow-up

On a separate sheet of paper, paraphrase Perry's answer to the last question in this interview. Be sure to include all of her important ideas, but state them in your own words.

✓Personal Checklist

Read each question and put a check (✓) in the correct box.

1. How well do you understand the information presented in this interview?
   - ☐ 3 (extremely well)
   - ☐ 2 (fairly well)
   - ☐ 1 (not well)

2. How well did the questions that you wrote in Building Background help prepare you for reading and understanding an interview?
   - ☐ 3 (extremely well)
   - ☐ 2 (fairly well)
   - ☐ 1 (not well)

3. How well were you able to complete the word map in the Vocabulary Builder?
   - ☐ 3 (extremely well)
   - ☐ 2 (fairly well)
   - ☐ 1 (not well)

4. In the Strategy Follow-up, how well were you able to paraphrase Margaret Perry's answer to the last interview question?
   - ☐ 3 (extremely well)
   - ☐ 2 (fairly well)
   - ☐ 1 (not well)

5. How well do you understand why Margaret Perry said that the Harlem Renaissance was a fascinating time?
   - ☐ 3 (extremely well)
   - ☐ 2 (fairly well)
   - ☐ 1 (not well)

Vocabulary Check

Look back at the work you did in the Vocabulary Builder. Then answer each question by circling the correct letter.

1. What is another word for *renaissance*?
   a. inspiration
   b. movement
   c. rebirth

2. Which definition of *culture* best fits the context of this selection?
   a. civilization of a given people or nation
   b. condition in which bacteria are grown
   c. behavior that is socially taught

3. Which word means the opposite of *unique*?
   a. one-of-a-kind
   b. common
   c. special

4. Which definition of *movement* best fits this selection?
   a. the moving parts of a machine, like a watch
   b. a distinct part of a musical composition
   c. a series of activities that have a common goal

5. When people talk about their heritage, to what are they are referring?
   a. what has been left to them by their ancestors
   b. what they enjoy most about life
   c. the place where they were born and grew up

Add the numbers that you just checked to get your Personal Checklist score. Fill in your score here. Then turn to page 219 and transfer your score onto Graph 1.

Check your answers with your teacher. Give yourself 1 point for each correct answer, and fill in your Vocabulary score here. Then turn to page 219 and transfer your score onto Graph 1.

Strategy Check

Review the paraphrase that you wrote in the Strategy Follow-up. Also review the interview if necessary. Then answer these questions:

1. What is an important rule to remember when you paraphrase?
   a. Reuse the exact words of the original source.
   b. Use your own original ideas.
   c. Put the main ideas into your own words.

2. What might be another fitting title for this interview?
   a. Writers and Artists
   b. The Life of W.E.B. Du Bois
   c. The Harlem Renaissance

3. Which of these ideas would you *not* have included in your paraphrase of Perry's last answer?
   a. The Harlem Renaissance helped instill a pride in one's heritage.
   b. The Harlem Renaissance helped linked the past and the future.
   c. People are still inspired today by literature of the Harlem Renaissance.

4. What does Perry say is one of the greatest contributions of the Harlem Renaissance?
   a. bridges that people built during that time
   b. literature that people can still study
   c. many widely known personalities

5. If you were to paraphrase the answer to the sixth question (about literary and artistic achievements), which of these ideas would you include?
   a. Renaissance achievements gave African Americans a sense of pride.
   b. African Americans did actually come from somewhere.
   c. The renaissance helped build a bridge to the past and future.

Comprehension Check

Review the interview if necessary. Then answer these questions:

1. What was the first name given to the movement now known as the Harlem Renaissance?
   a. the "New Negro" movement
   b. the American Renaissance
   c. the African American movement

2. What years does Perry say the Harlem Renaissance covered?
   a. 1905 to 1914
   b. 1919 to 1934
   c. 1914 to 1928

3. How did their time in other countries change African American soldiers during World War I?
   a. They discovered that Europe was more dangerous than the United States.
   b. They realized that they wanted to travel to Europe more often.
   c. They realized how poorly they had been treated in the United States.

4. Which of these artists does Margaret Perry consider to be a major figure in the Harlem Renaissance?
   a. Waring Cuney
   b. Gwendolyn Bennett
   c. Langston Hughes

5. According to Perry, what is one lasting outcome of the Harlem Renaissance?
   a. It helps people know where Harlem is.
   b. It is an inspiration for today's writers.
   c. It gives historians an interesting topic to learn about.

Check your answers with your teacher. Give yourself 1 point for each correct answer, and fill in your Strategy score here. Then turn to page 219 and transfer your score onto Graph 1.

Personal	
Vocabulary	
Strategy	
Comprehension	
TOTAL SCORE	✓ T

Check your answers with your teacher. Give yourself 1 point for each correct answer, and fill in your Comprehension score here. Then turn to page 219 and transfer your score onto Graph 1.

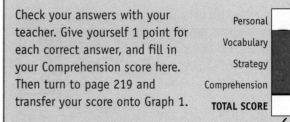

Personal	
Vocabulary	
Strategy	
Comprehension	
TOTAL SCORE	✓ T

Extending

Choose one or both of these activities:

PRESENT A HARLEM RENAISSANCE PROGRAM

This interview mentions several writers who became popular during the Harlem Renaissance. Choose one of those writers and locate some of his or her works. The resources listed on this page will give you a place to start. Choose one or two pieces to share with the rest of the class. Then, with other class members, present a program of oral readings from the Harlem Renaissance. Be sure to share your reasons for choosing the pieces that you did.

WHERE IS HARLEM?

You have read that Harlem was the "cultural capital of black America." But do you know exactly where it is? Get a map of New York City and locate the area called Harlem. Identify the borough in which it is located. If possible, use other resources to find out a bit of the history of Harlem, and present that information in a short report.

Resources

Books

Bloom, Harold, ed. *Major Black American Writers Through the Harlem Renaissance.* Writers of English. Chelsea House, 1996.

Giovanni, Nikki, ed. *Shimmy Shimmy Shimmy like My Sister Kate: Looking at the Harlem Renaissance Through Poems.* Holt, 1996.

Lewis, David L., ed. *The Portable Harlem Renaissance Reader.* Viking, 1994.

Web Sites

http://www.nku.edu/~diesmanj/harlem_intro.html
This Web site contains links to information on writers and artists of the Harlem Renaissance.

http://www.si.umich.edu/CHICO/Harlem/text/introduction.html
This Web site is an online historical exhibition about Harlem from 1900 to 1940.

Videos/DVDs

Against the Odds: The Artists of the Harlem Renaissance. PBS Home Video, 2001.

From These Roots. William Greaves, 1974.

The Dozier Brothers

chords

Eskimo pies

guitar

harmonica

instruments

popsicles

sorghum

strings

washboard

water ices

Building Background

In the interview that you read in Lesson 19, Margaret Perry mentions Arna Bontemps (1902–1973), a poet and author whose works were quite popular during the Harlem Renaissance. His wide body of work includes novels, poems, literary criticism, biography, and children's stories. With the help of fellow writer Countee Cullen, he even wrote a musical comedy called *St. Louis Woman*, which was an adaptation of his first book, *God Sends Sunday*.

In addition to being a writer, Bontemps was a schoolteacher, a principal, and a college librarian and professor. The story you are about to read is from one of his books called *Sad Faced Boy*.

Vocabulary Builder

1. The words in the margin are all found in "The Dozier Brothers." Which of these words are related to music? Which are related to foods that people eat on hot days? List each vocabulary word on the appropriate clipboard. Use a dictionary if you need to.

2. Save your work. You will refer to it again in the Vocabulary Check.

CLIPBOARD
Music Words

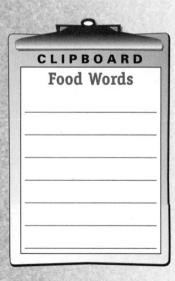

CLIPBOARD
Food Words

Strategy Builder

Mapping the Elements of a Story

- As you know, one of the main elements of every story is its **plot**, or sequence of events. In most stories, the plot revolves around a **problem** that the main characters have and the steps they take to solve it.

- Another element is the **setting**—the time and place in which the story takes place. Writers choose the setting with care because they know that it can greatly influence what happens in the story. For example, the characters in a story that takes place in a jungle are not going to be practicing their downhill skiing.

- In the story you are about to read, the setting determines what the characters do and think—and even how they speak. You will notice that the three brothers speak in a dialect. A **dialect** is a pattern of speech used by people from a certain group or area of the country. Using a dialect helps the author make the setting and the story more authentic.

- A good way to keep track of a story's major elements is to record them on a **story map**. The story map below lists and defines the elements that you should look for as you read a story.

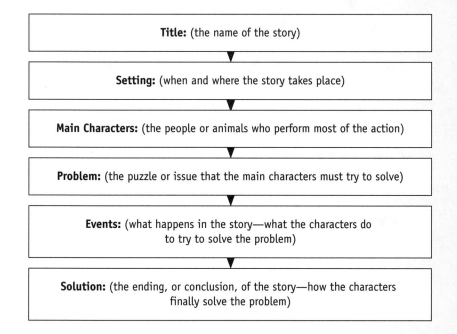

Title: (the name of the story)

Setting: (when and where the story takes place)

Main Characters: (the people or animals who perform most of the action)

Problem: (the puzzle or issue that the main characters must try to solve)

Events: (what happens in the story—what the characters do to try to solve the problem)

Solution: (the ending, or conclusion, of the story—how the characters finally solve the problem)

The Dozier Brothers

by Arna Bontemps

As you begin reading this story, apply the strategies that you just learned. Keep track of the setting, the main characters, and other elements. You may want to underline them as you read.

The days grew hotter and hotter. . . . A great many men came out on the streets of Harlem with little white wagons and sold **water ices** to the children. And it was not long before Slumber and Rags and Willie had spent all the nickels that Uncle Jasper Tappin could afford to give them.

Then when the nickels were all gone, they found themselves still thirsty for water ices, and the days were still hot. Where would they get more nickels for water ices?

 Stop here for the Strategy Break.

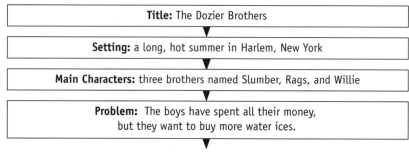
Strategy Break

The author has quickly introduced the setting, the characters, and the problem in this story. If you were to make a story map for this information so far, it might look like this:

> **Title:** The Dozier Brothers
>
> ▼
>
> **Setting:** a long, hot summer in Harlem, New York
>
> ▼
>
> **Main Characters:** three brothers named Slumber, Rags, and Willie
>
> ▼
>
> **Problem:** The boys have spent all their money,
> but they want to buy more water ices.
>
> ▼
>
> **To be continued . . .**

As you continue reading, look for the way in which the brothers work to solve their problem. You will complete the story map in the Strategy Follow-up.

Go on reading to see what happens.

Slumber worried a great deal during the long afternoons. Harlem was surely no place to be without money. Harlem made you want things you never wanted before—like water ices and **Eskimo pies** and **popsicles**— but it didn't help you to get the money to buy these things. Slumber began to wish again that he were at home with his mama.

"If I was back home," he told Willie and Rags as they stood against the iron fence, looking down into the park, "I wouldn't be wanting no water ices or nothing like that. I wouldn't be studying about nothing such like. I'd just be chewing on a stalk of **sorghum** and feeling good."

"No, you wouldn't be feeling good," Rags said. "You going to always be wanting what you seen up here in Harlem. Even when you get back home again, you'll be wishing you had some popsicles. Once you start in wanting things, you can't never get over it. You shouldn't of come to Harlem."

"I reckon I shouldn't, but I want to go home just the same," Slumber said softly.

He did not fully agree with Rags about how he would keep on wanting the things he had seen in Harlem, even when he was home again. No, Slumber felt quite sure that when he reached home again, stretched himself out on the shady side of the house, scratched his bare feet in the cool

ground and started chewing his stalk of sorghum cane, he would forget all about Eskimo pies and water ices and popsicles. But, of course, they were now a long way from home, and Uncle Jasper Tappin didn't seem to be in any special hurry to carry them back.

Slumber tried crossing his fingers and making wishes, but he found that nothing like that would work in Harlem. Those good luck tricks worked very well when he was at home in Alabama and in the country, but they didn't do a bit of good in New York. He found that in the big city to which he and his brothers had come even a rusty bent horseshoe or a rabbit's left hind foot wouldn't help you to get a cool water ice when you didn't have the nickel.

Little Willie finally thought of a wise thing. While they stood there, looking sorrowfully down into the park, he touched Rags on the back and said, "Listen, big shorty. I know what."

"What you know, little half-pint?" his brother said, smiling.

"Let's us go play some music and forget about what we has and what we hasn't got."

Slumber snapped his fingers, mocking his Uncle Jasper Tappin.

"Dogs my cats," he said. "That's just the ticket."

So they went across the street and down into the furnace room where they did most of their playing nowadays. And there was no question about it—playing music did help a great deal.

That night when they were in bed, Slumber opened his eyes suddenly with a bright thought.

"Let's us start a band and call it the *Dozier Brothers Band*," he said.

"Start a band with what?" Rags asked. "Just your **harmonica** and a tin can and a **washboard**?"

"Sure," Slumber said. "We can start with that and then look around and see what else we can find. Maybe Uncle Jasper Tappin will let you use that old **guitar** he got hanging on the wall."

Rags did not answer. The next afternoon, however, when their cleaning was done, he began to look around. Slumber kept his eyes open, too, and his thoughts were busy all morning.

"I seen some folks come in the air shaft with a old no-account band and play till people commenced throwing money at them from out the windows," he told Rags once. "We might could get us some nickels like how they did."

Rags was interested, but he was a little uncertain about the **instruments**. He wouldn't be satisfied with just a washboard to play on, and he was almost afraid to ask Uncle Jasper Tappin to let him take the guitar from off the wall. Yet, when the work was done, he made up his mind to try his luck.

In the meantime Willie found a broken drum in an ash can. Slumber repaired the old thing and painted the name of the band in big letters, *Dozier Brothers*. He struck the instrument a few strong booms, then handed it to his little brother.

"There now," he said. "You and me is fixed. If Rags will go ask Uncle Jasper Tappin for his guitar, we'll be ready for business."

Rags left the others in the furnace room and went to see about the instrument. While he was gone, Slumber and Willie went over a song or two, Slumber playing the tune on his harmonica and Willie beating the heavy part on the drum.

"How it sound?" Willie asked.

"Not so bad," Slumber said. "Not so bad."

About that time Rags came running through the door.

"Here it is, bubbers. Here it is," he cried. "Now we's *ready*."

"I told you so, big shorty," Slumber said, trembling with joy. "I told you he might would let you use it."

"He say it wasn't doing nobody no good up on the wall, cause he never yet seen a guitar what was made to be looked at. This old box was made for music, and here it comes. You listen."

Rags tuned the **strings**. Then, when Slumber began another song on his harmonica, he began to chime in with **chords** that sounded mighty fine indeed. Little Willie kept the drum booming just right. And the more they played, the sweeter the music sounded. The old furnace room had never heard anything like it.

No, sir, not since the building was built had there ever been music such as that in the furnace room. Slumber got warmed up and commenced to bear down on his harmonica. And when Slumber was warmed up, mind you, he could play a harmonica like very few people can play one. Why the little old furnace room windows started quivering and rattling to the tune. Uncle Jasper Tappin's old coal shovel caught one of the notes and began humming it almost as if it had been struck by Willie's drum stick. Slumber was bearing down, and his brothers were keeping right with him.

"This coming Sunday we can get out and let the folks hear us," Slumber decided. "Soon in the morning, just about time they's getting out of bed good, they'll hear us down in the air shaft. Maybe they'll throw some money at us."

"Sometimes you think up some powerful smart things, Slumber," Willie said.

"He sure do," Rags said. "I don't see how he can do it and still be so dumb."

A smile came over Slumber's sad face.

"Sunday," he reminded the other two as they left the furnace room. "Sunday—soon in the morning." ●

Strategy Follow-up

Now complete the story map for "The Dozier Brothers." Use a separate sheet of paper if you need more room to write. Parts of the events have been filled in for you.

Problem: The boys have spent all their money, but they want to buy more water ices.

Event 1: First, Slumber tries

Event 2: Then Little Willie suggests that

Event 3: Next, Slumber suggests that

Event 4:

Event 5:

Solution: The boys agree to

✓Personal Checklist

Read each question and put a check (✓) in the correct box.

1. How well do you understand what happens in this story?
    - ☐ 3 (extremely well)
    - ☐ 2 (fairly well)
    - ☐ 1 (not well)

2. After reading this story and the information in Building Background, how well do you understand why Arna Bontemps was an important contributor to the Harlem Renaissance movement?
    - ☐ 3 (extremely well)
    - ☐ 2 (fairly well)
    - ☐ 1 (not well)

3. In the Vocabulary Builder, how well were you able to put the words on the appropriate clipboards?
    - ☐ 3 (extremely well)
    - ☐ 2 (fairly well)
    - ☐ 1 (not well)

4. How well were you able to complete the story map in the Strategy Follow-up?
    - ☐ 3 (extremely well)
    - ☐ 2 (fairly well)
    - ☐ 1 (not well)

5. How well do you understand the kind of relationship that the brothers have in this story?
    - ☐ 3 (extremely well)
    - ☐ 2 (fairly well)
    - ☐ 1 (not well)

Vocabulary Check

Look back at the work you did in the Vocabulary Builder. Then answer each question by circling the correct letter.

1. Which of these words is easily related to music?
    a. harmonica
    b. sorghum
    c. popsicles

2. Which of these words names something refreshing to eat on a hot day?
    a. guitar
    b. water ices
    c. instruments

3. When you play a guitar, which part of it vibrates?
    a. its washboard
    b. its sorghum
    c. its strings

4. On which instrument would most people say it is not possible to play a chord?
    a. a drum
    b. a guitar
    c. a piano

5. Which of these is a tall grass used for making molasses or syrup?
    a. strings
    b. sorghum
    c. Eskimo pie

Add the numbers that you just checked to get your Personal Checklist score. Fill in your score here. Then turn to page 219 and transfer your score onto Graph 1.

Personal
Vocabulary
Strategy
Comprehension
TOTAL SCORE
✓ T

Check your answers with your teacher. Give yourself 1 point for each correct answer, and fill in your Vocabulary score here. Then turn to page 219 and transfer your score onto Graph 1.

Personal
Vocabulary
Strategy
Comprehension
TOTAL SCORE
✓ T

Strategy Check

Review the story map that you completed in the Strategy Follow-up. Also review the story if necessary. Then answer these questions:

1. What does Slumber try first to solve the boys' problem?

    a. pretending that it's not hot outside

    b. crossing his fingers and making wishes

    c. looking for some instruments to play

2. Who comes up with the idea of starting a group called the *Dozier Brothers Band*?

    a. Willie

    b. Rags

    c. Slumber

3. What happens when the boys start playing music on their new instruments?

    a. They sound terrible, and people yell at them.

    b. The more they play, the sweeter they sound.

    c. The more they play, the worse they sound.

4. Where do the boys practice their music?

    a. in the furnace room

    b. in the attic

    c. in front of their apartment

5. What is the final solution to the boys' problem?

    a. They agree to play music on Sunday to try to get people to throw them some money.

    b. They agree to ask Uncle Jasper Tappin to take them back home to their mama.

    c. They agree to ask Uncle Jasper Tappin to be the singer in their new band.

Comprehension Check

Review the story if necessary. Then answer these questions:

1. Where do the boys usually buy their water ices and popsicles?

    a. from men with white wagons on the street

    b. from other kids in the neighborhood

    c. from the freezer case at the corner store

2. Where were the boys before they arrived in Harlem?

    a. New York

    b. Alabama

    c. Chicago

3. Why do the boys decide to make music at first?

    a. to make money

    b. to annoy the neighbors

    c. to lift their spirits

4. Why does Uncle Jasper Tappin allow Rags to play his guitar?

    a. The guitar is cheap, so he doesn't care what happens to it.

    b. He feels that guitars are made for playing, not just looking at.

    c. He is tired of it and wants to hang something else in its place.

5. How do the brothers feel while they are planning their performance and practicing their music?

    a. hopeful

    b. worried

    c. angry

Check your answers with your teacher. Give yourself 1 point for each correct answer, and fill in your Strategy score here. Then turn to page 219 and transfer your score onto Graph 1.	Personal		
	Vocabulary		
	Strategy		
	Comprehension		
	TOTAL SCORE		
		✓	T

Check your answers with your teacher. Give yourself 1 point for each correct answer, and fill in your Comprehension score here. Then turn to page 219 and transfer your score onto Graph 1.	Personal		
	Vocabulary		
	Strategy		
	Comprehension		
	TOTAL SCORE		
		✓	T

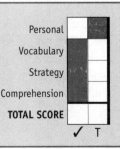

Extending

Choose one or more of these activities:

RESEARCH MUSIC OF THE HARLEM RENAISSANCE

African American music thrived during the Harlem Renaissance movement. Two types of music that became especially popular were blues and jazz. Using some of the resources listed on this page, locate recordings by African American musicians of the period, such as W. C. Handy, Louis Armstrong, and Duke Ellington. Play recordings of their music for the class as part of a Harlem Renaissance presentation.

RESPOND TO A MUSICIAN'S WORK

After listening to some songs that you researched for the activity above, choose the one that appeals to you most. Respond to the song in one of the following ways:

words—write a poem, song, descriptive paragraph, or critique

pictures—work in water colors, oils, or a medium of your choice

shapes—make a sculpture or a three-dimensional scene, using the medium of your choice

music—play or sing a song that you or someone else composed

movement—perform a dance to the song you have chosen

READ MORE BY ARNA BONTEMPS

Using the books listed on this page or ones you find yourself, read (or listen to) more books, stories, or poems by Arna Bontemps. Respond to what you have read in an oral or written book report. If other students have read the same materials, you might hold a panel discussion during which you all share your insights and opinions.

Resources

Books

Bontemps, Arna Wendell. *Lonesome Boy.* Beacon Press, 1988.

———. *Sad Faced Boy.* Houghton Mifflin, 1937.

———, and Jack Conroy. *Sam Patch, the High, Wide, and Handsome Jumper.* Houghton Mifflin, 1951.

Audio Recordings

Arna Bontemps, ed. and narr. *An Anthology of African American Poetry for Young People.* Smithsonian/Folkways, 1990.

Louis Armstrong Plays W. C. Handy. Sony, 1997.

Up in Duke's Workshop. Duke Ellington, perf. Original Jazz Classics, 1991.

Learning New Words

Suffixes

A *suffix* is a word part that is added to the end of a root word. When you add a suffix, you often change the root word's meaning and function. For example, the suffix -*ly* can mean "in a _____ way, or manner." So the adjective *cautious* changes to an adverb meaning "in a cautious way, or manner."

-ship

The suffix -*ship* can have different meanings. It can mean "quality or condition of being _____." Or it can mean "position, title, or job of _____." In the legend "Turkey Girl," White Moon lives a life of loneliness and hardship when she is taken captive by the Chippewa. *Hardship* means "quality or condition of being hard to bear."

Write the word that each definition describes.

1. position or title of champion _____

2. condition of being an owner _____

3. position or title of governor _____

4. position or title of member _____

5. quality of being sportsmanlike _____

-ment

The suffix -*ment* is another suffix that can mean "quality or condition of being _____." However, it also can mean "act, process, or fact of _____." For example, in Lesson 19 Margaret Perry discusses the Harlem Renaissance movement. In this context, *movement* means "the act or process of a group of people working together to reach a common goal."

Write the word that each definition describes.

1. act or process of arranging _____

2. condition of being content _____

3. act or process of settling _____

4. act or process of making amends _____

5. condition of being resentful _____

Multiple-Meaning Words

A single word can have more than one meaning. For example, two meanings for the word *culture* are "the civilization of a nation or group of people" and "condition in which bacteria are grown." To figure out which meaning of *culture* an author is using, you have to use context. Context is the information surrounding a word or situation that helps you understand it. When you read "An Interview with Margaret Perry" in Lesson 19, you used context to figure out that the *culture* she was referring to meant "the civilization of a particular nation or group of people."

Now use context to figure out the meaning of each underlined word. Circle the letter of the correct meaning.

1. There's nothing like the challenge of a good game of chess.

    a. a doubting or questioning of the truth

    b. thing that commands effort or interest

2. From the corner of my eye, I detected a subtle movement behind the bushes.

    a. the rhythm and tempo of a piece of music

    b. motion; change of place or position

3. Listening to Robert describe the death of his dog struck a sympathetic chord in all of us.

    a. emotion or feeling

    b. combination of musical notes

4. My dentist sterilizes her instruments as soon as she finishes with each patient.

    a. devices for producing music

    b. the tools of one's trade

5. Melissa tuned her strings before the concert.

    a. wire, nylon, or gut used on a musical instrument or a tennis racket

    b. numbers of things in a line or a row

Graphing Your Progress

The graphs on page 219 will help you track your progress as you work through this book. Follow these directions to fill in the graphs:

Graph 1

1. Start by looking across the top of the graph for the number of the lesson you just finished.

2. In the first column for that lesson, write your Personal Checklist score in both the top and bottom boxes. (Notice the places where *13* is filled in on the sample.)

3. In the second column for that lesson, fill in your scores for the Vocabulary, Strategy, and Comprehension Checks.

4. Add the three scores, and write their total in the box above the letter *T*. (The *T* stands for "Total." The ✓ stands for "Personal Checklist.")

5. Compare your scores. Does your Personal Checklist score match or come close to your total scores for that lesson? Why or why not?

Graph 2

1. Again, start by looking across the top of the graph for the number of the lesson you just finished.

2. In the first column for that lesson, shade the number of squares that match your Personal Checklist score.

3. In the second column for that lesson, shade the number of squares that match your total score.

4. As you fill in this graph, you will be able to check your progress across the book. You'll be able to see your strengths and areas of improvement. You'll also be able to see areas where you might need a little extra help. You and your teacher can discuss ways to work on those areas.

Graph 1

For each lesson, enter the scores from your Personal Checklist and your Vocabulary, Strategy, and Comprehension Checks. Total your scores and then compare them. Does your Personal Checklist score match or come close to your total scores for that lesson? Why or why not?

Go down to Graph 2 and shade your scores for the lesson you just completed.

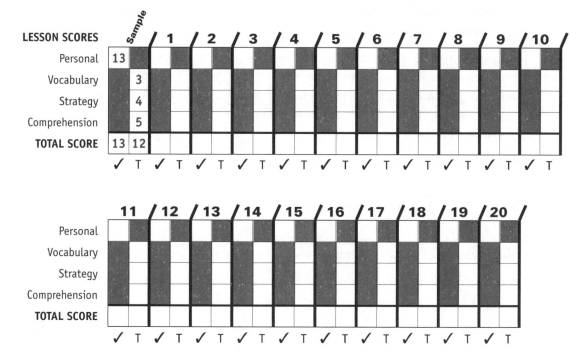

Graph 2

Now record your overall progress. In the first column for the lesson you just completed, shade the number of squares that match your Personal Checklist score. In the second column for that lesson, shade the number of squares that match your total score. As you fill in this graph, you will be able to check your progress across the book.

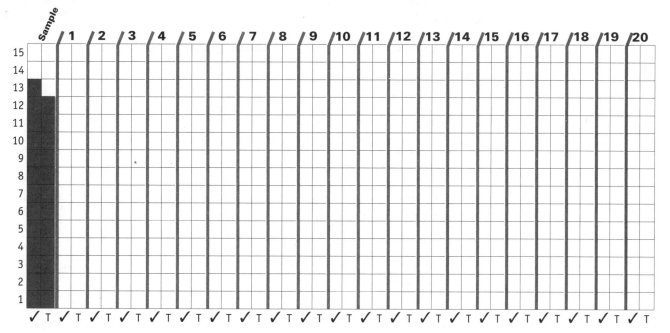

Glossary of Terms

This glossary includes definitions for important terms introduced in this book.

antonym   a word that means the opposite of another word. *Quickly* and *slowly* are antonyms of each other.

author's purpose   the reason or reasons that an author has for writing a particular selection. Authors write for one or more of these purposes: to *entertain* (make you laugh), to *inform* (explain or describe something), to *persuade* (try to get you to agree with their opinion), to *express* (share their feelings or ideas about something).

autobiographical sketch   the story of a part of a real person's life, written by that person.

biographical sketch   the story of a part of a real person's life, written by someone else.

biography   the story of a real person's life, written by someone else.

cause-and-effect relationship   the relationship between events in a piece of writing. The cause tells why something happened; the effect tells *what* happened.

characters   the people or animals that perform the action in a story. Static characters stay the same from the beginning to the end of a story. Dynamic characters change in some way.

comparing   looking at how two or more things are alike.

compound word   a word that is made up of two words put together. *Weekend* and *baseball* are examples of compound words.

conclusion   a decision that is reached after thinking about certain facts or information.

context   information that comes before and after a word or situation to help you understand the word.

contrasting   looking at how two or more things are different.

end result   the solution that a character or characters try that finally solves the problem in a story.

fantasy   a make-believe story with imaginary settings, characters, and/or events.

fiction   stories about made-up characters or events. Forms of fiction include short stories, science fiction, fantasy, and legends.

first-person point of view   the perspective, or viewpoint, of one of the characters in a story. That character uses words such as *I, me, my,* and *mine* to tell the story.

flashback   an event that is told out of sequence and describes something that happened in the past.

informational article   a piece of writing that gives facts and details about a particular subject, or topic.

interview   a piece of writing that records the questions and answers given during a conversation.

legend   a traditional tale that has been passed from generation to generation by word of mouth. Legends often contain magical elements, such as talking objects or animals, or characters that can change form.

main idea   the most important idea of a paragraph, section, or whole piece of writing.

narrator   the person or character who is telling a story.

nonfiction   writing that gives facts and information about real people, events, and topics. Informational articles and biographies are some forms of nonfiction.

outline   a framework for organizing the most important ideas in a piece of writing. Some outlines are organized according to a system of Roman numerals (I, II, III, and so on), capital letters (A, B, C, and so on), and Arabic numerals (1, 2, 3, and so on).

paraphrase   to retell the gist, or main idea, of a selection in one's own words.

plot   the sequence of events in a piece of writing.

prediction   a kind of guess that is based on the context clues given in a story.

prefix   a word part that is added to the beginning of a root word. Adding a prefix usually changes the word's meaning and function. For example, the prefix *un-* means "not," so adding *un-* to the root word *even* changes the word to its opposite, *uneven*.

problem   a difficulty or question that a character must solve or answer.

science fiction   fiction that is often based on real or possible scientific developments. Much science fiction is set in outer space, in some future time.

sequence   the order of events in a piece of writing. The sequence shows what happens or what to do first, second, and so on.

setting   the time and place in which a story happens.

signal words   words and phrases that tell when something happens or when to do something. Examples of signal words are *first, next, then, finally, after lunch,* and *in 1893.*

solution   the things that characters or people do to solve a problem.

suffix   a word part that is added to the end of a root word. Adding a suffix usually changes the word's meaning and function. For example, the suffix *-less* means "without," so the word *painless* changes from the noun *pain* to an adjective meaning "without pain."

summary   a short description. A summary describes what has happened so far in a piece of fiction, or what the main ideas are in a piece of nonfiction.

supporting details   details that describe or explain the main idea of a paragraph, section, or whole piece of text.

synonym   a word that has the same meaning as another word. *Fast* and *quick* are synonyms of each other.

third-person point of view   the perspective, or viewpoint, of someone outside the story. That narrator uses words such as *he, she, his,* and *her* to tell the story.

topic   the subject of a piece of writing. The topic is what the selection is all about.

Acknowledgments

Acknowledgment is gratefully made to the following publishers, authors, and agents for permission to reprint these works. Every effort has been made to determine copyright owners. In the case of any omissions, the Publisher will be pleased to make suitable acknowledgments in future editions.

"Amusement-Park Rides." Copyright © 1998 by Consumers Union of U.S., Inc. Yonkers, NY 10703-1057, a nonprofit organization. Reprinted with permission from the July/August 1998 issue of *Zillions* from *Consumer Reports for Kids.* To be used for educational purposes only. No commercial use or photocopying permitted. Visit us at http://www.zillionsedcenter.org/.

"The Clever Thief" by Sophie Masson as appeared in *Cricket,* September 1994, Vol. 22, No. 1. Reprinted by permission of the author.

"Another Cinderella" by Norman Stiles from *Free to Be . . . A Family* conceived by Marlo Thomas. Copyright © 1987 by Free to Be Foundation, Inc. Used by permission.

"The Challenge" by Margaret Roberts. Reprinted by permission of *Cricket* magazine, November 1998, Vol. 26, No. 3. Copyright © 1998 by Margaret Roberts.

"The Dozier Brothers" excerpt from *Sad-Faced Boy* by Arna Bontemps. Copyright 1938, © renewed 1965 by Arna Bontemps. Reprinted by permission of Houghton Mifflin Company. All rights reserved.

"Freaky Food" by Nancy Shepherdson from *Boys Life,* September 1998. Used by permission of the author and Boy Scouts of America.

"It Wasn't Always Called Baseball" by Vicki McClure from *Child Life.* Copyright © 1985 by Children's Better Health Institute, Benjamin Franklin Literary & Medical Society, Inc., Indianapolis, Indiana. Used by permission.

"Just Once" by Thomas J. Dygard from *Ultimate Sports* by Donald R. Gallo. Copyright © 1995 by Donald R. Gallo. Used by permission of Random House Children's Books, a division of Random House, Inc.

Adaptation of "The Quick Little Fellows" by James Cross Giblin from *From Hand to Mouth.* Copyright © 1987 by James Cross Giblin. Used by permission of HarperCollins Publishers.

"Scream, Too" by John Kontakis from *Contact KIDS,* July-August 1998, Issue #189. Copyright © 1998 Sesame Workshop (New York, New York). All rights reserved. Reprinted with permission.

"The Squid" adapted from *Twenty Thousand Leagues Under the Sea* by Jules Verne as appeared in *Read for Your Life,* 1998. Reprinted by permission of Millbrook Press, Inc.

Supergrandpa by David M. Schwartz. Lothrop, Lee & Shepard Books, 1991.